The Rise and Fall of
Nicolae and Elena Ceauşescu

Mark Almond is a lecturer in Modern History at Oriel College, Oxford. He was Theodor Heuss Research Fellow at the Alexander von Humbolt-Stiftung in Bonn from 1982 to 1984 and was a Junior Research Fellow of Wolfson College, Oxford, from 1985 to 1989. While living in West Germany, he began to travel widely in Eastern Europe and developed an interest in the peculiar society and politics of what was still then called 'Real Existing Socialism'. He is one of the few Westerners to have experienced the oppressive nature of the Ceauşescus' regime at first hand, during his many visits to Romanians willing to defy the former ban on meeting foreigners. In 1988 he published *Decline without Fall: Romania under Ceau*

The Rise and Fall of
Nicolae and Elena Ceauşescu

MARK ALMOND

The expense of spirit in a waste of shame . . .
Savage, extreme, rude, cruel, not to trust . . .
Past reason hunted, and no sooner had
Past reason hated, as a swallow'd bait
On purpose laid to make the taker mad;
Mad in pursuit and in possession so; . . .
Had, having and in quest to have extreme . . .
All this the world knows well
To shun the heaven that leads to this hell.

Shakespeare, SONNET CXXXIX

CHAPMANS

Chapmans Publishers Ltd
141–143 Drury Lane
London WC2B 5TB

First published by Chapmans 1992
This paperback edition first published by Chapmans 1992

© Mark Almond 1992

The right of Mark Almond to be identified as the author
of this work has been asserted by him in accordance with
the Copyright, Designs and Patents Act, 1988.

ISBN 1 85592 573 7

Printed and bound in Great Britain by
Clays Ltd, St Ives plc

For
'C'
who sent me there

Happy Christmas
Paul,

from B——

Acknowledgements

In the course of researching this book, many people in Romania were very helpful. Not all wish to be publicly acknowledged but they should accept my gratitude in every case. I should like to thank Gheorghe Apostol, Silviu Brucan, Pavel Câmpeanu, Sergiu Celac, Virgil Cândea, Grosz Karoly, Kiraly Karoly, Ion Gheorghe Maurer, and Mircea Trofin for talking to me, sometimes about painful or embarrassing subjects.

Anyone writing about modern Romania or the Ceauşescus must owe a lot to the previous researches of Mary Ellen Fischer, Michael Shafir and Vladimir Tismaneanu. I am sure that my debts to their work will be obvious.

I owe the transformation of my interest in Ceauşescu's Romania into a serious involvement with the country to Jessica Douglas-Home, Noel Malcolm, and Christine and Norman Stone. The Mihai Eminescu Trust which the first three established to aid the persecuted intellectuals of Romania gave me and others the opportunity of meeting and helping in a small way some of the most impressive people there (or anywhere else): Marianna Celac, Doina Cornea, Andrei and Katrinelle Pleşu, and Andrei Pippidi.

It was Gerry Frost of the Institute for European Defence and Strategic Studies who first encouraged me to write about Ceauşescu's Romania and he has generously allowed me to re-use here some material from my study, *Decline without Fall* (whose unprophetic title was my choosing in 1988). I am very grateful to him for his support over the years.

Charles Moore, then of the *Spectator*, Will Ellsworth-Jones of the *Independent Magazine* and Philippa Ingram of *The Times* encouraged me to write about Romania and thereby helped to facilitate the research towards this book.

Claudiu and Cornelia Secaşiu have given assistance well beyond the call of friendship. I hope this book is at least not completely unworthy of their time and trouble.

Christian Mititelu and the staff of the BBC Romanian Section have always been ready to help me and many others despite the heavy burdens of their own work, which deserves better recognition.

Peter Robinson has been generous in his support and confidence. Mark Crean encouraged me and then waited with the patience of several saints for the completion of the manuscript.

My parents and friends have patiently put up with the ghosts of Nicolae and Elena for long enough. I hope that I have laid them suitably to rest, but any flaws and errors in the execution remain my responsibility alone.

Contents

Preface

> 'A history without tyrants would be
> like a zoo without hyenas.'
> Emil Cioran

Christmas 1989 saw the climax of the East European revolution with the overthrow of the Romanian dictator Nicolae Ceauşescu. The events in Bucharest took on an almost mythical stature as the collapse of a tyranny was played out before a world-wide television audience with the inevitability of a Greek tragedy. The subsequent revelations about the rule of Nicolae and Elena Ceauşescu, and the contrast between their extraordinary life-style and the poverty and deprivation of their fellow Romanians, caught the imagination and aroused the sympathy of countless people in the West.

Anybody who saw pictures of the squalor in asylums for orphans, the handicapped or insane in Romania, let alone smelled them, or who learned about the dissemination of AIDS among infants because of the refusal of an insanely proud government to admit that the virus existed in the country, could be forgiven for taking a simple moralistic view of the regime that had brought about such conditions. The squandering of uncounted resources on a vast palace for a Communist dynasty which ignored even the most basic needs of its subjects seemed to be a sin as much against reason as common decency.

Such was the disgust with the Ceauşescus' last desperate efforts to keep themselves in power by shooting down unarmed demonstrators that even people in the West who scarcely knew where Romania was a few days earlier shared the exultation of the Romanian television announcer on Christmas Day who gave the news of the execution with the words 'the Antichrist is dead'. Unlike Romanians, Westerners did not know that the announcer-turned-avenging-angel had been a regular voice extolling the virtues of the dead couple until three days before.

What had seemed a simple moral tale of sin and retribution to Westerners – even the then Archbishop of Canterbury, Robert Runcie, used that most un-Anglican term, 'Antichrist' to denounce the Ceauşescus – turned out for Romanians to be more complicated. The heroism of unarmed demonstrators in Timişoara and Bucharest brought to power not 'The People' but some of the former politburo colleagues of Ceauşescu. The new president, Ion Iliescu, had been the number two in the Communist Party in the early 1970s. The Romanian revolution, so much more violent and dramatic than the other East European uprisings, seems to have changed less than met the eye in December 1989.

The rise of both Nicolae and Elena Ceauşescu from poverty in rural Romania to unrivalled power and wealth is an extraordinary story. But their biography is not just an account of how a most unlikely pair came to dominate a poor Balkan country. If their lives had simply been a rags to riches tale of political *nouveaux riches*, it would have only passing interest: they would have been the Marcoses of the Balkans, nothing more. What adds a more profound importance to their lives was their peculiar lifelong commitment to Communism.

To the bitter end, the Ceauşescus pursued power as inseparable from fulfilling their ideological purpose – the creation of a new type of humanity in an entirely transformed society. At the last Communist Party Congress only a month before his execution, Nicolae Ceauşescu still talked of Communism in his quaintly romantic way as 'the Prince Charming of Humanity' and asserted his determination to achieve the dream of creating the new society. Were these ideals simply a smokescreen for personal ambition? Or did Ceauşescu's commitment to fulfilling the ideology of Marx and Lenin actually contribute to making Romania into the moral and social disaster-area it had become by 1989?

Other recent biographers have sought to find the key to Nicolae Ceauşescu's repulsive behaviour either in medical disorders which affected his mental stability[1] or in his outspoken nationalism[2]. If poorly treated diabetes caused Ceauşescu's megalomania, then it must have been a rampant disease in the twentieth century: insulin must have been withheld from Stalin, Mao and Kim Il Sung, among others.

The expropriation of nationalism, like everything else, by Communist regimes is an important phenomenon, but the 'Great Leaders' have seen it as a tool to support their projects of human transformation rather than as an end in itself. By sponsoring a contradictory and repetitive Romanian nationalism which insisted on the unique antiquity and continuity of the Romanian state for more than two thousand years from pre-Roman times, Ceauşescu was trying to legitimize his regime with his people, but also to insulate it from the reformism of his neighbours and from Western influences as well. Of course, this policy actually persuaded impeccably democratic Western statesmen that the Romanian regime was really liberal at heart.

The story of Nicolae and Elena Ceauşescu is a depressing one not least because their disappearance from the scene has solved very little in Romania. Freaks of twentieth-century history they may have been, but they were not alone. They had role-models in the Communist world, and more depressingly they had influence as worthy objects of imitation with a score of Third World rulers who envied them their power, their caprices and the (simulated) adulation of their people. Nicolae and Elena Ceauşescu are dead, but like some vampire spirit, their mentality and ambitions live on in others. At least their downfall makes a cautionary tale.

Mark Almond,
Oxford, June 1991

A Chronology of Modern Romanian History

1859	Unification of Moldavia and Wallachia: first Romanian state.
1878	Full independence of Romania recognized by the Congress of Berlin.
1912–13	Balkan Wars: Romania expands at the expense of Bulgaria.
1916	Romania's entry into the First World War.
7 January 1918	Birth of Elena Petrescu (Ceauşescu).
26 January 1918	Birth of Nicolae Ceauşescu.
May 1918	Treaty of Bucharest: Romania accepts German terms.
November 1918	Defeat of Germany and Austria-Hungary by Allies; Romania rewarded with Transylvania and the Banat from Hungary; later Romania receives Bessarabia from Soviet Russia.
December 1918	Proclamation of first state containing all Romanians.
May 1921	Defectors from Romanian Socialist Party form Communist Party.
June 1940	Soviet Union occupies Bessarabia and Northern Bukovina.
30 August 1940	Vienna Award: Romania loses Northern Transylvania to Hungary.
September 1940	Abdication of King Carol; dictatorship of Antonescu.
22 June 1941	Germany invasion of USSR supported by Romania.
23 August 1944	Soviet troops having entered Romania, King Michael arrests the pro-German dictator, Marshal Antonescu.

March 1945	Imposition of pro-Soviet government led by Dr Petru Groza.
November 1946	Communist-dominated National Democratic Front wins 'elections': 347 seats to 36 for the opposition.
30 December 1947	King Michael forced at gunpoint to abdicate.
1948	Romania becomes a People's Democracy.
1948–	Suppression of non-Communist parties: mass imprisonments of scores of thousands; forced labour on Danube–Black Sea Canal.
1952–54	Show trials; purges inside Communist Party.
April 1964	Declaration of Romanian Workers' Party's independence from Moscow.
March 1965	Death of Gheorghe Gheorghiu-Dej, the first post-war leader of Communist Romania; Nicolae Ceauşescu succeeds him.
21 August 1968	Soviet-led invasion of Czechoslovakia.
1971	Nicolae and Elena Ceauşescu visit Mao's China and North Korea; start of Ion Iliescu's decline from favour.
1974	Nicolae Ceauşescu becomes President of Romania as well as General-Secretary of the Party.
4 August 1977	Coal-miners strike in Jiu Valley.
June 1978	Nicolae and Elena Ceauşescu pay a state visit to Britain; knighthood of Ceauşescu at Buckingham Palace.
1982	Mysterious death of Virgil Trofin.
1984	Iliescu finally removed from Central Committee of Communist Party.
15 November 1987	Braşov protests against Ceauşescu's regime.
April 1989	A letter attacking Ceauşescu from 'the Six', is published.
9 November 1989	Opening of Berlin Wall and the fall of Todor Zhivkov in Bulgaria.
16 December 1989	Beginning of anti-Ceauşescu protests in Timişoara.
22 December 1989	Flight of Nicolae and Elena Ceauşescu from Bucharest.
25 December 1989	Execution of Nicolae and Elena Ceauşescu.

Who Was Who in Modern Romania

Apostol, Gheorghe: veteran Communist; leader of trades unions; Ceauşescu's rival for the succession to Gheorghiu-Dej in 1965; one of the Six (see below).

Bârladeanu, Alexandru: veteran head of central planning; ousted by Ceauşescu; one of the Six; president of the Senate after the revolution.

Bobu, Emil: Second Secretary of Romanian Communist Party under Ceauşescu; a passenger in the couple's last helicopter ride.

Brucan, Silviu: pre-war Communist; leading Party journalist; diplomat; member of the Six and a key figure in plotting Ceauşescu's downfall.

Ceauşescu, Ilie: brother; Deputy Minister of Defence; historian.

Ceauşescu, Nicolae Andruţa: brother; Deputy Minister of Interior.

Draghici, Alexandru: head of the secret police under Gheorghiu-Dej; later disgraced by Ceauşescu.

Gheorghiu-Dej, Gheorghe (1908–1965): the first post-war leader of Communist Romania.

Iliescu, Ion: Ceauşescu's first heir-apparent; fell from grace slowly after 1971; today the President of Romania.

Kiraly, Karoly: Hungarian member of Romanian Communist Politburo; a dissident after 1974.

Magureanu, Virgil: Securitate officer; judge of Ceauşescu at his trial; current head of the Romanian Information Service (security service).

Manescu, Manea: Prime Minister under Ceauşescu.

Maurer, Ion Gheorghe: Prime Minister under Dej and Ceauşescu until 1974.

Milea, Vasile: Defence Minister until 22 December 1989.

Pauker, Ana: leader of 'Muscovite' group of Romanian Communists; purged in 1952.

Postelnicu, Tudor: Minister of Interior under Ceauşescu.

Roman, Valter: veteran Communist; died in 1983; father of Petre Roman, the current Prime Minister of Romania.

Stanculescu, Victor Athanasie: Army General; sometime Deputy Defence Minister and Defence Minister before and after the revolution of December 1989; one of Ceauşescu's judges at his trial.

Six, the: former leading Communists, who signed an open letter attacking Ceauşescu in April 1989: Apostol, Bârladeanu, Brucan, Corneliu Manescu, Constantin Pîrvulescu and Mircea Raceanu.

Trofin, Virgil: early favourite of Ceauşescu; disgraced after a dispute with him; died in mysterious circumstances in 1982.

Vlad, Iulian (Colonel-General): head of the Securitate in the last years of Ceauşescu's rule; reputed to like modern art and classical music.

The Ceauşescu Family Tree

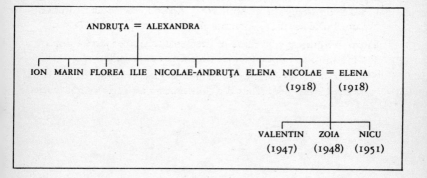

I

The Fall

First newspaper reader: Why do you read the front page first
                            every day?
Second newspaper reader: I'm looking for an obituary.
First newspaper reader: But the obituaries are on the back
                            page.
Second newspaper reader: Not the obituary I am looking for!
                            (Romanian joke before 22 December 1989)

Rarely can a great moment in history have been captured so precisely as the instant at which Nicolae Ceauşescu's hold over Romanian society crumbled before his very eyes on the morning of 21 December 1989. As ever, his speech to the assembled working people of Bucharest from the balcony of the Central Committee building, facing the old royal palace, was being broadcast live by Romanian state radio and television. The carefully marshalled delegations from the individual factories and offices around the capital had been let into the square through cordons of militiamen – as the police were known – watched over by plainclothes members of the Securitate. The same hurrahs which had always greeted his appearance before the people over the last twenty-four years roared out for the last time. The placards with the inevitable slogans in his honour – 'The Party – Ceauşescu – Romania' – jostled with the perennial portraits of an ageless president and his rejuvenated wife. Elena Ceauşescu was by his side. Everything was in order. It might almost be called normal.[1]

Two decades before, a similar-sized crowd (minus winter overcoats but carrying the same portraits of a youthful General-Secretary, who was still only fifty) had gathered on the afternoon of 21 August 1968 in the same square in front of the concrete monstrosity which housed the offices of the Communist Party's top bureaucrats. Then too great tension hung in the air. Soviet tanks had entered Czechoslovakia only hours before to begin the process of crushing the Prague Spring. A few days earlier, Nicolae Ceauşescu himself had flown to the Czech capital to demonstrate his support for Alexander Dubcek's policies of reform. The Romanian leader's presence at the side of Dubcek seemed to align Romania with the idea of 'Socialism with a Human Face' and with the idea that each country in the Warsaw Pact should be free to pursue its own internal policies as it saw fit without Moscow's veto or intervention. When the Soviet troops crossed into Czechoslovakia, all Moscow's other allies in the Warsaw Pact, except one, sent contingents with the Red Army to show their support for Brezhnev and his doctrine denying 'fraternal allies' the right to act against the Kremlin's wishes even in their internal affairs. Romania alone refused to participate in the invasion of Czechoslovakia. So at the end of August 1968, the Romanians feared Soviet intervention in their own country too.[2]

Despite anticipation that he would buckle under Soviet pressure, when Ceauşescu spoke, he made it clear that the Romanians, unlike the Czechs and Slovaks, would resist any invasion of their country. He spoke briefly, apparently from the heart. He called the Warsaw Pact's intervention 'a great mistake and a grave danger to peace . . . a shameful moment in the history of the revolutionary movement'.

Ceauşescu went on: 'It is said that in Czechoslovakia there was a danger of counter-revolution; maybe tomorrow there will be some who say that here too, *at this rally*, counter-revolutionary tendencies were manifest. We will answer all of them: the entire Romanian people will not allow anybody to violate the territory of our homeland . . .' He concluded with a promise which was also a warning to Moscow: 'Be sure, comrades, be sure, citizens of Romania, that we shall never betray our homeland, we shall never betray the interests of our people!'

Some of Ceauşescu's phrases may have been stilted, but his message of patriotic defiance was clear. Communist and anti-Communist Romanians alike could agree on the need to preserve their country's independence. Indeed, the less sympathetic a person was to communism the more they might endorse Ceauşescu's speech. Certainly, the scores of thousands in the crowd cheered wildly. For the first time, a Communist leader in Romania tasted the intoxicating brew of genuine popular admiration. Ceauşescu's words seduced many otherwise sceptical Romanians into seeing in him a Communist of a new type, at heart a reformer and patriot. Their response to his resolute stand convinced him that he was the people's hero now and for ever more.[3]

Twenty-one years later, those who could remember the atmosphere of trepidation before Ceauşescu emerged onto the balcony that late summer afternoon, had other things on their minds. They shared with those born or grown to maturity since 1968 more bitter and depressing experiences. As they waited for Ceauşescu to speak on a cold winter's morning, they knew that they could not expect a short speech or a rousing one. Too many speeches had been made from the same balcony for the memory of 1968 to count for much against the deluge of words, promises, and breaches of faith which had cascaded on them since. Some even perhaps regretted that Brezhnev had not invaded after all. Since they knew that after Brezhnev at last came Gorbachev and reform, even in the month before to Czechoslovakia itself. While they shivered in their independence and waited for the appointed moments to cheer or clap in unison.

For once the content of the General-Secretary's speech was not going to be his standard recitation of statistics showing the ever-improving standard of living for ordinary Romanians and the ceaseless increase in industrial output. The day before, Ceauşescu had made a television speech from the studio reserved for presidential utterances inside the Communist Party's massive headquarters on Bucharest's main square. In that speech, he had admitted the existence of a serious problem in Romania for the first time since he came to power in 1965.

Although the people in the square did not know for certain what was happening in the western city of Timişoara, everyone understood that the greatest crisis ever faced by the Communist regime in Romania was under way. Foreign radio stations had given only the vaguest information, rumours in fact, of demonstrations against Ceauşescu in Timişoara and then of shootings by his troops and secret police. But Ceauşescu's television address to the nation immediately after his return from a state visit to Iran the day before had aroused far more excitement than any illicit news from the BBC Romanian Service or Radio Free Europe. He had admitted protests had taken place and were still going on. For forty years, nothing like it had been admitted before.[4]

Now in the open air before 80,000 people, Ceauşescu was going to repeat his television speech of the night before. The crowds had been summoned from the morning shifts in the factories and offices of Bucharest. The standard banners and protraits of both the President and his wife had been brought out. At about nine, people were told that, after all, there was not going to be a spontaneous meeting of the working people. Was it a sign of internal dissension among the Communist Party leaders? Certainly, it was evidence of indecision, because hardly had the unwilling audience begun to relax and to return to their normal tasks than they were summoned out again to assemble in the main square before the Central Committee building.[5]

Unusually large numbers of plainclothes, as well as uniformed, policemen controlled all the entrances to the E-shaped double square which the populace had to fill even though

4

many of them would not be able to see the speaker on the balcony or even hear clearly what he said through the huge but tinny system of loudspeakers. Each individual entering the square was checked to make sure that he or she was a member of an official delegation from a specific workplace.

Even before the rally began, there was a dispute at the northern end of the square where the Calea Victoriei entered it between the two luxury hotels for foreigners: the Hotel Bucuresti, barely seven years old; and the Athénée Palace, made famous in English literature by Olivia Manning. The Calea Victoriei was Bucharest's main street but no private traffic was allowed to use it: it was reserved for use by the presidential motorcade and a few other favourites. On the morning of 21 December, the militia cordon refused to permit some women workers to cross into the square. Not only did they not have the right papers, but their demeanour suggested that they intended to participate at the 'Working People's Meeting' in an all too spontaneous fashion. Their arguments with the militiamen were out of sight and earshot of the dignitaries on the balcony, but they added another unprecedented element to the event.

However sullen the bulk of the crowd appeared, as usual a claque of enthusiastic minor Party officials had been placed at the front of the crowd, just behind the row of plainclothes Securitate agents who always stood as the first row of the 'People'. Another cordon of militiamen right at the front kept everyone a good thirty yards back from the front of the Party Headquarters itself. The Party dignitaries came onto the balcony and were greeted by ritualized applause. There were deep, throaty cheers for the two Ceauşescus, accompanied by the waving of pictures of them not looking younger, but perhaps drawn from another incarnation. After heartfelt thanks from the head of the Bucharest Communist Party organization for gracing the rally with his presence, Nicolae Ceauşescu began to speak.

What happened next remains mysterious. Its impact was obvious. Shortly after Ceauşescu began to speak, even before he had warmed to his subject – a condemnation of the outbreak of anti-Communist protests in the western city of Timişoara – there was an explosion, or at least a loud bang. People were screaming, and some were even chanting 'Timişoara' and other indistinct but obviously hostile slogans.

The face of the tyrant registered the dissolution of his power before his own eyes. Confusion came over him. Ceauşescu stuttered a few sounds. He made the strange window-wiping gesture that usually silenced applause when he had wearied of it, but to no effect. Then he looked anxiously to his wife. The other dignitaries on the balcony shuffled in their winter boots and looked down at their feet. The window door behind Ceauşescu was opened and the chief of his personal security guard manoeuvred him inside the building as the television transmission was cut and replaced by martial music.[6]

A strange anti-climax ensued. After a few minutes the radio broadcast was resumed. Elena's voice had already been heard urging her husband to 'offer them something'. Now Ceauşescu's voice carried on lifelessly through a speech which mingled inducements to loyalty with threats against the 'hooligans' in Timisoara. Pensions to go up 10%, wages too. But nobody was listening any more. The crowd was drifting away from the Palace Square back down the Calea Victoriei towards the university a few hundred yards to the south. Elsewhere workers drifted back home or to their factories. Some dragged their banners and slogans along in the gutter behind them, some had thrown them away at the height of the confusion. Television viewers and radio listeners scattered to share the news with neighbours who had missed the broadcast or to discuss the significance of the interruption. Until a few minutes before hardly any of these people would have dared to discuss a political event more or less openly with people they hardly knew. Now everyone knew that it was the beginning of the end.[7]

Even before the resumed transmission of the speech had finished, passengers arriving at Baneasa Airport could see busloads of troops from the neighbouring Securitate base setting out in the direction of the city centre. They were equipped with riot-shields – clear evidence that popular protest had begun in the capital too. The columns of buses split up at the Piata Victoriei in front of the harsh neo-classical concrete of the Foreign Ministry. It was obvious to the actor, Ion Caramitru, who had returned to Bucharest from Cluj and was driving down from the airport amid the military vehicles, that they were splitting up into three groups to encircle some as yet invisible crowd of protesters.[8]

Ceauşescu had sensed trouble coming. Everything in November was calm, but it was the tense stillness before a storm. Before he left Bucharest to travel to Iran on 18 December, he called the Political Executive Committee together and issued his instructions for what was to be done in his absence. During this meeting it became clear that Ceauşescu had ordered both a show of force to intimidate the protesters in Timişoara and the use of firearms if the parade of armoured vehicles failed to quieten the situation. He left a committee of three, headed by his wife, Elena, to run the country while he was away. The others were the nominal number two in the Party, Emil Bobu; and Manea Manescu. He also ordered the borders of Romania to be closed to all tourists, except visitors from China, North Korea, and Cuba – his only reliable allies left. Since the meeting between US President George Bush and Mikhail Gorbachev in the stormy seas off Malta only two weeks before, Ceauşescu was increasingly convinced that the two superpowers were redefining their spheres of interest in the world, and, more to the point, the Soviet Union was conceding its hegemony over Eastern Europe to Washington. How else could the turmoil and 'counter-revolutions' throughout the region over the last six months be explained?[9]

The trouble in Timişoara worsened dramatically during the two and a half days Nicolae Ceauşescu spent in Iran. By the time he returned on 20 December the city was largely in the hands of rebels. The army and the Securitate had failed to suppress the discontent. By that Wednesday evening, some troops had already gone over to the rebels in Timişoara. Others had withdrawn from the city in response to threats by workers to blow up their factories if the security forces continued to shoot at the demonstrators. Ceauşescu had underestimated the scale of protest in the western city, but more importantly, he could not see that Romanians throughout the country, as well as the Hungarian-speaking minority in Timişoara itself, had turned against his regime. In his weary and rambling television speech on 20 December, the day of his return from the gruelling visit to Teheran, Ceauşescu blamed 'foreigners' – clearly meaning the Hungarian government – for the trouble.

He had hardly begun to repeat the charges in his speech the next morning when the crowd began to heckle him. Even the moronic chanting of his name by the Party loyalists at the front of the crowd could not drown out the abuse hurled at him. The demonstrators' words were indistinct to radio listeners, but they were clearly the voice of the people.

Ceauşescu carried on to the end of his speech and then returned indoors to take stock of the situation. Crowds were already gathering half a mile away in the University Square. Partly by instinct, partly following the examples they had heard from elsewhere in Eastern Europe on Western radio, or even seen on Bulgarian television broadcasting only eighty miles away, the students and others began to chant slogans demanding the resignation of Ceauşescu and the end of communism. Despite the spectacular fiasco they had just witnessed, many of the first few thousand to risk their lives by open defiance expected that it would take a prolonged confrontation to bring about the downfall of their rulers. The example of the six-week-long sit-in in Tiananmen Square in Peking was in a few minds, though they were perhaps a little more confident that their own demonstration would end triumphantly if not quickly. Their slogans were the universal cries of 1989: 'We are the People' and 'No violence' ('Fara violenţa').

The Minister of the Interior, Tudor Postelnicu, was sent down to talk to some of the crowds gathered at the northern end of the square. Together with the Securitate general, Bucurescu, he tried to find out who was in charge of the demonstrators. (Somebody had to be in charge; spontaneous demonstrations did not happen in a country like Romania.) They suggested that the leaders of the demonstrators come forward and then join them in the Central Committee building for 'a discussion'. Wisely, no one took the bait.[10]

By dawn, after a night of confrontation, violence, and some bloodshed, it seemed that the security forces had regained control of the University Square area. Demonstrators continued to skulk around the edges of the district and in the side streets, but some semblance of 'normality' had begun to reappear. Workmen were dispatched to paint out the anti-Ceauşescu slogans which the demonstrators had scrawled on the walls of the university buildings. Even today, neat blocks of green paint can be seen where the diligent rewriting of history had started. Removing the signs of discontent was always the first step to denying that it had ever existed. But the 'normalization' of life had hardly begun when it was rudely shattered.[11]

Radio Bucharest announced that the 'traitor' General Milea had committed suicide. The death of the Minister of Defence was the signal for an about-turn in the allegiance of the army. Certainly during the night many of the soldiers had been unwilling to shoot at the demonstrators, and troops in barracks around the capital had made their feelings felt. These sentiments were usually shared by their officers and NCOs. But there is no evidence of any desertions or of troops turning their guns on those shooting at the demonstrators, whether fellow soldiers, militiamen, or *securiştii*. Discipline remained intact until late in the morning of 22 December, when, acting as if one man, the troops and tanks turned their weapons to face a new enemy: their old boss in the Central Committee building.

Vasile Milea had never been popular with the troops. He was not a regular soldier but really a Party general. For many years he had commanded the Patriotic Guards, the glorified 'Dad's Army' of Communist Romania which was supposed to organize the civilian population into a partisan force to resist foreign invasion. The Patriotic Guards were also seen as a way in which the Communist Party could divide control of military power between several organizations. In addition to the army and the Patriotic Guards, the secret police had powerful para-military units, especially the four thousand strong so-called anti-terrorist squad, USLA. Milea had risen to the rank of Minister of Defence largely through the patronage of Elena Ceauşescu. He was a sycophantic creature given to gossip and drink.[12] He was very different from his smooth, well-groomed, almost aristocratic deputy, Victor Stanculescu.

Stanculescu was the odd-man-out among Ceauşescu's favoured men. He was not self-consciously low-born and uncouth in his habits or manner of speaking. He was cultivated and well-read. His military expertise lay in chemical warfare and psychological operations. Like any high-ranking officer in the Warsaw Pact, he knew a great deal about the arts of deception in warfare.[13] In the last few years, Ceauşescu had relied upon him more and more, but not in military matters proper. As the efficiency of the Romanian economy declined in the 1980s, increasingly unable to meet the unrealistic targets for production set by Ceauşescu, he had resorted to bringing in the generals to run industry in a disciplined military fashion. Stanculescu found out at first hand the real causes of Romania's desperate economic problems during his tenure as what was, in effect, managing-director of much of Romanian heavy industry and power production. Even as he rose in Ceauşescu's favour, Stanculescu saw the evidence of the catastrophic consequences of his policies. By bringing the military into the economy, Ceauşescu brought the generals closer to becoming involved in politics.[14]

With the outbreak of the trouble in Timişoara, Stanculescu suddenly and shrewdly became incapacitated with a broken leg. In the tense days leading up to the climax of 22 December, Nicolae Ceauşescu allowed himself a rare moment of jocularity when he saw the Deputy Minister's plaster-encased foot. Whistling in the dark to try and keep up the drooping spirits of his subordinates, he laughed 'Victor, what a time to break your leg!' This injury was cosmetic: by Christmas Day, it had been cured. In the meantime, it justified the Deputy Minister's absence from the scenes of bloodshed and even from his master's sight. Stanculescu had left the supervision of the troops in Timişoara to the Chief of Staff, Stefan Gusa, and General Mihai Chiţac. Ion Coman, Ceauşescu's Secretary for Security in the ruling Political Executive Committee, had also been in Timişoara in charge of the overall operation on the spot. Stanculescu had an alibi to answer any questions about his part in the shootings on the streets of Timişoara or the capital itself.[15]

During a sleepless night, both Nicolae and Elena Ceauşescu could hear the rattle of tank tracks across the square in front of the Central Committee building. The steady rumble of military vehicles suggested that the situation could still be controlled. An overwhelming armed force was being assembled. It would teach the *agents provocateurs* on the streets a lesson, but a powerful military force in the capital would also discourage any attempt by Gorbachev and the Soviet Union to intervene. The demonstration of force, which Ceauşescu had ordered should take place in Timişoara itself at the start of trouble but which Milea had failed to organize, was at last under way.

When they woke – if they slept – Nicolae and Elena Ceauşescu soon realized that fresh troops had not arrived from the provinces. It was equally clear that the army was not using its full available power to suppress discontent. The streets immediately around the Central Committee building had been cleared but the city had not returned to calm. On the contrary, in the working class districts, strikes and protest marches seemed to be getting under way. Milea was the guilty party: he had failed to order the necessary measures again. Whether he did so on his own, or after consulting his deputy is not known. Equally unknown is who persuaded Ceauşescu that Milea had betrayed him. All that is certain is that Stanculescu was appointed to replace the 'traitor'. Milea had been one of Elena's favourites: if he did not commit suicide as the official version proclaimed, he was probably 'executed' by one of his mistress's bodyguards.

The belief that Milea was murdered by the Ceauşescus quickly became universal in Romania. It fitted the psychological image that people had of their rulers. Probably nothing can shake the conviction of Romanians that Milea was done away with in the last moments of the regime (thereby metamorphosing from villainous minion of the tyrants into their innocent victim), but his successor as commander of the Patriotic Guards, Colonel Corneliu Pircalabescu, gave evidence at the trial of the Big Four of Ceauşescu's politburo, which suggests that Milea did in fact kill himself. Milea told Pircalabescu that he could not order the troops to fire on the people; Pircalabescu was outside the Minister's office when a shot was fired at 10.42 a.m.[16] Of course, this evidence fitted the myth of an army innocent of responsibility for civilian deaths that was assiduously promoted by the new government. Whatever the cause of Milea's death, within twenty-four hours Stanculescu, who briefly took his place, was a minister in the new government which proclaimed Milea to be a 'national hero'.

In the meantime the death of Milea was having its effect on the troops. Suddenly, on the streets where tanks and cordons of armed men confronted the crowds, the gun-turrets reversed their aim. One soldier in a dramatic gesture emptied the cartridge of his automatic rifle. The excited people began to chant 'Armata cu noi' ('the Army is with us'), and to sing the song of the Army's football team, Steaua, the rivals of the Securitate's team, Dinamo. At the time, no one knew whether the secret police would follow the soldiers' example. The troops and their tanks, together with the people, began to move on the Central Committee building. Within a few minutes, the inhabitants of the Communist Party head-quarters knew that their fears of yesterday had come true: the crowd was about to break in. Pandemonium erupted inside the Central Committee building when, as if by intuition, the normally stolid apparatchiks and their secretaries and servants realized that the end had come. The collapse of order inside the building resembled an ants' nest which had been kicked over. People rushed through the dimly lit corridors. Now the lights flickered as if the current was about to fail. There was a general movement throughout the offices towards the roof where one of the fleet of presidential helicopters had landed.

In the chaos, neither Nicolae nor Elena Ceauşescu seems to have given much thought to rescuing their colleagues apart from Manea Manescu and Emil Bobu, both long-time political supporters of the couple. Even their accompanying the Ceauşescus into a lift heading for the roof was perhaps fortuitous. In fact, far too many people crammed into the lift along with their boss. It stalled between floors five and six on its way to the top of the building. Whether the lift came to a stop because it was overloaded or because the electricity supply inside the Central Committee building was shut down is not clear. The bodyguards had to force open the doors of the lift to release everyone after several minutes which must have been anxious ones. Even before their departure from the roof by helicopter, the escape of Nicolae and Elena Ceauşescu had already made the flight to Varennes by Louis XVI and Marie Antoinette seem the very model of a dignified retreat. Every vestige of authority and rank, all pretence of loyalty to them, was being stripped away. Soon nothing would be left.[17]

By now the crowds had broken through the doors six floors below and were swarming through the building. Many were diverted in the dim corridors into the myriad offices or ran out onto the balcony facing out across the square from Ceauşescu's office. Others reached the roof as the presidential party was being bundled into the helicopter. Many of the revolutionaries seem to have been more anxious to wave to the people below them than to prevent the escape under way further along the roof-top. There is some suspicion that many of the first people to reach the top of the building were in fact bureaucrats who had scattered pell-mell looking for refuge. They now took the chance to assume the air of ardent revolutionaries cheering the crowds on.

Once inside the helicopter, the situation did not get any clearer. With bulky politburo members breathlessly perched on each other's knees, conditions were not exactly suitable for a calm and rational analysis of the options open to the passengers. As the helicopter slowly climbed into the air above central Bucharest, giving its occupants a last glimpse of the huge building site dominated by the unfinished colossus of the Palace of the Republic, one decision at least was taken. Nicolae Ceauşescu had no intention of trying to flee the country. Although Otopeni International Airport was within easy reach, the helicopter flew northwards past it to land at the presidential residence at Snagov. (Press reports on 22 December claimed that the Lufthansa engineers who serviced the presidential Boeing 707 had bravely refused to prepare it for take-off, but in fact their courage was never put to the test.)

At Snagov, the Ceauşescus' arrival caught the staff off their guard. They had not expected the couple until after Christmas. The refugees were not interested in the obeisance of the housekeepers. The two disappeared inside the palace. When they re-emerged they had bags full of something, but bedclothes pushed on top of the luggage disguised whatever it was. Speculation suggests that as true-born peasants they had hidden cash and valuables in the mattresses of their beds at Snagov. Certainly, the beds were disturbed but, after the capture and trial, nothing was revealed of what they had taken with them. All that was put on display was Elena's handbag and the pathetic pouch containing Nicolae's insulin for his diabetes, and the expensive Western disposable syringes that he used. Whatever they collected at Snagov either got lost in the course of their last few chaotic hours of liberty, or was of no value and not worth displaying after their capture to add to the testimonies of infamy against them.[18]

During the hour or so they spent inside their summer residence at Snagov, the two did not just rifle drawers and rip up mattresses. They also tried to contact loyalists by telephone. When they had flown from the roof of the Central Committee, Nicolae Ceauşescu's intention was to rally loyal forces *around* Bucharest. He seems to have thought that his younger brother, Nicolae Andruţa, might still be in control of the Securitate base at Baneasa. Even if the conspirators had managed to suborn all the troops around the capital, the General-Secretary and his wife could make for Sibiu where his son, Nicu, was the head of the Communist Party. From beyond the Carpathians, it should be possible to organize his own counter-*coup* against the rebels, as he regarded them, in Bucharest. It was only after all his telephone calls were refused, or met with incredulity and insubordination that it must have become clear that the situation was still more serious than he had imagined.[19]

Manescu and Bobu were waiting for them. It was decided that they should remain behind. The helicopter had after all hardly managed to take off with them on board when they had fled from the Central Committee an hour and a half before. Manescu and Bobu would have to shift for themselves. When they parted, Manescu knelt to kiss his master's hands, making the gesture of oriental servility for the last time. In the circumstances, when all his other minions were scurrying to distance themselves from him and to pour abuse on him, it was perhaps the only, and certainly the last, sincere act of homage that Ceauşescu ever received. (At his trial, one month later, Manescu tried to excuse his action by saying that he was grateful to Ceauşescu for having given him the 'lift' in the helicopter.)[20]

Returning to the helicopter, it became clear that the pilot, Lt-Colonel Vasile Malutan, was not willing to fly on. Afterwards he exaggerated his defiance of the fallen dictator, but his insistence that the radar control of the Romanian Airforce would detect any flight and certainly try to co-ordinate an attempt to shoot them down if they set off by air again, nearly persuaded the dignitaries to leave Snagov by land. The pilot suggested, gallantly, that if he flew off, the helicopter would act as a decoy to mislead anybody who was pursuing them. His somewhat contradictory suggestions were not disputed very strongly, but since the helicopter was the only means of continuing their escape they were unwilling to abandon it.

When the helicopter took off again, it may have appeared on the radar screens at the airforce headquarters, but one of the bodyguards had the presence of mind to stop the pilot making verbal contact. If the pilot was involved in a plot to whisk the fallen dictator away from the hands of the crowds and into a place of secure confinement, things went rapidly wrong. Even the commander of the airforce was unwilling to issue clear orders that chaotic day. The helicopter's image was probably permanently on the screens of the Romanian Airforce's radar operators, but whether they kept at their posts in the excitement of the revolution is open to doubt. Events had overtaken everyone involved – from the dazed Ceauşescus, still not comprehending the extent of the collapse of their power, through to the group of old Communist leaders and military men hoping to take advantage of it.

The pilot, Malutan, had clearly recognized the symptoms of universal desertion even before taking off for the second time. His object was to get away from his passengers without risking becoming their last victim. Eventually, he managed to persuade Ceauşescu that the helicopter was in danger of being shot down by the rebels. They were near the airforce base at Boteni, which Malutan seemed to think was the best place to land. Perhaps suspecting his pilot's loyalty or fearing anti-aircraft fire, Ceauşescu decided to land at once so that the party could continue their escape by car. Passing motorists on the road to Titu below stopped to watch the helicopter land. Its four passengers disembarked. One of the bodyguards went onto the road to flag down a passing vehicle.[21]

The disappearance of the helicopter left the group of fugitives with no choice but try to proceed by car. But that little white French-built helicopter was much more than a means of fast get-away. It was one of the most potent symbols of Ceauşescu's power. For almost two decades, he had flown above his people like a god, choosing when and where to descend from the heavens and go among them. How often television had shown pictures of the 'greatest son of the Romanian people' arriving to advise the peasants on their planting or harvesting. How many Romanians had waited obediently for hours for that little white machine to come down to earth so that they could cheer in rhythm the approved slogans. Ceauşescu's loss of his helicopter not only sealed his fate. It stripped him of the last and most peculiar outward sign of authority.[22]

The two bodyguards halted passing cars. Since the only available vehicles were the Dacia 1300 – a Romanian-built version of the Renault 12, modified to make it less comfortable and more inefficient – it was obvious that they could not all travel together. Nicolae and Elena Ceauşescu decided to continue their flight with one of their bodyguards in the first car, while the second guard came after them in the next car. The hijacked drivers have described the combination of hysteria and depression which marked the mood of their passengers. Elena seemed to preserve more composure, perhaps because she still had hopeful illusions of escape or even restoration in her mind. One bodyguard, Marian Rusu, who had served them for years, abandoned the two old people. In a panic at one brief halt, the Ceauşescus drove off without their last loyal follower. Probably, Florian Rat counted himself lucky. Alone, except for their hijacked, Seventh-Day-Adventist driver, Nicolae Petrisor, the fallen pair trundled on into the late afternoon darkness through their erstwhile realm.

Already their capture had been announced several times by radio and television. The threesome heard the poet, Mircea Dinescu, announce Ceauşescu's downfall and proclaim, 'We are free!' It was the moment at which Nicolae Ceauşescu seemed to despair, but Elena, pistol in hand, kept Petrisor driving with the radio switched off. In villages and towns as they passed they could see that other people had heard the news too: they were dancing in the streets. At one point, Ceauşescu had the idea of making for Tirgovişte where he seemed to think that he would find loyalists to help him. Why he thought of going to Vlad Dracul the Impaler's former capital, he never had time to explain, but he was soon to meet the man who probably put the idea into his head there. Petrisor had the impression that neither of his passengers much cared where they were taken so he drove them on into the gathering gloom, desperately hoping he would be able to ditch them before too long.[23]

II

The Making of a Communist

The slave begins by demanding justice and ends by wanting to
wear a crown. He must dominate in his turn.

Albert Camus

The father was a brutal, self-centred, disreputable drunkard.
The mother was pious, self-sacrificing, concerned only for the
well-being of her nine children. Nicolae Ceauşescu's family
background seems to have been constructed out of a psycho-
biographical textbook for tyrants. Was any twentieth century
dictator born to a sober and considerate father? Certainly the
circumstances of Nicolae Ceauşescu's childhood were reminiscent of the upbringing of the greatest tyrants of modern
times – Hitler and Stalin. They were to be the shapers of the
new world which grew out of the chaos and collapse of the old
Europe, into which the third child of Andruţa and Alexandra
Ceauşescu was born on 26 January 1918. If wicked fairies
were present at the christening of the newborn Nicolae Ceauşescu in 1918, they were the spiritual representatives of Fascism and Communism, battling for the possession of his soul.

The Bolsheviks had seized power in Russia three months
earlier. The impact of their revolution was hardly yet felt in
the Balkans, but its effects would shape the whole life of the
new-born child. The span of Nicolae Ceauşescu's three score
years and eleven from 1918 until Christmas Day 1989, will

probably be seen in retrospect as the communist era: he grew up with it and died as Lenin's legacy went through its own death-throes. But in the winter of 1918, the villages of the Oltenian plain to the south of the Carpathians were more affected by war and enemy occupation: the presence and demands of German troops were the main intrusions of the outside world into peasant life. Romania had entered the First World War on the side of the Allies and had paid a bitter price. By the winter of 1917–18, most of the country had been occupied by the Germans and their Austro-Hungarian allies. Although the Romanian army's generals were perhaps less distinguished than their contemporaries and it possessed a few comic-opera aspects – such as the restriction of the use of make-up to the officer corps – the ordinary soldiers earned a reputation for stubborn resistance and with it the respect of their German enemies.[1] Andruţa Ceauşescu was an exception to this honourable rule, as might have been expected. According to village myth in Scorniceşti, he deserted the army and presumably fathered Nicolae while AWOL.[2]

When the new Communist rulers of Russia made peace with Germany at Brest-Litovsk in March 1918, the Romanian government was forced to abandon its commitment to the Western Allies and made peace with Germany in May. By the Treaty of Bucharest, Romania gave up control of its greatest single asset in the modern world, its oil-fields (the largest in Europe), but the dramatic reversal of the fortunes of war in the autumn of the same year turned the treaty into a dead-letter. With the collapse of Germany's ally Austria-Hungary, Romanian troops were able to drive forward even to Budapest, where they helped to suppress the would-be Soviet regime of Bela Kun. For its perseverance in the Allied cause Romania received the formerly Hungarian provinces of Transylvania and the Banat with their Romanian majorities, plus the Bukovina, but each with its own patchwork of non-Romanian minorities.[3] At the same time, the Russian Civil

War meant that the largely Romanian-speaking province of Bessarabia could be reunited with the rest of Romania. For the first time in modern history, all the Romanians lived in a single state. It was, however, a far from happy time: famine threatened in the winter of 1918–19 and fuel was short. The peasants in the Old Kingdom demanded, 'Give us food. Give us wood.'[4]

Fear of a peasant revolt was not far from the minds of the Romanian government. The example of Bolshevik Russia was near at hand and at the end of 1917 agitators had been sent by the Soviet Communists into the area around Iaşi still controlled by the Romanians after their defeats at the hands of the Germans. Unease at the progress of defeatist propaganda among the ranks of the Romanian peasant-soldiers promoted by Soviet Russia compounded the government's deep-seated fear of rural unrest.

In 1907, the last great peasant revolt in European history had swept through Romania. It was a savage Jacquerie-like nightmare from the Middle Ages. Both sides had behaved brutally. The peasants of Wallachia and Moldavia were hungry for land, not least because of the rapid growth of the population. In fact, the higher the birthrate in a district, the more likely it was to rebel.[5] In addition to the pressure of ever more mouths to feed, the peasants felt that changes in the way their landlords ran their estates meant they were more exploited than before. The role of new land agents and new owners who bought out traditional landlords was particularly resented. Peasants who could not pay their rents were sometimes even deprived of their clothes.

A powerful current of anti-Semitism ran through the rebellion. Just as the liberal regime in Romania encouraged the free market in everything, so it released Jews in particular from the legal restrictions upon them. As elsewhere in Europe, legal emancipation did not mean the end of prejudice against Jews. Often the very people who denounced Jews as urban creatures when they were prevented from buying land, now attacked them as parasites moving into agriculture as profiteers. Mutual antagonism spurred both sides to unreasonable actions. When peasants in arrears with their rent were forced to pay up with their own clothes if necessary, their violent outbursts were not entirely inexplicable – though the ritual slaughter of landlords' favourite horses or pets added a macabre and sinister quality to their indignation.

Pre-war Romania was undoubtedly the scene of spectacular social and economic change, but even the rapid pace of development could not match the growing expectations of the population and their feeling that they were losing out through the process of modernization. The fact that the gainers were often from the religious and ethnic minorities sharpened the tensions. As a reaction to centuries of oppression and exploitation, the Romanian Orthodox Church had tended to encourage a special sense of Romanian-ness, the unique value of being Romanian. The fact that national independence did not immediately produce prosperity for all, but in practice only for a few (albeit a growing minority) was compounded by the fact that many of those few were the traditionally despised religious deviants, the Jews. The new oil-wealth, so vital to the German war-effort in 1918 (and in the Second World War) was largely in the hands of foreigners. Many Romanians resented the dominance of their economy by Westerners and overlooked the investment which they made in local industries and the stimulus which was given to development by alien capitalists.

Resentment of foreign beneficiaries of economic development was a key part of the appeal of the radical critics of Romanian society after 1918: those critics of the new market economy could be found on both left and right of the political spectrum. They may have hated each other, but their common attacks on capitalism helped to undermine the stability of post-war Romania, even before the Great Depression dealt a body-blow to agriculture as well as trade and industry after 1929.[6]

Romanian peasant farmers were already in difficulties before 1929. King Ferdinand's land reform after 1918 was a major achievement, but inadequate to satisfy the land-hunger of the rapidly growing rural population. By the mid-1920s, agricultural prices throughout the world were in decline, which made life still harder for the predominantly rural economies of Eastern Europe. A feckless peasant like Andruţa Ceauşescu was not suited to meeting the economic challenges of his times. Resort to the bottle seems to have been his chief response. Neither poverty nor *tuica* inhibited Andruţa's fathering of children. Like peasants the world over, Andruţa would have seen sons as his insurance policy for the future. They would help him work his land – perhaps even make it unnecessary for him to work at all – and then provide for his security in his old age. Middle-class urban reformers have always found it difficult to come to terms with why poverty-stricken peasants breed ever more mouths to feed. Instinct taught the ignorant peasant that a house with few children could lose everything if disease carried off the heirs, as it easily might: a father with one son had no guarantee of protection in old age or infirmity.

By contrast with her husband, though like a model for the mothers of dictators, Alexandra Ceauşescu was a religious, conscientious, family woman, who always put herself last. Unlike other mothers of famous communists, neither history nor legend has attributed to her any insight into the nature of her son's ambition, nor the consequences of his fulfilling it. Stalin's mother Ekaterina Dzhugashvili, lived long enough to regret that her Iosif did not become a priest after all. Alexandra Ceauşescu seems not to have comprehended the enormity of the changes to everyone's life in Romania, not only her own, which young Nicolae's rise to power involved. Even popular wit, which was never short of apocryphal stories, did not fasten any good jokes on her name. Leonid Brezhnev's mother did better with a story that could equally have been laid at Alexandra's door: According to legend, the successful Leonid Ilych showed the elderly Mrs Brezhnev the fruits of his office as General-Secretary of the Soviet Communist Party, first of all, the Kremlin itself, followed by his palatial residence outside Moscow and another dacha in the Caucasus and then one on the Black Sea. 'What do you think, mother?' Brezhnev asks. 'Well, Leonid,' she replies, 'it's all very fine, but what if the Reds come back?'

Despite her own silence in the historical record, at times, Alexandra's life sounds uncannily like Ekaterina Dzhugashvili's in Georgia a generation earlier: 'She worked in the house at her sewing machine, took in washing, and did domestic work in other households in order to supplement the family income, much of it evidently sacrificed to Vissarion's drinking habit.' But the two pious mothers of future tyrants were fundamentally different on one point: Stalin's mother upbraided her drunken husband in the presence of her son and fought back against his blows. (The comparison with the Ceauşescu family also does not hold fully on another – ironic – point: Ekaterina would not let her husband make the young Iosif into a shoemaker.)[7]

Andruţa Ceauşescu inherited some land around the hamlet of Tatarai on the edge of the village of Scorniceşti, but he was on the downward spiral of drinking, borrowing and quarrelling with the neighbours. However much his boys stuck by him, it is difficult to believe that they did not feel the humiliation of his decline. They may have resented the other villagers scoffing at their father – who wouldn't? – but the shadow of his failings was also upon them. When he grew up, unlike many of his contemporaries, not least the other high-ranking apparatchiks of the Communist Party, Nicolae Ceauşescu was remarkably self-controlled in his drinking of alcohol until his development of diabetes brought an end to his consumption of alcohol altogether.

It is easy to scoff at the old hagiographic accounts of the young Nicolae's childhood and schooldays in which he was always the born leader. The individual episodes in the official version may be false, but certain elements ring true. No doubt the story of how the older children were afraid to go into the woods as shepherds, only to be assured by the little Nicolae that they would be safe with him, is too prophetic, but in all probability, the young boy was able to assert an unusual authority over his older brothers.[8] They were revealed by the events of December 1989 to be complete nullities without his charismatic authority. Even their direct subordinates (in fact, precisely those in constant contact with Nicolae Andruţa or Ilie) seem to have been without any respect for them. When the people's fear of Nicolae Ceauşescu disappeared, so did any subordination to his siblings.

The officially sponsored biographies of Nicolae Ceauşescu, which appeared in Western countries as well as in Romania once he was firmly in power, often relate absurd 'memories' of his childhood and youth allegedly freely given by his surviving contemporaries. Not all these hagiographies could, however, avoid giving revealing insights into the family life of the Ceauşescus. For instance, Heinz Siegert quoted reports that Alexandra would 'often' insist: 'My children must learn so that others won't make fun of them.' This suggests that she was sensitive both to her husband's reputation and to her children's speech defects and poor grammar. Although she herself was illiterate, Alexandra made sure that the children went to school regularly. She knew that they would not spend many years there. They had to learn while they could. Nicolae left school at eleven. The family could no longer afford his upkeep. Instead, his labour was needed to help with its maintenance.

The child's playing and fantasy-life were normal. He admired stories about medieval Romanian princes, particularly Michael the Brave who had defeated the Turks. Later his official biographers claimed the boy knew patriotic poems and legends by heart. Perhaps this is true, after all even in his old age Stalin could recite the Rustaveli's Georgian epic, *Knight in the Panther's Skin*[9], but the *Vozhd* never went so far in his adult years as to recreate his schoolboy fantasies. Shortly after becoming General-Secretary, Ceauşescu revived the games of his childhood in a series of pageants celebrating the heroes of the Romanian past, with himself dressed up in the title role.

The young Nicolae, who identified himself with the heroes of Romania's struggle against centuries of Ottoman oppression, must have suffered on account of the dubious origins of his family's surname. His grandfather, Andrei, still bore the name 'Ceauşu', which suggests that his forebears, possibly even Andrei's father, were minor cogs in the administration of the Ottoman Empire. A *ceauşu* could be a court official of lowly rank, but in their case it was more likely that the name came from the common function of the *ceauşu* to act as an overseer. In fact, there is a local story that Andrei Ceauşu's father was precisely that. It is said that he passed through the area of Scorniceşti in the 1820s and set up home there. Whether the dynasty was founded by a servant of the Muslim rulers of the Christian Balkans or not, the Turkish root of the name was instantly recognizable to inhabitants of the former Ottoman territories. (In the 1970s, when Stalin's most faithful disciple, the Albanian Enver Hoxha, wanted to denounce his Romanian counterpart for toadying to the US imperialists or the Soviet 'revisionists', he would contemptuously accuse the *chaush* of being a typical Romanian pimp going to Washington, Moscow or Peking to pander to the *bashchaush*, his Ottoman boss.)[10] It must have been difficult at times for a patriotic small boy who liked to play 'Romanians versus Turks' to have such a name.

By the end of the 1920s, Andruţa Ceauşescu was having ever more difficulties making ends meet. In practice, this meant that his wife had to take in ever more washing to earn what she could to keep the family's finances afloat. With so many mouths to feed, the answer for the Ceauşescu family, like so many others in Romania, was to begin the despatch of one child after another to find work in the big city and to learn to shift for itself. By the time Nicolae was ten, his elder sister, Maria, and brother, Marin, had already made their way to Bucharest. He followed them, sent as an apprentice to a shoemaker in the Calea Victoriei. This was not a bad site for a shop and suggests that the Ceauşescus had better connections than many really destitute peasant families, whose offspring sank without trace into the squalor and vice of the capital's seedier districts.

Gheorghe Klein remembers meeting the fourteen-year-old Ceauşescu outside Bucharest's main railway station, the Gara de Nord. He was selling newspapers, like Klein. The boys talked; Ceauşescu with his noticeable stammer. He told Klein that he came from Oltenia and then to the boy's surprise insisted, 'I am a communist'. Klein had no idea what a communist was, and suspected that his new acquaintance was little better informed, but the vehemence of Ceauşescu's assertion made a deep impression on him. By the early thirties, Marin Ceauşescu seems to have been on the fringes of the Communist Party and probably introduced Nicolae to it. After he came to power, Nicolae found it useful to backdate his membership of the Party and usurped his older brother's record for that purpose.[11]

Romania under Carol II was in some ways like a comic-opera prefiguring of the Orwellian nightmare that was to come to full fruition fifty years later. Unlike Ceauşescu, the king lacked the energy to push through some of his more grandiose plans. Half a century before the laying of the foundation stone of the enormous Palace of the People, Carol II's government toyed with the idea of building a new administrative centre for Bucharest in the very quarter which Ceauşescu demolished in the early 1980s. Conscious of the threat of a *coup d'état*, the king had several tunnels constructed beneath the Royal Palace and other key installations like the Ministry of the Interior, to enable him to escape from an uprising or to bring in loyal troops to surprise mutineers or rebellious subjects. These tunnels did Carol II little good in 1940 when he was forced to abdicate after conceding Bessarabia to Stalin and a large portion of Transylvania to Hungary; but they survived unknown to the pòpulation of Bucharest until revealed as the labyrinthine lair of the Securitate's last defenders of Ceauşescu. The great square in front of the Royal Palace, stretching up to the Athénée Palace Hotel and across to the University Library and the brand-new Ministry of the Interior (the future Central Committee building), and the scene of the most dramatic moments of the Romanian revolution, was also the work of Carol II. One critic remarked that the square looked as if it had been designed as the stage-set for a *coup d'état*.

The Romanian government in the 1930s had a highly developed network of informers serving its secret police, the *Siguranţa*. Under the Communists, carefully edited extracts from police reports and informers' tales were published to glorify the underground activities of the few early communist agitators like Nicolae Ceauşescu during the clandestine years. All sorts of people served as informers, sometimes whole professions, like prostitutes and hotel porters, were more or less in the service of the *Siguranţa*. In 1936, the Romanian guild of chimney-sweeps emphasized their value to the state when they demanded that members of the suspect national minorities (Jews, Hungarians, etc.) should not be permitted to practise a trade whose members 'can see everything, hear everything and go freely anywhere'.[12]

Of course, the average person was unaffected by the security concerns of the government. They had other more pressing concerns. Despite the Great Depression, Bucharest remained the 'wickedest city in the world', with Carol II the most notorious monarch in Europe.[13] Economic hardship drew thousands of peasants from the land to the capital every year. Behind the scenes of the glittering social life of Bucharest which drew Western visitors in search of adventures and thrills, the tenements of the city filled up with discontented young people who had found that the capital's streets were not paved with gold. Petty crime and the extremist politics of resentment flourished in this atmosphere – and not only in Romania.

There is an old, and certainly apocryphal story about how Nicolae Ceauşescu first came into contact with both communism and King Carol's police. It is said, quite plausibly, that the communist underground used the main railway station, the Gara de Nord, as a dropping-off point for propaganda brought into the capital from a clandestine press. A communist activist would wait at a specific place inside the large station building, watching the spot where the next consignment of illegal pamphlets or posters would be placed for collection. The courier would deliver his contraband to the spot and pass on without making direct contact with the collector in case one or other was already under observation by the *Siguranţa*. According to the story, one evening in the early 1930s, an out-of-work, hungry but alert teenager noticed a traveller put down a suitcase on the floor of the ticket hall and disappear. The lad, thinking that the luggage might contain something of value which he could sell, or perhaps just for the sake of taking the case to pawn it, went over and grabbed it. He was immediately seized by plain-clothes policemen who had been tipped off by an informer about the delivery. Thus, it was long whispered in Romania, had Nicolae Ceauşescu, the petty thief, become a hero of the working class, since naturally the Party played up his youth in order to make him a sympathetic victim of the quasi-fascist state.

Unfortunately, as with all the best stories, there is no evidence to corroborate this legend, but it might contain a grain of truth since he himself came to act as just such a courier. In any case, it is highly unlikely that even in his early teens Nicolae Ceauşescu regarded the property of the bourgeoisie as sacrosanct. Petty theft was probably one way he eked out his living, just as selling newspapers was another source of income. Certainly, when he first came to the attention of the courts, he was a skinny lad, healthy but not well-fed, who had got into fights.

By the time he was sixteen, Ceauşescu had become involved with the Romanian Anti-Fascist and Anti-War Committee. Like similar bodies elsewhere in Europe, the Romanian Anti-Fascist Committee was in effect a front for the Communist Party, although that may not have been known to many

29

of its members. One of Ceauşescu's future rivals, Gheorghe Apostol, was among the chief organizers of the Committee. The teenage Ceauşescu was one of its couriers. At the turn of 1935–36, he was arrested by King Carol's police when he was found to be in possession of a pamphlet, *Against War and Fascism*. (Perhaps this was the basis for the apocryphal story about the origin of Ceauşescu's involvement with the Communist Party.) He was interrogated by the *Siguranţa* in Tirgovişte and then sent to await trial in the Transylvanian town of Braşov.

In May 1936, Ceauşescu went on trial there. He made an impression on his judges, confirmed the *Siguranţa's* view of him, but also was noted by several of the journalists present as a youth of striking character and fire. He was sentenced to an extra six months for contempt of court because of his insubordinate behaviour. His original sentence of two years of imprisonment was reduced to a matter of months plus a restriction for a year after release to his home village, Scorniceşti. He was sent to the prison at Doftana. There he was supposed to have met not only fellow communists, but even peasant rebels still imprisoned almost thirty years after the great revolt of 1907. In retrospect, the communists may have romanticized their experiences in Doftana and the other prisons of Carol II's Romania. Conditions were certainly severe but in comparison with the hard labour imposed by the former inmates of Doftana on their opponents after 1948, they were nonetheless well within the bounds of the survivable.

Apostol and others recall beatings by the guards in Doftana. Ceauşescu's hagiographers claim that he was fearless about facing the terrors of cell 'H'. His defeated rival, Apostol, says the youth was a coward, who could not prove his claims to have been beaten with any bodily evidence. Perhaps Ceauşescu persuaded the guards to refrain from brutalizing him by pleading or by offers to act as an informer as Apostol suggests. Or perhaps the surviving witness is taking his long-hoarded revenge on the reputation of his nemesis. If

Ceauşescu had wanted to take the easy way out of his difficulties, there were many opportunities then and later. Bad men are not necessarily cowards. If Ceauşescu had merely been ambitious, he might have attached himself to another party which offered more prospects and fewer dangers.[14]

Many nationalistic and rootless young men were attracted to the Iron Guard at this time. Founded by the would-be Romanian messiah, Corneliu Zelea Codreanu (whose parentage was German-Ukrainian, though his father was his model as a Romanian ultra-nationalist), the Iron Guard attracted the support of many more Romanians, particularly young men, than its rival on the ultra-left, the Communist Party. Although in its early days the Iron Guard was able to commit violent, and even murderous, acts without severe punishment, by the time the young Nicolae Ceauşescu was active in street-politics in Bucharest, the Iron Guard's combination of growing popularity and brutal, frequently sadistic violence was making the authorities look less favourably on it. By the outbreak of the Second World War, about 500 legionnaires (as Codreanu's supporters were called) had been killed, as had their *Conducator* – 'shot attempting to escape' from police custody.[15]

By the late 1930s, there were supposed to be about 34,000 local groups or 'nests' of Iron Guardists, amounting to about 350,000 supporters. Their rhetoric stirred up resentment against foreign influences over Romania and against the resident minorities, particularly the Jews. Xenophobia was a natural product of Romania's long history of occupation and exploitation. Even Romania's greatest poet, Mihai Eminescu had given voice to it in his poem 'Doina': 'If any shall cherish the stranger may the dogs eat his heart, may the weeds destroy his house; and may his kin perish in shame.' What Codreanu and his followers did was to carry over, and intensify, the traditional Romanian resentment of alien domination into the new, united state established after 1918, in which the Romanians were the great majority. To Codreanu, one of the most virulent anti-Semites in Romania (if not Europe), the mere existence of minorities was an offence against his 'super-sensitivities' – he even claimed to be able to sniff out Jews. His creed required total assimilation to his model of mystical Romanian peasant-traditions, now challenged by the modern world rather than threatened by foreign overlords.[16]

Of course, like the great majority of Romanians, Ceauşescu did not join the Iron Guard but, unlike that silent majority, he went instead into the politics of resentment marketed by the left. It is difficult to avoid the suspicion, however, that the relentless rhetoric of the Iron Guard did not influence him (and Elena) to a degree. Perhaps it seeped into them unconsciously but, fifty years later, much of the propaganda put out to glorify Ceauşescu and the new Romania recalled the Iron Guard's cult of Romania's specialness and its *Conducator* Codreanu. Even before Ceauşescu was in a position to give free rein to his own definition of Marxism-Leninism and to include virulent nationalism as one of its tenets, he clearly possessed some ability to appeal to the nationalist sentiments of people otherwise unsympathetic to his cause.

By joining the Communist Party, Ceauşescu was associating with the most un-Romanian body of men, which again seems strange in retrospect, given the cult of the unique and undefiled Romanian race he was later to sponsor. With the exception of Dej and Apostol, most of the other leading Communists in Romania were from non-Romanian stock. The Communist Party was the party of disgruntled minorities *par excellence*: it was disproportionately composed of Hungarians, Germans, Ukrainians, and Jews. Just as Jews and the other persecuted minorities of Imperial Russia had very often formed the backbone of the revolutionary groups there before 1917, so in Romania the minorities were much more prone to support communism than their Romanian fellow-citizens. As, at best, second-class citizens, the minorities had less to lose from upheaval than others. Of course, despite their discontent, out of the total number of Jews, Hungarians

and Germans only a few joined the Party, but their dispro-
portionate prominence in its ranks encouraged the counter-
attacks of the government and the openly fascist right that
the Communist Party was an 'un-Romanian', indeed 'anti-
Romanian', conspiracy. The leaders of the Party recognized
the need to extend their support among the ethnic Romanian
population and welcomed any pure Romanian recruit with
open arms. Nicolae Ceauşescu was a godsend to them.[17]

In the autumn of 1940, Romania experienced a profound
political crisis. King Carol had tried to buttress his quasi-
dictatorial regime not only by imitating some of the pomp
of his fascist contemporaries, and even some of their methods,
but also by shifting Romanian foreign policy more in line
with the Rome-Berlin Axis and away from Romania's French
alliance. Unfortunately, King Carol's new friends were no
more inclined to protect Romania's interests than the French
and British appeasers. At the end of June 1940, Stalin
(Hitler's *de facto* ally at that time) demanded that Romania
cede Bessarabia to the Soviet Union. Germany had just
humiliated France, and Romania had nowhere to turn for
help. Stalin got what he wanted. The Hungarians were not
slow in learning the lesson. Admiral Horthy demanded the
return of Transylvania. Hitler and Mussolini agreed to
mediate in the dispute: their foreign ministers, Ribbentrop
and Ciano (Mussolini's son-in-law), summoned the Hungarians and the Romanians to Vienna where on 30 August
1940, they proceeded to award Northern Transylvania to
Hungary. The humiliation of King Carol and of Romania
was complete.

. King Carol was forced to abdicate in favour of his
seventeen-year-old son, Michael. He departed the country
unregretted, accompanied by his mistress, Madame Lupescu
(whose unpopularity was increased by the fact that she was
Jewish), and a baggage train containing, it was rumoured,
much of the national treasury. A military regime under Marshal Ion Antonescu took power. Somewhat unfairly, Anton-

escu blamed what communists called the 'bourgeois democratic', and what the legionnaires called 'cosmopolitan', politicians for the national humiliation. They were retired or put behind bars. The Marshal favoured military men or right-wing nationalists, and even flirted with Hora Simia, Codreanu's successor as leader of the Iron Guard. Eventually, in January 1941, Antonescu decided to crush his Iron Guard allies. They were bidding for complete power, trusting that their virulent anti-Semitism and purer form of Fascism would make them more acceptable to the Germans than the more conservative Antonescu. In fact, Hitler trusted Antonescu and gave military support to the Romanian Army's liquidation of the legionnaires. (Of course, Hitler's confidence in Antonescu was not total – which future events showed was unjust – and he kept Hora Simia and other Iron Guard leaders in Germany as insurance against any disloyalty by the Marshal. Fascist politics were often as convoluted and dishonest as Balkan politics were supposed to be.)

Even before the decisive clash in 1941, it was clear that the legionnaires were dissatisfied with their place in the new order. They hoped to force their way into full control, but at the very least to get rid of their political opponents whom Antonescu had treated too mildly. In November 1940, some of the Iron Guard went on the rampage. Some murdered and plundered Jews, while others broke into the Jilava prison, where Ceauşescu and other Communists were held along with bourgeois critics of the new dictatorship.[18]

According to Hamelet's biography, the Communist prisoners were saved from the butchery inflicted on Antonescu's less radical opponents by Ceauşescu's tactic of making friends with the guards and his 'awakening in them of the sentiment of national dignity and pride'. The guards protected the Communist wing of the prison from the ferocity of the Iron Guard. Whether the prison warders had a feeling of national humiliation after the Vienna Award which Ceauşescu had been able to play on, is something now impossible to discover.[19] Did he share it? Almost certainly he did: in the final crisis of his life, he returned to the iniquity of the border revisions resulting from the Nazi-Soviet Pact as one of his last rallying cries to the Romanian people. If Ceauşescu had publicly decried the loss of territory to Hungary and the USSR, even if only within the prison walls, it was an early sign of his break with the party line directed from Moscow. Like Communists throughout the world, the few Romanian comrades had dutifully fallen in line with Stalin's anti-Western policy after 23 August 1939. They had sung the praises of the Nazi-Soviet Pact and decried the 'imperialists' in London, Paris, and Bucharest who denounced the cynical collusion between Hitler and Stalin. Since that collusion involved German acceptance of Soviet annexations of Romanian territory (Bessarabia), the Romanian communists' approval of the Pact made them less popular than ever inside Romania.[20]

Perhaps Ceauşescu was protected by the guards in Jilava because he possessed a charismatic personality which later vanished, but which then, combined with a patriotic message, turned their stone-hearts to kindness. However, it is just as likely that Ceauşescu was a prison 'trusty', or even informer, as has been alleged. To understand the ambiguity and deviousness inherent in the position of Communist prisoners of fascist regimes in this period, a look at the example of Erich Honecker, Ceauşescu's East German ally, may be instructive.

Honecker survived ten years in Hitler's prisons. The rigours of life under the control of the SS were infinitely more destructive than anything that Antonescu contrived. Yet a communist like Honecker, and he was not the only one, could survive a decade, when the average life expectancy of Himmler's charges was well below six months. Magdeburg Prison was not Auschwitz, but even so, it was not surprising that after the fall of the East German regime, documents came to light indicating that Honecker had given information to the Gestapo after his arrest and had been regarded as a 'trusty' by prison officials.

It is easy to understand that the young man gave way to

the fear and pain that the Gestapo could inflict, but that is not the whole explanation. A man like Honecker (or Ceauşescu) was drenched in Marxist-Leninist propaganda. Serving the cause of the revolution was the definition of morality and also of heroism. Futile self-sacrifice was discouraged by the Party. What mattered was living to fight another day, always for the cause. If survival depended on betraying others, non-Communists, albeit anti-Nazis, then so be it. In any case, such people would be a threat to the Communists once Fascism was defeated. Better to let them die heroes at the hands of Hitler than to have to kill them oneself as miserable class enemies in the future. The success of Stalin's disciples cannot be understood if the source of their combination of complete self-righteousness and total cynicism is not understood. Men like Ceauşescu took deceit on behalf of their cause as not only necessary, but as the only type of virtue.[21]

In inter-war Romania, the combination of social and economic upheavals and rapid change from the old ways of life combined to produce widespread alienation and yearnings for both a better future and nostalgia for a better past. Although the extremists of right and left tried to capitalize on them, in practice much of the emotional dislocation produced by change expressed itself in religious forms. The biggest popular phenomenon of the pre-war period was not political but an almost medieval millenarian outburst: in 1935, the shepherd, Petrache Lupu, like countless simple religious men through the generations all over Europe, had a vision, near the village of Maglavit. An 'old man with a white beard' told him, 'Go and preach love and peace to your sinful countrymen.' Huge crowds came to hear the prophet – which was more than they did for the preachers of political extremism – but even so, few paid any attention (as is usually the case). Most Romanians may not have been tempted by either old-time peasant revivalism or by the new pseudo-religious faiths offered by the Iron Guard or the Communists, but soon they would not be asked to make a choice.[22] Ceauşescu rejected religious renewal, but his faith in communism had almost mystical overtones.

When he emerged from the Doftana prison, Andruţa asked his son why he had chosen to risk his liberty. Nicolae replied (according to his cousin, Florea): 'I went to jail so we can work the land with heavy machinery and we can raise production.'[23] This has the ring of grim, banal authenticity. It was the point of view he stuck to for the rest of his life. Although hardly a man yet, the young Ceauşescu had already formed in his mind a set of ideas about what a future communist society would be like: they were unshakeably crude and simplistic, and all the more powerful for that. Unlike liberal democratic politicians, who change their ideas to suit their audience, the ideologically driven tyrant wants to change people to fit them into his vision of the world. What the young Hitler, as an almost down-and-out in pre-1914 Vienna and Munich, called the 'granite foundations' of his outlook were fully formed at an early age. Ceauşescu's dogmatic formulae were also fixed even before the Second World War.

What Ceauşescu had yet to learn was how to put them into practice. It was Romania's quasi-Fascist regime which was to give him the opportunity to learn all about Lenin's unrivalled methods for taking power and keeping it. Antonescu's government made the same mistake as countless others in dealing with militant subversives. Like the British government's disastrous policy of concentrating IRA prisoners in Ulster, Antonescu's decision to lock up the Romanian Communists together merely provided the Party's leaders with the opportunity to indoctrinate their less well-trained followers at leisure and to plan the Party's future strategy. In the mid-sixties, the new rule book of the Communist Party introduced by Ceauşescu gloated that the 'prisons and camps in which communists were imprisoned were transformed into genuine Marxist-Leninist universities'.[24]

Throughout his life, Ceauşescu looked back on his time in

the Doftana and at Tîrgu Jiu as a key episode. It was during his long periods in prison that he met and became the protégé of Gheorghe Gheorghiu-Dej. Like the young Ceauşescu, and unlike most of the other leading communists of the day, Dej was from a poor Romanian-speaking family. He had worked with his hands and was a self-taught Marxist. In 1933, his moment of glory came when he organized a strike at the Griviţa railway works in Bucharest. The violence accompanying the breaking of the strike secured Dej's revolutionary reputation.

Ceauşescu became Dej's reliable aide during the war years and it seems likely that Dej regarded the younger man as a substitute son. Certainly, he fostered his career after the war. Ceauşescu did not repay Dej's patronage with kindness to his memory after his death in 1965, but Dej was not a sentimentalist and would have recognized in his protégé's dismantling of his reputation an unwelcome but necessary political step: Ceauşescu should be seen to rule in his own right. According to his acquaintances, Ceauşescu gradually transformed the picture of his relationship with Dej in the prison years and afterwards in power: at first, he had been the loyal disciple of Gheorghiu-Dej; later, after Dej's death, Ceauşescu became – in his own eyes and anecdotes at any rate – the dominant figure.

Ceauşescu may have shown scant loyalty to the memory of his most important patron, but he treated his fellow prisoners no better. The chief rivals to Ceauşescu's succession to Dej in 1965 were also incarcerated with him: Chivu Stoica, Gheorghe Apostol, and Alexandru Draghici. They all fell from grace soon after the death of their mentor, leaving no one to share the glory of the anti-Fascist struggle with Ceauşescu. The experience of prison life may have strengthened their loyalty to the Party, it certainly did not encourage solidarity with each other. During the long years of incarceration, these men developed the rivalries and animosities out of which so much of Romanian history from 1944 until 1989 was made.[25]

Gheorghe Apostol is the only one of the major prisoners to have survived the 'Epocha Ceauşescu'. His memories of Ceauşescu as a coward and informer are naturally coloured by his future disappointments and humiliations at the hands of the younger man, for whose talents and character he never possessed a high regard. But Apostol's testimony about Ceauşescu's personality is supported by other prisoners who never rose to challenge him for supreme power. The young Communist, Pavel Câmpeanu, for instance, shared a cell with Ceauşescu in the camp at Caransebeş. They passed the time playing chess with homemade figures. Despite spending months together, Câmpeanu learnt next to nothing about his fellow prisoner's background or life to date. The only emotions which Nicolae Ceauşescu readily revealed were bitter frustration when he lost a game of chess and a more generalized resentment against the world inside and outside the camp.

The self-contained nature of Ceauşescu's character and his indifference to others, even those close to him through shared personal or political experiences, was brought home to Câmpeanu a few years after the war was over. By now Ceauşescu was one of the high-flyers in the new Communist order and Câmpeanu was ordered to report to him with regard to some matter of no great consequence. Despite many months in the same cell, Ceauşescu did not greet him with any sign of particular recognition, let alone ask after him or about what had happened to him in the intervening period. He just got straight down to business.[26]

Ceauşescu's impersonality struck many of his contemporaries from this period of clandestine activity. In retrospect, it was seen as a fatal flaw in his character. At the time, it was what marked him out as one of the new type of Stalinist activists who had no personal feelings and who did not allow sentiment to get in the way of fulfilling his duty to the cause. The only hint of normal youthful emotions came in the spring of 1939, when Ceauşescu met the only woman who seems to have attracted him.

*

Elena Petrescu was born in an inn. Her father was the publican of 'La Briceag' – literally, 'The Penknife'. It was a simple three-room establishment, which doubled as bar and home. Unlike her husband, Elena never wanted to glorify her birthplace. The fate of Scorniceşti did not befall the village of Petreşti: it was not transformed into an agro-industrial centre worthy of its famous offspring. On the contrary, it was left to rot. The villagers were convinced that Elena intended to have it destroyed as part of the systemization. No trace would remain of her rural roots. Unlike her husband's birthplace, her own childhood house remained pretty much unchanged. It did not become a museum, but nor was it demolished. Instead her mother lived on in it for much of the year, guarded at the door by the militia, who discouraged people from disturbing her solitary games of draughts. She spent her time alone with her West-German television set and a bottle of imported brandy. Probably Elena intended to wipe the place off the face of the earth after her mother's death, but she did not live to see the day.[27]

The future 'world-ranking scientist and academician' attended the one-class village school along with all the other children within four years of her age. Today her contemporaries remember Elena Petrescu as a solitary and shy child, who kept herself to herself. They recall the difficulties she had with spelling even her name on the slates used for writing exercises. In retrospect, their bitter criticisms of her and their contempt for her later scholarly pretensions are understandable. The school records for 1929 survive and seem to confirm the memories of the elderly women who never left the village. Each subject was marked out of ten: music 6/10, writing 5/10, memory 5/10, composition 4/10, religion 4/10, history 4/10, geography 4/10. Her best subject was handicraft: 7/10. She had to remain behind and retake the class.[28]

Perhaps her poor performance at school was not entirely due to the stupidity which all of her contemporaries insist was all too evident at an early age. On market days, Elena had to help out by selling sunflower seeds and so she missed school. Her future husband also failed to complete his statutory schooling. They were certainly not alone – probably the great majority of their contemporaries failed to achieve much at school. Long before communism made the disparity between official rules and regulations and the realities of life in Romania almost complete, the limitations of a peasant society made the liberal pieties enshrined in the laws passed in Bucharest irrelevant. It is their future aspirations to erudition which make the actual school records of Nicolae and Elena Ceauşescu so revealing.

The other children nicknamed Elena, 'the little bird'. Her elderly contemporaries disagree about the origin of the name: perhaps it came from her ungainly way of walking, throwing the weight from one hip to the other, or perhaps because she used to raid birds' nests for their eggs – a useful supplement to the family diet. Elena retained her manner of walking, despite her affectation of regal refinements in later life. The more cosmopolitan wives of her husband's later colleagues and subordinates in Bucharest commented on it behind her back and away from prying ears.

Unlike other girls in the village, the young Elena Petrescu was not a church-goer. Her family lived on the margins of village society. On the one hand, their inn made them slightly better off than most of their neighbours, but it was also the source of their near ostracism. Inn-keepers were tainted by their trade's poor reputation. Parents kept their children away from the publican's daughter. Since the Petrescus were not a family of church-goers, their daughter was not invited to dance with the other girls on Sundays either. She grew up lonely and isolated from her peers at least until she moved to the big city to earn her living like countless other girls of her generation.

According to the Party legend Elena met Nicolae for the first time at a May Day rally in 1939. In almost every museum in Communist Romania before December 1989, a widely displayed photograph apparently showed them in the same crowd at the anti-war and anti-fascist demonstration held in

Bucharest on 1 May 1939. Unfortunately, the picture is an obvious forgery: the two portraits of Nicolae and Elena looking seraphic have clearly been superimposed on the bodies of other, unhistoric demonstrators. What is more peculiar still about this photograph is that several of their fellow demonstrators appear to be making fascist salutes with their right arms outstretched. This incongruous bringing together of two intrepid underground communists and several fascists suggest that the picture editors in communist Romania finding that there were no pictures of the Communist May Day rally at all, let alone photographs of Nicolae and Elena together at it, decided to make the best of a bad job by utilizing a picture of an enthusiastic but now forgotten demonstration by the fascist Iron Guard from about the same time, or of King Carol's officially sponsored rally.

Elena's brother, Gheorghe Petrescu was also involved with the Communist Party in the late 1930s. It may be that Gheorghe Petrescu knew either Marin or Nicolae Ceauşescu through his subversive connections and introduced his sister to her future husband. The hagiographies have various romanticized versions. The most improbable, almost evangelical story, claims that the youthful activist, Nicolae Ceauşescu, passed through Elena's home village on his way to one of many prisons. His glance fell upon the virgin Elena, who was standing with her mother watching the prisoners pass by, full of sympathy for their plight and with revolutionary ardour beating in her breast. The mother and daughter took pity on the youngest and most handsome of the convicts and gave him some food; he in return took the girl to his heart.

Another more plausible official story has it that the dark-eyed Elena was chosen 'queen of the May Day parade' in 1939 thereby coming to the attention of the heroic young agitator during one of his brief spells outside prison. Cynical interpreters suggest a different version. At that time in the late thirties, young male workers often came to the capital in search of work. Fresh from the countryside where they had relatives and perhaps a fiancée, they found themselves alone in Bucharest. Naturally they sought out female company and the local prostitutes were often recent arrivals to the city, forced by their poverty to make a living as best they could. According to local legend it was the custom of the clients in certain bars-cum-brothels either to draw lots for the girls or to elect the prettiest, or for the man who bid the most to get the girl of his choice. It may well be that Elena, as a poor, single girl, frequented such bars, where she met Nicolae.

During the Second World War, Elena was separated from Nicolae for years and the question naturally raises itself as to whether she remained faithful to him. At his trial after the revolution (when he had every reason to distance himself from his sister-in-law), Nicolae Andruţa claimed, 'One day [in 1943] I found her and her sister-in-law, Adela, naked with two German officers.' Andruţa remarked that unnaturally, 'She did not like that too much. She asked me: "Why did you come, Nicu? Look, we are with two friends."' Possibly Andruţa exaggerated the degree of intimacy which he witnessed between the two young women and the Germans. But since he also went on to make clearly absurd claims that he himself had been 'persecuted' by his brother and sister-in-law, his testimony has to be treated with scepticism. Whatever her past career, there is no evidence that Elena was ever attracted to another man after she was reunited with Nicolae in 1944 and their marriage in 1945.[29]

The anti-fascist demonstration on May Day, 1939, was an important part of the Communists' myth of themselves after the war. Ceauşescu's part in it may have been small, and the demonstration itself hardly significant, but the Party's need for a record of opposition to the previous regime after 1944 gave its few pre-war activists a retrospective place in the limelight. Ceauşescu was to exploit it ever afterwards. Fifty years on, special postage stamps recorded Nicolae and Elena's participation. By 1989, the cult of the couple had come to overshadow all other Communists, or indeed Romanians, so that the official media simply ignored other demonstrators.

One participant was especially forgotten: a metallurgist and Party member, Alexandru Iliescu. He was dead, but his son, Ion, lived on and was not in favour with the 'hero of the nation's heroes'.[30]

Nicolae Ceaușescu was hardly out of prison during the war years. The long periods of confinement strengthened his relationship with Gheorghe Gheorghiu-Dej. Although Ceaușescu was not part of the Party leadership in jail, he was certainly well informed about the divisions among Antonescu's Communist prisoners. He would also have experienced the major development of the war years from the point of view of clandestine Communists: Stalin's dissolution of the Comintern in May 1943. For the internal Romanian Communists, the Comintern's interference in their Party's affairs had been a recurrent disaster. The men in Moscow had imposed their choice of leaders on the Romanian Party with serene indifference to the realities of life in the country. Repeatedly, they chose non-Romanian general-secretaries to guide a tiny party trying to appeal to a majority which had just achieved its ethnic reunion after centuries of division and foreign occupation. The consequences of the Nazi-Soviet Pact had been calamitous: the Party's few activists at large had had to try to defend the loss of territories to Hungary and the Soviet Union itself. After 1941, when Antonescu joined Hitler's invasion of Russia, many Romanians felt Stalin was getting what he deserved for his aggression against their country. Of course, Romania's revenge turned into a nightmare as Hitler's blitzkrieg went terribly wrong: more Romanians than Germans were lost during the Soviet counter-offensive around Stalingrad.

The end of the Comintern's formal authority over the individual Communist parties was used by Dej and his allies in prison to bring about a change in the Party's leadership. As the Red Army advanced towards Romania in spring 1944, Dej organized the removal of Stefan Foris, the Comintern's nominee, from his office as general-secretary on the charge that he was a 'traitor'. Foris might well have been co-operating in some way with the authorities, but that was not the real basis of the charge. Dej had already worked out the essential precept of any would-be Stalinist leader: What communism is, I embody; therefore anybody who is against *me* is against Communism.

Doing away with Foris was an essential step in the restoration of Dej's authority over the Party inside Romania. It was also an important preparation for any rivalry with the Communists who had taken refuge in the Soviet Union during the years of royal dictatorship and war. The return from exile of émigré Communists like Ana Pauker who had survived Stalin's purges could easily threaten the prospects not only of Dej himself but the others in the 'internal' group of Romanian Communists. Whatever their own rivalries, they would need to form a common front against the returning men – and woman – from Moscow. They did not need reminding what the consequence of losing a power struggle with the 'exiles' might mean for them. The great problem was that Dej and his comrades were in prison camps while Ana Pauker and her allies could be expected to arrive in the baggage-train of the all-conquering Red Army. Even the defeat of Fascism did not make that an altogether welcome prospect.[31]

III

The Rise

Inferior minds were as a rule more successful . . . Their enemies despised them, were confident of detecting their plots and thought it unnecessary to effect by violence what they could achieve by their brains, and so were taken off their guard and destroyed.

Thucydides

Everywhere in Eastern Europe, the victory of the Red Army over Hitler's *Wehrmacht* was decisive for the fortunes of the local Communist Parties. Even the partisans in Yugoslavia or Albania could not have liberated their countries by themselves if the Germans had not retreated to avoid being cut off in the Balkans by the rapid advance of Stalin's troops to their north through Poland, Hungary and Romania. The tiny Romanian Communist Party was the greatest beneficiary of the Soviet Union's conquest of Hitler and his allies. With fewer than one thousand members, the Romanian Party was in no position to seize power by itself or even to play an influential role. Alone, their past mistakes and allegiance to a foreign power would have precluded the Romanian Communists from any share in government. But as the ally of Stalin, the minuscule Party took on an altogether greater significance.[1]

By the late summer of 1944, it was clear that Antonescu was dragging Romania down to defeat by sticking to his alliance with Nazi Germany. The huge losses of Romanian troops on the Eastern Front had long since overshadowed any gains in national pride and territory that Antonescu had made by reoccupying Bessarabia in 1941. Stalingrad was as much a Romanian disaster as a German débâcle. War-weariness and fear of the consequences of fighting to the end on the losing side led most senior Romanian politicians and King Michael's personal advisers to conspire to overthrow Antonescu much as the king of Italy and his generals had ditched Mussolini a year earlier. Since it was the Soviet Army which was pouring into Romania, good relations with the Communists seemed essential if a deal was to be struck with Stalin that preserved any kind of Romanian independence.

More than forty years of myth-making have obscured exactly what role the Communists played in the *coup* against Antonescu on 23 August 1944. Even in exile, their defeated rivals had every reason to play down the Communists' part, just as Dej and then Ceauşescu wrote and re-wrote the glorious history of their own role in the overthrow of the dictator. What seems fair to say is that some Romanian Communists played an important but subordinate role in the fall of Antonescu – though they were not always the ones who got the credit in future years. The Communists were determined to get rid of Antonescu and their influence therefore reinforced the 'bourgeois' politicians' resolve. With their aid, King Michael's arrest of Antonescu was a success and not a fiasco like the July Plot against Hitler only a month before.[2]

The German response to Antonescu's fall was swift and brutal. If Hitler could not rescue Antonescu, as his para-troopers had freed Mussolini from the Gran Sasso in September 1943, then he could at least take his revenge. He bombed Bucharest and laid waste to as much of Romania as his troops could destroy as they retreated before the Red Army. The savagery of the Nazi reaction to Romania's 'betrayal' of their cause helped legitimize the new government's claim to have become an Ally against Germany. It also encouraged ordinary Romanians to support a new war, now against Germany. Six hundred thousand Romanian troops changed sides and opened fire on their erstwhile comrades-in-arms.[3]

King Michael and his advisers knew that they would have to deal with the Soviet Union and thought that the local Communists would provide intermediaries acceptable to Stalin. The fallen dictator and his brother were taken prisoner by King Michael's own guards but then handed over to Communist-led soldiers of the 'Patriotic Guards' organized by Emil Bodnaraş, who had spent the war years until 1943 in a military prison for deserting the Romanian Army a decade earlier. Soon this primitive force was supplemented by the Tudor Vladimirescu Division. This was a unit of Romanian prisoners of war captured during the fighting in Russia who had agreed to serve with the Soviet Army. They were to provide much of the muscle behind the Communists' successful rise to complete power over the next three years.

Dej's escape from prison appears to have been engineered on 9 August. Soon afterwards Apostol and others hurried to follow him to Bucharest where they found the Ukrainian-born Bodnaraş already in charge of Communist para-militaries. He was recruiting more supporters and – to those Romanians of an opportunistic nature or with a shady past to hide – the Communist Party and its various affiliated groups offered the best chance of getting in with the winning side early on. It was clear that Stalin's army was going to occupy Romania and that the Western Allies were not going to have any power over developments there. Joining up with the Communists was to side with Stalin's friends, whom he was likely to favour in the future.[4]

Whilst the flood of new recruits hastened to join the Party, the exact whereabouts of Nicolae Ceauşescu and Elena Petrescu remains unknown. Certainly, unlike most of the other prisoners in Tîrgu Jiu, Ceauşescu did not go straight to the capital on 23 August. The evidence is that Nicolae and Elena were reunited soon after 23 August and that Nicolae Ceauşescu only reappeared in Bucharest at the end of the month. Their official biographies resumed their love-story on the symbolic day of liberation from Fascism, but in fact a famous picture of them together on 23 August was taken at a demonstration about ten days later.

They were soon married, but their mutual devotion to the cause left them little time together. They were a couple of model apparatchiks. Whatever Elena's behaviour during the dictatorship of Antonescu, she certainly set about making up for it now. Nicolae Ceauşescu resumed his work in the Communist Youth organization. Elena entered the Party bureaucracy too. At this time she was still content to move in the shadow of her husband and her main educational concerns seem to have been practical: to improve her basic attainments gained at school so that she could master her office chores.[5]

King Michael was not allowed any leeway by the Soviet authorities who backed the local communists. What delayed the takeover of complete power by the Romanian Communist Party was its numerical weakness, though Stalin also hoped to promote the spread of communism in Western Europe by appearing moderate. If Communists participated in coalition governments in the newly 'liberated' countries of Eastern Europe, why shouldn't they play a part in government in the West too? Stalin anticipated that the French and Italian Communists, who still looked to him as their model and hero, would be able to make at least as much headway as their Czechoslovak comrades were doing in the genuinely restored democracy in Czechoslovakia. After all, about a quarter of Frenchmen and Italians voted for the Party after the war. Many others were sympathetic to their victorious ally in the war against Nazi Germany.[6]

The Soviet leaders appear to have had a low opinion of the Romanian Communists. Stalin was inclined to be dismissive not only about the indigenous leaders, like Dej, but also those sent from Moscow like Ana Pauker. The Yugoslav Communist, Milovan Djilas, travelled to Moscow in January

1947 and passed through Romania. He noted the servility of the Romanian Communists towards their Soviet masters, who were, in effect, still occupying the country. For their part, the Soviet officials openly abused the Romanians as 'not a nation but a profession'. Trade between Romania and the USSR was conducted on the principle of 'heads we win, tails you lose' with the Romanians selling raw materials and industrial products to the Russians at below the world price and buying goods from them at above their market value. Djilas felt that only Ana Pauker shared the Yugoslavs' rejection of the idea that the Soviet Union was the absolute and binding model for the 'building of socialism', whereas Bodnaraş opposed the Yugoslav heresies.[7]

Stalin's foreign minister, Andrei Vyshynsky, arrived in Bucharest on 23 February 1945, and proceeded to dictate the composition of a new government to King Michael. The appointment of Petru Groza, the leader of the Communist front organization, 'The Ploughman's Front', marked the end of real coalition government. The Communists controlled the Ministry of the Interior, which in turn supervised the elections held on 6 March 1945. Stalin had remarked to Kalinin twenty years earlier: 'It does not matter who votes, what matters is who counts the votes.' So it was in Romania: the elections returned a massive majority for Groza's Communist-dominated Front of Popular Democracy.[8]

It took another eighteen months before every last vestige of Romania's old order was eliminated. Opposition politicians were either intimidated into silence or, like the veteran leader of the National Peasants' Party, Iuliu Maniu, tried on trumped-up charges and imprisoned. King Michael remained on the throne, but his attempts to assert his constitutional prerogatives were brusquely ignored by Dej and his comrades. On 30 December 1947, the king was forced at gunpoint, and with threats of reprisals against loyal monarchists, to agree to leave the country. He left with hardly any possessions, but was allowed to take the Order of Victory which Stalin had bestowed on him in 1945 during the period of false friendship. The lavishly diamond-encrusted medal turned out to be worth about $60,000 in the currency of the time: it was all the money the king had. Unlike Soviet recipients, King Michael had been allowed to keep his genuine example of the Order of Victory: Stalin's subjects had to return the medal after the ceremony of award and received cheap paste in exchange.[9]

The knowledge that they were only a small group, divided by personal rivalries, and helped by a motley crew of opportunists and ex-Fascists to rule over a more or less unwilling majority, gave the Communist leadership in Romania a peculiar atmosphere – even by the standards of the time. The sense of conspiracy and suspicion felt by the Romanian communist élite is revealed in Enver Hoxha's memoirs. In 1948 he paid a secret visit to Bucharest at the start of Stalin's campaign against Tito. He was met at the airport by Dej himself:

> I got into a big Soviet ZIS car together with Dej . . . When I was about to enter the car the driver opened the door for me and I did not notice that it was a [bulletproof] car. I saw this when I got out and opened the door from inside. Never before had I had the occasion to see such a thing . . . Such cars were used by kings and dictators to protect themselves from attempts on their lives, and by gangsters . . . Once in the car, it seemed to me I was not in a car, but in a real arsenal: both on my side and Dej's side we had a German twenty-round automatic pistol, each with two spare magazines, under our feet we each had another German twenty-round pistol with spare magazines and, of course, the guard and the driver had the same.[10]

Enver Hoxha has left us the reaction of a militant Stalinist to the state of affairs that existed in Romania at the moment of the Communist takeover. The full rigours of Stalin's social and economic system had not yet made themselves felt. Despite the enormous loss of soldiers' lives on the Eastern Front, the war had acted as a stimulant to production in Romania itself. A naturally fertile country was well able to provide foodstuffs still rationed in London, let alone elsewhere in Eastern Europe or the Soviet Union. The abundance of food and the continuing escapism of the fashions of the ladies of the capital enabled Bucharest to enjoy a last fling — living up to its pre-war reputation as the most wicked city in Europe. It did not please the Communists. After the discussions to co-ordinate anti-Tito activities among Stalin's loyal henchmen, Hoxha took time off to play the tourist in the Romanian capital: 'The Romanians called Bucharest "the little Paris" . . . When you looked around the city, you formed the impression that it had never seen the war . . . What there was to see! The shops were full of strikingly luxurious goods . . . It seemed as if you were not in a city which had just emerged from the war, but in [the] Champs-Élysées of pre-war Paris.'

Hoxha was accompanied by the Soviet Ambassador to Albania, Dmitri Chuvakhin, who seems to have shared Comrade Enver's outrage and disgust at the un-communist affluence visible in Romania:

> Chuvakhin and I looked at the shop windows with curiosity and astonishment. As always I thought of the empty shops in Tirana, while Chuvakhin thought of those in Moscow which certainly were not full of goods like these . . . We went to a café and sat down to rest. There were many people there strikingly well-dressed . . . This was one of those cafés which Dej told us were frequented by the bourgeoisie, where he 'with his revolver in his belt and surrounded by security men went to provoke them in their own lairs.'![11]

Hoxha was convinced that Romania would never be a proper communist country until all the fashionably dressed women, and full shops and cafés with coffee and cream, were swept away. It was done soon enough.

The first task for the Communists after they had dispensed with both bourgeois parliamentary democracy and the king was to revoke many of the concessions which they had made to important sectors of Romanian society in order to persuade them to side with the new order against those who wanted to revive Romania on a Western model. The most important group who had to be thoroughly subordinated to Communist rule on the Soviet model was the peasantry. Peasants still made up the great bulk of the population and without controlling them, economically as well as politically, the Romanian Communists would have failed to meet Stalin's test of orthodoxy and loyalty to him. Nobody needed reminding what happened to Eastern European Communists who did not meet Stalin's expectations. After 1948, wave after wave of show trials controlled by Soviet 'advisers' swept through the new Soviet satellite states. Ultra-loyalty to Stalin did not guarantee immunity from arrest, torture and humiliating confession, but it reduced the risks of falling victim to the machinery of terror.[12]

Nicolae Ceauşescu was set to work encouraging collectivization of agriculture. The advantages to the peasantry of abandoning their own farms and working together in co-operatives were never so self-evident that vigorous persuasion was not needed to put the case over effectively. Peasant resistance was widespread as it had been in Soviet Russia twenty years before. Even the poorer peasants were not always easily convinced that it was to their advantage to join a collective farm. The whole arrangement sounded too much like serfdom for many peasants' liking. On the other hand resistance was not easy and its consequences almost certain to be bad.

Ceauşescu's reputation as a man personally capable not only of ordering killings in support of the Communist cause but of committing the crime as well depends on two incidents. The first took place in 1946, immediately after the rigged elections to the national assembly. Ceauşescu had been sent to Slatina, an important town to the west of Bucharest, to oversee the voting there. The day after the polls, he fatally stabbed a local bank manager, Vasile Lupu, in broad daylight after the man obstinately refused to make a 'voluntary' contribution to Communist Party funds and was even bold enough to criticize the Party activists' behaviour during the campaign.[13]

The murder of Lupu was followed a dozen years later by an incident during the renewed collectivization drive in the late 1950s. He was often out in the fields encouraging and cajoling the peasants to go along with collectivization and to vote to pool their land, their animals and their tools. On occasion these meetings did not run according to script. At least once, the peasants shouted back. Ceauşescu went into his official car and drew out a machine gun to intimidate the recalcitrant people. When they failed to take the hint, he encouraged his guards to shoot, firing the first shots himself. There are reports that several people were killed. Similar incidents occurred all over the country, and in all the countries within Stalin's sphere of influence, whenever peasants were required to learn the virtues of collective farming on instructions from above. The 1950s saw repeated waves of arrests and persecutions in Romania with little let-up.

Even before the last months of his life when Stalin became more or less openly anti-Semitic, the members of the Romanian Communist Party of Jewish origin began to face purges by 'anti-cosmopolitan' enthusiasts. But they were held in check by the apparently high regard with which Ana Pauker was held in Moscow. Only if Stalin lost his respect for her could the local leadership risk a purge – or rather a pogrom. After 1946 Stalin's regime campaigned against 'cosmopolitan' tendencies in the arts. At first these were as much campaigns against Western influences on Soviet culture as Jewish ones, but before long the specifically anti-Semitic element became plain. It was not long before it entered the political sphere, and not only in Soviet Russia.

In January 1953, in the Soviet Union itself, a group of the Kremlin's special doctors were accused of plotting to poison the Soviet leaders and to have already done away with several of them. Almost all those accused were abused as 'rootless cosmopolitans'. Naturally, Jews everywhere in Stalin's empire were at risk. Only his early death on 5 March 1953 saved the Soviet Jews from deportation far into Siberia. In most East European countries, the death of Stalin marked the end of an era. The thaw set in even before Khruschev's famous 'Secret Speech' to the Twentieth Congress of the Soviet Communist Party in February 1956. All the Party leaders of Eastern Europe felt the thaw and the fallout from the power struggle among Stalin's successors in the Kremlin. They had to fall in line with the new collective style of leadership in Moscow. After shooting Lavrenty Beria, the head of Stalin's secret police, his other henchmen could not decide who should rule. Fearing each other, they co-operated in an uneasy troika, Khruschev, Malenkov and Molotov. Collective leadership therefore became the norm in the Bloc. Romania was an exception – 'de-Stalinization' never really caught on there.

Stalin had supported the removal of Ana Pauker. He told Apostol in late 1952 that it was up to the Romanian Communists how they settled rivalries within their leadership, but if they took his advice – which they were hardly likely to ignore – 'they would drop her'. Even today, Apostol remembers Stalin's hand coming down firmly on the table and rattling the vodka glasses as he expressed his advice to the Romanian delegation.[14] Although Ceauşescu was always associated with Dej's coterie, he had also co-operated closely with the Jewish members of the leadership. Early issues of *Scînteia*, the Party newspaper, often carried pictures showing him on public platforms with Jewish Communists.

Silviu Brucan, the acting editor of *Scînteia* helped Ceauşescu prepare several articles for publication under Ceauşescu's name. It was important for any ambitious Communist hoping to rise to leadership in the Party to produce some theoretical writings, which could then be quoted in turn by his supporters. Ceauşescu's lack of formal education left him dependent on the expert aid of men like Brucan who did the donkey-work and handed on drafts of speeches or essays to him for final approval. At this stage in his career Ceauşescu was already adept at plagiarism. (It was a skill which his wife was to prove expert in too.) He was also clever enough to avoid showing any resentment towards his ghost-writers, who were also politically influential like Brucan. So long as he needed them, Ceauşescu was a good colleague.[15]

It seems that Dej, like various other leaders of satellite states, felt threatened by Khruschev's policy of reform and its implication that new men were needed at the top of the individual parties. Dej had no intention of surrendering power, but he recognized that he had to follow the Soviet lead. Dej knew that all the current leaders of the Party were implicated in the purging of his rivals like Pauker, and the judicial murder of Patraşcanu. He had ensured that they were tied by guilt rather than affection to him. If the Soviet model of collective leadership had to be adopted, Dej preferred to share power with his own cronies. In 1955, he formally handed over leadership of the Party to Gheorghe Apostol, but kept the premiership. It was left to Dej's young protégé, Nicolae Ceauşescu, to announce to the Communist Party Congress that collective leadership was the method of their Party, which otherwise they might not have noticed.

According to Ceauşescu, 'Collective work prevents us from making unilateral decisions, wrong decisions . . .'[16] But in case anyone missed the cosmetic nature of this new tone of self-criticism, Ceauşescu went on to reiterate the importance of Party discipline, i.e. the subordination of the members to the leadership, which meant in practice to his patron, Dej. Ceauşescu clearly enjoyed Dej's trust, and earned it through subservience to the older man and ruthlessness towards the lesser members of the Party and the Romanian people. By the end of the 1950s, Dej entrusted Ceauşescu with the most sensitive matters: he became in effect head of the Party's disciplinary and recruitment body. Apart from Dej himself, Ceauşescu had the final say in matters of promotion and demotion: ambitious Communists were wise to look to him as a patron.[17]

In late 1956, Dej entrusted Ceauşescu with probably the most sensitive task ever given to a Romanian Communist. Ceauşescu was put in charge of the crisis-management team which had to supervise the handling of the Nagy case when the Hungarian Prime Minister was abducted by the KGB in Budapest after the Soviet forces suppressed the anti-Communist revolution there in November 1956. It was not just a delicate issue in relation to world opinion and Romania's relations with the Soviet Union – and Hungary, for that matter (though Hungarian opinion did not count for much that autumn); the whole case of Imre Nagy had implications for Dej's standing with Khruschev and his chances of surviving the Soviet leader's de-Stalinization.[18]

Khruschev had given his support to the opponents of the Eastern European allies of his own rivals for power in the Kremlin. The Soviet Party leader's policy had its most dramatic results in Hungary, but they were hardly what Khruschev had intended. The events in Hungary in October – November 1956, were a turning point in the history of the Soviet bloc, especially for Romania. Any intention Khruschev might have had of endorsing a rival to Dej disappeared after his protégé, Imre Nagy, let the situation in Hungary get out of control, forcing Khruschev to send in troops to reimpose a Communist government. In many ways, the collapse of communism in Hungary in the autumn of 1956 prefigured the events of 1989 throughout the region. A reformist Soviet leader unwittingly and unwillingly opened the floodgates of popular anti-Communism by undermining the stability of the hard-liners. Faced by open revolt, Khruschev reacted very differently from Gorbachev: while his ambassador in Budapest, Yuri Andropov, played on Nagy's loyalty and affection for the Soviet Union to deceive him about the

Kremlin's real intentions, the Red Army regrouped for its devastating counter-attack on the Hungarian freedom fighters.[19]

Under Stalin, Hungary had been ruled by Matyas Rakosi, who was one of the few people whose physical ugliness and brute strength matched his character to perfection. Rakosi's most famous contribution to posterity was his sinister term 'salami tactics' to describe the universal divide-and-rule tactics used by Communists throughout Eastern Europe. They would form insincere coalitions with foolish or frightened parties, use them until they had nothing more to give and then slice them off the ruling coalition until only the Communists remained. Rakosi's abilities as a subtle salami slicer belied his appearance: he looked like the sort of man who would instinctively use a rubber truncheon to slice meat.

In the new climate after Stalin, Rakosi was pushed aside to make way for the more scholarly Nagy. In practice, Nagy as Rakosi's Minister of Justice was as responsible for the mass murders and tortures before 1953 as any of Rakosi's underlings, but his academic appearance, horn-rimmed glasses, walrus moustache (clearly modelled on Stalin's, but quickly forgotten only three years after his death), made him seem the human face of communism. To be fair to Nagy, he was one of those communist reformers who wanted to make a break with the past, not least his own. But he had difficulty forcing himself upon the Hungarian Party even with Khruschev's help. As so often the hardliners were greedy but not stupid. They recognized that too much relaxation of control would enable the profoundly anti-Communist sentiments of the bulk of the people to rise to the surface – and explode.

The explosion at the end of October 1956, was beyond Nagy's power to control. He had to run along with the crowds to avoid being trampled underfoot. Suddenly, it became clear that everybody had been conforming while secretly yearning to revolt. Once the Hungarian people started to attack government and Party buildings the apparently total control of the Communist state began to wither. Secret policemen hung from the lampposts and the Hungarian flag flew proudly with the communist symbol cut from the centre. His own deep emotional ties to the Soviet Union meant that Nagy never came to terms with the Hungarian people's rejection of everything Soviet. He trusted the assurances of the Soviet Ambassador, Yuri Andropov, that the Soviet troops in Hungary were converging in the north-east of the country in order to withdraw as a body. When they returned to suppress the Hungarian people, Nagy fled to the Yugoslav Legation. Tito, in the first of many acts of reconciliation with the Soviet Union, persuaded Nagy to leave under a promise of safe conduct. He was immediately seized and taken to Romania.

The revolution in Hungary was followed closely in Romania. Although the Romanian Communists denied that it had any repercussions inside the Hungarian-speaking parts of their country (and Ion Maurer, who was Prime Minister under both Dej and Ceauşescu, continues to deny this), in fact in several towns, people demonstrated in sympathy with their cousins across the border. Disturbances were quickly suppressed, but the fact of their existence was to have important consequences. But they came later. In the winter of 1956–57, the most important problem was how to deal with Nagy.[20]

Janos Kadar, even though he had betrayed Nagy and joined the Soviet invaders, hoped that the Hungarian people would still accept him as the least of all evils. Kadar presented the image of a man who was at least not a blood-thirsty Stalinist like Rakosi, but nor was he a suicidal opponent of the Russians. Kadar's message was that it was better to collaborate with him than fight to no purpose. But Kadar needed Nagy out of the way. At first Kadar tried to persuade Nagy to resign his premiership in his favour in order to give the Soviet-installed regime a semblance of legality. Nagy refused to co-operate despite the less gentle persuasions of his Soviet and Romanian captors. In the end, Kadar demanded Nagy's death. Nagy had become a symbol of resistance: Kadar preferred a dead martyr to a living hero.

To balance Nagy's judicial murder, Kadar asked Khruschev to hand over Rakosi, who had taken refuge in the Soviet Union, so that he could be punished for his crimes. By executing one innocent and one guilty man, Kadar hoped to make himself acceptable. Khruschev refused to co-operate: at first, he tried to save even Nagy. In the end, Rakosi survived, but Nagy went to the gallows and then was buried among the remains of zoo animals in wasteland on the edge of Budapest.

To be fair to Kadar, he was haunted Macbeth-like to the end of his long years by the murder of Nagy. Although various Western statesmen and academics said many foolish things in honour of Kadar and forgot the circumstances surrounding his elevation to power, Kadar himself lived long enough to see Nagy reburied triumphantly in June 1989, and to die abandoned by his own protégés-turned-reformers within the month.[21]

Dej put Ceauşescu in charge of the Romanian side of the dealings with the doomed Nagy. Ceauşescu and Bodnaraş had already overseen the Romanian side of the intelligence and security co-operation with the Soviet forces operating inside Hungary against the revolutionaries. Ceauşescu had not been long out of the Frunze Military Academy in Moscow and that, along with his association with Bodnaraş, made him a natural choice for the role of gaoler. Dej trusted him too of course. Nagy was kept in desperately poor conditions in a safe-house of the Securitate outside Bucharest. He was interrogated by KGB officials, who rewarded him with blankets and food when he co-operated, and denied the necessities of life during a bitter winter if he resisted.

The pay-off for Romanian assistance in suppressing the Hungarian Revolution and dealing with Nagy was the withdrawal of Soviet troops from Romanian territory in 1958. The agreement was negotiated by Bodnaraş, who had been Ceauşescu's superior as Minister of Defence during Ceauşescu's period as chief political commissar of the Romanian armed forces. Bodnaraş was trusted by the Soviet leadership and may well have functioned as its eyes and ears in the

Romanian politburo. Perhaps he was sincere when he argued that Romania's capacity to control anti-Communist forces had been displayed in 1956 when she had not needed the Red Army to put down protests (unlike the Hungarians) and that therefore the USSR could score a propaganda victory over the West by withdrawing her troops from Romania. After all what more spectacular refutation of Western claims that communism in Eastern Europe depended upon Soviet bayonets could there be than the sight of the Red Army going home? Khruschev seems to have accepted these arguments.

For Dej, the removal of Soviet troops was a vital step in his strategy of stablilizing his regime. Unlike the Polish, or even the Hungarian Communists, Dej did not try to curry favour with his people by making partial liberalizations. Instead, he tried to appeal to their nationalism as his best card in an effort to legitimize his rule. Dej knew how unpopular the Russian connection was inside Romania. By distancing himself from Moscow, he might gain support in Romania. It was a risky manoeuvre and depended on the removal of the immediate Soviet presence in the country. Otherwise it would be easy for the Kremlin to intervene against him.

In the late 1950s, Mao Tse-tung in China was also irritated by Soviet presumptions of the right to direct the affairs of communism throughout the world. Mao flirted with de-Stalinization only briefly before returning to a fully Stalinist policy of trying to industrialize China through revolutionary willpower alone. The Great Leap Forward was a catastrophic set-back to China's development. The humiliation of its failure was compounded by Khruschev's unwillingness to pick up the pieces or to give the secrets of nuclear weapons to so rash a statesman as Chairman Mao. The Sino-Soviet split provided the best possible scenario for Dej's plans to assert Romania's independence *vis-à-vis* Moscow.

China could be a powerful ally against Soviet hegemony, but was far enough away to be unable to interfere in Romania directly. China would not be pleased if the Soviet Union too obviously meddled in Romanian affairs and for Moscow such intervention would have the unpleasant consequence of proving Mao's claims that the Soviet Union aspired to imperial control over its 'brother states'.

Nicolae Ceauşescu did not play a prominent part in the making of foreign policy under Dej. Although he participated in a few ritual delegations to Moscow and Peking, his field of activity was essentially domestic. He was building up his power base inside the Communist Party's apparatus. Using his position as secretary in charge of cadres, Ceauşescu was promoting men who would be loyal to him when Dej finally departed the scene. A high profile was not necessary for this task.

Despite his domestic policy concerns, Ceauşescu must have attended the politburo meetings where Romania's relations with the Soviet Union were discussed. According to Silviu Brucan, Ceauşescu clashed with Dej over Romania's assertion of its independence against Moscow. Brucan is the only source for this claim, but says that he was commissioned to brief the politburo on its foreign policy options and so was present at the relevant meetings. Perhaps Ceauşescu had grown impatient of his role as heir-apparent and thought that he could push Dej aside with Soviet help. However, his very survival in the leadership suggests that any disagreement between him and Dej was not very serious. In the conspiratorial atmosphere of the Romanian Communist Party élite, Dej may have even used Ceauşescu as a reliable *agent provocateur* to flush out his real opponents. Nonetheless, on his death-bed, it is said Dej proposed that the politburo should choose not Ceauşescu but Gheorghe Apostol as his successor.

The story that Dej preferred Apostol to Ceauşescu is told not only by the loser. Both Brucan and Maurer suggest that the old man came to foresee the likely faults of his successor. This is a rather dramatic interpretation of the dying man's state of mind. Both Brucan and Maurer are still anxious to protect the memory of Dej and tend to play down his crimes, if they admit them at all. If Dej did reject Ceauşescu as his successor, the reason is less likely to have been a sudden rueful and prophetic fear, in the style of Greek tragedy, of what his protégé would do with absolute power than the realization of what would be done to his own memory.[23]

In fact, it would be difficult to think of any major area of policy inherited from Dej which Ceauşescu abandoned immediately after 1965. To be sure, he dragged Dej's reputation through the mud by denouncing the show-trials of communists in the early 1950s. He rehabilitated some of the victims, and gave their widows pensions. But Ceauşescu neither then nor later revised the verdicts on the non-Communist victims of Dej's terror. He built on the secure foundations of a generation of Romanians intimidated by the experience of mass terror under Dej. He could afford to be lenient himself because the lesson of what happened to the insubordinate had been learnt during the previous twenty years. Preserving Dej's foreign policy legacy was a useful tool in consolidating Ceauşescu's hold on power. It gave the new Party leader the aura of independence and liberalism which the method of his coming to power did not justify.

The two rivals for the succession to Dej were very different characters. Gheorghe Apostol's appetite for power can be judged from the fact that Dej had entrusted the Party's First Secretaryship to him in the mid-1950s. Apostol had then given up the position when Dej felt secure enough from Soviet intervention to take back all the top jobs in Romania into his own hands. Apostol was an old favourite of Gheorghiu-Dej, but not an ambitious, driven man like Ceauşescu, who was ten years younger than him. Whereas Ceauşescu had played the role of hard-man and trouble-shooter, Dej gave Apostol a role much more in tune with his ebullient character. He was used as the 'nice guy' of the regime to promote acceptance of its policies among the workers. As the head of the official trades union organization Apostol had to get the workers to fulfil the Five Year Plans.

Outside office hours, Apostol led a more interesting and varied social life than Ceauşescu. Unlike the puritan comrade from Scorniceşti, Apostol was a bon vivant, more in tune with the common Western image of a Romanian politician. His recent marriage to a much younger actress left him open to the charge that his private life did not conform to the grey stereotype which the ruling elite liked to project to the workers and peasants. The politburo Secretary for Security, Draghici, was happy to help Ceauşescu dispose of Apostol since he was a rival to his ambitions as well.[24]

The art of telephone-bugging has always been central to power struggles in the communist world since Stalin learnt how to listen in on his rivals Trotsky, Zinoviev, and Bukharin, and to play them off one against the other. Rumour has it that Khruschev personally initiated Ceauşescu into the mysteries of this vital weapon on any budding general-secretary's armoury. Certainly, Draghici would have had his own agents listening to what his colleagues in the leadership said on the telephone, or anywhere else for that matter. Like Stalin, Khruschev, Castro or (in all probability) Gorbachev, Ceauşescu had a personal tapping centre next to his office in the Central Committee building. No doubt it was not the only one. Whether he had already established his own 'plumbing department', as Nixon might have called it, before April 1965, is unclear, but he certainly would have inherited Dej's – and possibly the old leader's tapes. Knowledge is power; secret knowledge is doubly effective.[25]

With both the head of the secret police, Draghici, and the comrade in charge of the Party's organization, Ceauşescu, working against him, it was clear that Apostol had no chance. Most of the politburo knew which way to jump. Apostol was not, however, finally removed from high office until after Ceauşescu had dealt with his more serious rival, Draghici himself. He had to wait until 1968 before getting Draghici removed not only from the politburo, but from the Party itself. For that purpose the support of several old revolutionaries was useful. It was their final service to the cause. Afterwards, one after another they were sent off into comfortable retirement. Whether many of them willingly accepted seeing out their old age in peace and quiet away from the intrigues of the Central Committee building is another matter. Ulti-mately, after almost two decades of anonymity, their names never mentioned in the Romanian media (which increasingly mentioned few people other than Nicolae and Elena Ceau-şescu), the has-beens of the Romanian Communist Party were to engage in one last conspiracy.[26]

In the spring of 1968, one of those periodic great awakenings of hope for change and liberalization in communist states seemed under way. In Czechoslovakia, the new leadership under Alexander Dubcek was permitting press freedom and encouraging debate within the Communist Party and between its members and non-Communists. The Prague Spring seemed to herald a new form of liberal communism. It is difficult today to recall that Dubcek and Ceauşescu were often mentioned in one breath as the great hopes of reform. In April 1968, just as Dubcek was announcing the Czechoslovak Party's 'Action Programme' for reform (which before the end of the summer was to bring a quarter of a million Soviet troops into Czechoslovakia), Ceauşescu was presiding over a meeting of the Romanian Central Committee which seemed to make a decisive break with the past, Romania seemed to be de-Stalinizing twelve years after Khruschev had started the process.

Dubcek had no illusions about his Romanian colleague's attitudes towards internal liberalization, but Ceauşescu was firmly wedded to a principle of vital interest to the Czecho-slovak leadership. Dubcek had expected that Tito or Kadar might stand up for Prague's right to pursue 'socialism with a human face', but they disappointed him. Given Kadar's past, Dubcek's hopes seem naïve, but the cult of Tito (in the West at least) as an independent spirit surpassed even Ceauşescu's, so perhaps Dubcek had some grounds for putting his hopes in the Yugoslav leader's support against Brezhnev.

In fact, seven years after the Soviet-led invasion of Czechoslovakia, by which time Dubcek had long been degraded to a clerk in the Slovak Foresty Department, Tito made it clear to a Czechoslovak military delegation where his loyalties lay if ever there was a threat to communist rule in any Eastern European country. Tito told the men from 'normalized' Prague: 'Formally we are not members of the Warsaw Pact, but if the cause of socialism, of communism, of the working class, should be endangered, we know where we stand . . . we hold our aims in common with the Soviet Union.'[27]

Unlike Kadar and Tito, Ceauşescu came to Prague (twice in fact) but not to urge Dubcek to back down in the face of Brezhnev's bluster and threats. According to Dubcek, Ceauşescu 'stated that all this [the Prague Spring] was an internal affair of the Czechoslovak Communist Party . . . He kept to this policy, this stance of his, in contrast to the others who did not behave in such a way.' Ceauşescu's impact upon the Communist who most of all came to symbolize the very aspirations that Ceauşescu crushed in Romania, was such that even in April 1989 Dubcek told Hungarian television:

> So this is why I say, as you have asked about Ceauşescu, that I acknowledged then, and I acknowledge today also, that at that time, Ceauşescu found enough strength in himself to say no [to Brezhnev] . . . From what I discerned he was not such a naïve politician either, as not to realize what turn events were taking. And it is also very important that he did not really approve of our internal political development. Nevertheless, he said: 'This is the internal affair of the Czechoslovak Communist Party.'[28]

By then Dubcek was living in retirement in Bratislava, having had every humiliation of the un-person heaped on him. His Soviet-installed successors had long since made their peace with Ceauşescu. The Comrade himself seemed invincibly in power and Dubcek a shadow of yesterday's hopes, yet even then Dubcek still recalled his meeting in

August 1968 almost wistfully: 'I did not have the opportunity to meet him afterwards; there was no opportunity for the two of us to have a chat.' That Dubcek should still be taken in, twenty-one years later, is proof of the effectiveness of Ceauşescu's anti-Soviet stance.[29]

Ceauşescu's defiance of Moscow in August 1968, along with his removal of Draghici and his (often posthumous) rehabilitations of victims of the purges under Dej, was central to his sudden reputation as an anti-Stalinist, but this was completely unjustified even at the time. For instance, most of those he rehabilitated were as Stalinist as their persecutors: as everywhere else in the Soviet bloc, victim could easily have changed places with executioner and the story-line would have been no different. In 1964, even before the death of Dej, Ceauşescu still upheld Stalin as the guide for communist behaviour, albeit behind closed doors: he told students at the Romanian Communist Party's Academy that Stalin's *Problems of Leninism* should be obligatory reading for them if they wanted to understand Marxism-Leninism. Four months before his death, Ceauşescu defended Stalin's reputation telling *Newsweek* reporters (in a section of the interview originally unpublished) 'Stalin did everything a man in his position should have done.' After all 'in twenty years, Stalin raised Russia from an undeveloped country to the second most powerful country in the world . . . He won a war. He built nuclear weapons. He did everything a person should do in his job.'[30] It makes an interesting and revealing list of priorities.

In the late 1960s, Ceauşescu introduced several apparent reforms which convinced many Western observers that he had really embarked on a wholesale liberalization. First of all, he carried through the process of purging Dej's 'barons'. Not only did the new General-Secretary dismiss Draghici and Apostol, he also got rid of many of Dej's long-serving local Party bosses who had ruled Romania's seventeen districts with absolute authority so long as they had enjoyed the favour of the Boss in Bucharest. In 1968, Ceauşescu revised the boundaries of the counties, more than doubling their number to forty-one. At a stroke, he was able to both replace the old local leaders and to install a generation of district Party bosses who owed their promotion to him. It was a major step towards absolute power.

The squabbles and rivalries between Draghici, Apostol, and Maurer played into his hands. Ceauşescu had played them off one against the other, just as Stalin had defeated his better educated and apparently more sophisticated rivals for Lenin's heritage in the 1920s. Sometimes one has to wonder if Communists ever read their own history. Perhaps they were too busy making it. Probably Ceauşescu needed no lessons in intrigue from Stalin. But the peasant from Oltenia benefited from the same blind-spots on the part of his bourgeois colleagues which had prevented university-educated men like Trotsky, Zinoviev or Bukharin from taking the gruff Georgian seminarian seriously.[31]

One of Ceauşescu's master-strokes in his strategy of simulated liberalization was to introduce multi-candidate elections. To Western ears the idea of elections involving a choice of candidates sounds impeccably democratic. Who could ask for more? From Ceauşescu's point of view having a multi-candidate election (in which anyone standing for election had to be approved by the Communist-controlled Socialist Democracy and National Unity Front) served two purposes: it persuaded gullible Westerners – and they were legion, at least in foreign ministries, the media, and universities – that genuine democracy was under way; and they enabled him to remove neatly Communists whom he disapproved of – the People had spoken. (Remember – what matters is not who votes, but who counts the votes.) Of course, in the end it was a matter of indifference to the regime who won. Once elected to the Grand National Assembly the candidates would vote as they were told, so the local people could choose freely from the candidates put in front of them.

By 1971, Ceauşescu had eased all his old rivals aside, apart from Maurer who continued to act as prime minister until

1974, but who neither then nor later ever openly challenged the General-Secretary. In the place of the old guard, Ceauşescu brought into the key jobs in the Communist Party's Secretariat his own protégés, men younger than himself like Ion Iliescu, of an old communist family, and Virgil Trofin. He also promoted a token member of the Hungarian minority, Karoly Kiraly. These were to be the agents of his control over the Party and therefore over the rest of Romania. Each in his own way was a gifted man. They came from different parts of Romania. Their only connection was their link with Ceauşescu. One by one they fell from grace, each one quarrelling with their patron or falling under suspicion of ambition. It was a cardinal sin in the eyes of Ceauşescu.[32]

Karoly Kiraly, one of the few Hungarian-speakers among the top leaders in the Romanian Communist Party, gives an amusing account of how Elena came to join the inner council of the Party élite. Later on Kiraly fell from grace with his patron and became a dissident, but at the time he was one of Ceauşescu's closest and most trusted aides. Along with Virgil Trofin he was one of the small group of officials entrusted with the organization of the Party's National Conference in June 1972. They were responsible for the stage-management of the proceedings and for ensuring that any voting produced the right – unanimous – results.

Nicolae Ceauşescu was addressing the Party's National Conference in June 1972. He was anxious that women should play a more active role in politics at all levels, and therefore he wanted to be able to announce a list of women whom he proposed to promote into the top ranks of the Party. Trofin and Kiraly had to suggest the names of suitable candidates to the General-Secretary, but he only made up his mind to propose such a policy just before he began to speak. Since he intended to speak for several hours, this was not in itself a problem. In the interval of his speech, the back-stage committee could present the General-Secretary with the list of lucky ladies and he would simply proclaim their names at the end of his next hour and a half long session. Unfortunately, Trofin and Kiraly could not think of any remotely qualified candidate for the politburo. Ceauşescu was not impressed by their failure, though he accepted their other proposals. As he turned to go back to the podium, he said to them, 'Oh, put my wife in.' And so, according to Kiraly it was done, Elena rose from being the wife of the Comrade to being a comrade of no mean importance in her own right.[33]

Elena's ambition is said to have been sparked by the visit which she paid with Nicolae to China and North Korea in 1971. Whereas he was even more impressed by the cult of Kim Il Sung in Pyongyang than by the adoration of Mao on display in Peking at the height of the Cultural Revolution, Elena seems to have been deeply impressed by the sinister role played in Chinese politics by Madame Mao. Jiang Qing was at the height of iconoclastic influence. Through her virtual control of the Chinese media and arts, she had embarked on the destruction of traditional pre-revolutionary culture throughout the People's Republic, from far Tibet to the heartland of Han Chinese civilization. Today, she is probably best remembered for the proletarian operas which she sponsored (with plots of intentionally mind-bending monotony), but in China itself the ravages of her vandalism cannot be restored. Whatever ambitions Elena Ceauşescu had secretly harboured, in Peking in the early summer of 1971, she saw them lived out in all their megalomaniac crudity.[34]

Ion Iliescu was with the Ceauşescus on this visit. The old university contemporary of Mikhail Gorbachev was not as impressed, or so he would have us believe today. Certainly, the beginning of his fall from his position as number two in the Party hierarchy and *de facto* heir to Ceauşescu followed soon afterwards. That same summer, Mao's own most devoted disciple and official dauphin, Lin Biao, was suddenly exposed as a 'capitalist roader' and died mysteriously, allegedly trying to flee to the Soviet Union (in a British-built Trident). Iliescu's fall was less spectacular.[35]

Back in Bucharest from the Far East, Iliescu expressed

some private doubts about the mini-Cultural Revolution which Ceauşescu initiated in imitation of the Chinese. As Secretary for Propaganda, the new campaign was technically in his area of responsibility. Like Deng Xiaoping, Iliescu was one of those Communists who did not entirely subordinate technical competence to revolutionary zeal. Nicolae Ceauşescu thought differently: as late as April 1989, when experience was hinting something different, he told the Central Committee, 'One cannot be a good scientist without being a good revolutionary too.' Iliescu would have agreed with Deng's comment on the ideological purity of cats: 'It does not matter what colour the cat is. What matters is whether it can catch mice.'[36]

According to Kiraly, Ceauşescu said that he would think about Iliescu's reservations and turned to other business and Iliescu left to return to his own work. Once Iliescu was out of the room, Ceauşescu got his immediate cronies (i.e. Iliescu's colleagues and 'friends') to agree that the Second Secretary should be pushed sideways. He then telephoned members of the Central Committee to tell them that 'the others have agreed' and got the consent of one after another. Radio Bucharest then announced that the Central Committee had decided unanimously to redeploy Comrade Iliescu to new duties as first secretary of Timişoara county. Although Ceauşescu already made great play of the need for constant 'rotation of the cadres' and implied that movement from the central apparatus of control in Bucharest to the provinces did not imply demotion, everyone took Iliescu's new job as a sign that his star was waning. In fact, he remained a friend of the Ceauşescu family at least until the late 1970s, and on 22 December 1989, Nicu Ceauşescu was cheered up to hear that Iliescu had taken over from his father, thinking that he could talk to him, man to man as in the old days.[37]

In March 1974, Ceauşescu was 'elected' President of the Socialist Republic of Romania. It marked the culmination of his steady progress to absolute power since 1965. Slowly at first, he pushed aside, sometimes out of office altogether, his rivals and old comrades. By 1967, he had restored the title of General-Secretary of the Party to indicate his supremacy in it and then took over Chivu Stoica's job as President of the State Council. That made him head of state, but control of the government remained in the hands of the Prime Minister, Ion Maurer. Ceauşescu was not satisfied with the purely ceremonial functions of Chivu Stoica's job. He longed for executive authority too. It took him until 1974 to ease Maurer aside. By then, he had built up a sufficiently strong body of devoted supporters in the Central Committee that the older man could not resist the invitation to take a well-earned rest. Since the reforms of local government in the late 1960s, Ceauşescu had been aiming to get both Party and State authority in his hands. At the local level in each county (*judeţ*), as well as in towns, the local Communist Party leader was normally also the head of the local state adminstration. Now Ceauşescu united the functions of Party leader and head of state and government at the nationwide level. It was an unprecedented formal concentration of power in one man's hands.[38]

The ceremony of Ceauşescu's inauguration into office was also a break with tradition: the new President received not only a sash of office but also a sceptre! The fawning adulation with which his elevation to control of all the major offices of Party and State was greeted indicated that Nicolae Ceauşescu had achieved total control of Romania. He was now head of the Communist Party and head of the government, since the new presidency combined many of the powers previously divided between chairman of the Council of State and Prime Minister. He was also commander-in-chief and chairman of the Council of National Defence which gave him control of the armed forces. It was clear that neither the Politburo nor the Central Committee of the Communist Party, nor the Grand National Assembly exercised any effective brake on the decisions of the new Leader – the *Conducator*.

IV

Socialism in One Family

Pourvu que ça dure.
Madame Mère

It was some time after the crowds stormed the Presidential Palace compound in northern Bucharest in the late morning of 22 December 1989 that they found a confused old lady in a bungalow in the grounds. Elena Ceaușescu's mother was by then one hundred and two years old. Abandoned by her family and deserted by her servants, Elena Petrescu was incapable of grasping that a revolution had happened. Her long life had witnessed so many incredible events, but as the final twist of fortune engulfed her, she was already too decrepit, mentally and physically, to come to terms with it. She died a few days later. Her last nurses did not tell her about her daughter's terrible fate. Unlike Napoleon's mother, Elena Petrescu left no memorable quotation or hint that peasant-wisdom had perhaps already prepared her for her world to be turned downside-up again.[1]

Nobody since the first Napoleon made his Corsican brothers kings of half Europe had made the political code of the Latin world of the Mafia so obviously the basis of his policy as Nicolae Ceaușescu. Like any political *arriviste*, he could not be sure whom he should trust among his colleagues, but the

73

faction-fights of the previous thirty years must have taught Ceauşescu that in the Romanian Communist Party ideological affinity or even past services counted for little. Loyalty could only be guaranteed by fear or by family ties. Ironically, the effect of communism in the Balkans was to reinforce much older social attitudes and mores. In a perverse way, the new utopia dredged up ancient ways of doing things which capitalism a few decades earlier had threatened to abolish.

In Romania, politicians' reliance on relatives was a strong tradition long before the Communists came to power. Much of liberal politics before they were snuffed out by the Dej regime had been dominated by the Bratianu family. But the Bratianu family abided as often as not by the principles of its imported Western liberalism as its inherited clannishness. This was because the Bratianu dynasty flourished at the top of an increasingly Westernized society, whose new value it symbolized. The Ceauşescus, of course, were underdogs who rose despite the new capitalist system – or at least as its enemies. The disruption of agrarian society encouraged by modern industry and commerce pushed people like Nicolae Ceauşescu into the new world against their will, but also supplied them with a new ideology to explain their anger and frustration, and to make use of them. Marxism rationalized Ceauşescu's resentments against the new Romania of the inter-war period, but it did not abolish his pre-modern attitudes.[2]

Under centuries of Ottoman rule, throughout the Balkans, the individual had counted for nothing unless he had connections, 'family'. At the very least, in face of the hardships of peasant life under an alien and demanding regime, the Romanian peasant needed to be able to rely absolutely on his clan, the network of extended family relations, bound by blood and mutual obligations. In difficulties, members of a family could look to each other. In prosperity, the fortunate assisted their less well-off relatives. Instinct reinforced calculation in building bonds between members of a given clan, but also in preserving traditional enmities and feuds.

Ottoman rule had in effect atomized society. Theoretically,

every person was subject to the whim of the sultan, which in practice meant they were at the mercy of his capricious subordinates. Only people who could rely on an extended family network could hope to have the friends and connections necessary to protect themselves from the avarice of the sultan's lesser officials. At worst, one could fall back on the immediate family of brothers and cousins to protect the individual, if only by helping to pay up to meet the demands of the tax collector. Throughout the Ottoman world, centuries of arbitrary and frequently oppressive rule reinforced age-old peasant tendencies towards looking to the clan as the mainstay of life and regarding everybody outside with suspicion and hostility. Life in Takrit in Iraq fifty years ago was based on similar principles for the young Saddam Hussein as it had been in Scorniceşti a generation earlier for Nicolae Ceauşescu. Both came to lead theoretically revolutionary parties, which they staffed at the higher levels with relatives or friends from their home region. (The same could be said of Hafaz Assad in Syria, or Todor Zhivkov in Bulgaria, though perhaps to a lesser degree.)[3]

Throughout the Balkans for two generations after the Second World War, the initials 'PC' had two interchangeable meanings: 'Communist Party' and 'Friends and Connections' (*Prietini si Connexiunei*). By the late 1970s, Romanians talked of their Party, 'PCR', as 'Petrescu – Ceauşescu – and Relations'. The most famous joke was 'In the Soviet Union under Stalin, they achieved "Socialism in One Country", but in Romania under Ceauşescu we have achieved "Socialism in One Family"!' No one knows who first made the quip but it soon had universal currency. What Ceauşescu managed was to marry the traditions of conspiracy and tight discipline, developed by Lenin and Stalin to bring the Communist Party to power, with the local legacy of Ottoman rule: the methods and the morals of *cosa nostra*. Some historians and anthropologists have argued that the Sicilian Mafia began as a form of resistance by poor peasants against their harsh alien landlords. The Mafia was supposed to be originally a subversive secret society. If that was the case, then the example of the rule of the Ceauşescus suggests what the People's Mafia might have turned into had it ever succeeded in gaining power in Sicily.[4]

Only in Albania was the scenario of dynastic communism and vendetta carried on with more brutality and verve than in Romania, but at least there were two rival clans struggling for control of the Albanian Communist Party. In 1981, Enver Hoxha, whose wife Nexhmije controlled ideology, suddenly denounced his prime minister of a quarter of a century's standing, Mehmet Shehu, as an agent of Yugoslavia, the CIA, and the Gestapo. The cause of Hoxha's suspicion against a communist who had fought in the International Brigades in Spain and with him as a partisan during the Second World War was Shehu's consent to his son's marriage into the family of an exiled critic of Hoxha. Shehu committed 'suicide', though rumours suggested Hoxha shot him personally. Shehu's fall took his nephew Feçor Shehu, the Minister of Interior, and his brother-in-law, Kadri Hazbiu, the Minister of Defence, with him into the grave.[5] Politics in the Balkans always involved small interrelated élites: what communism did was to reinforce this tendency, and not just in the Balkans.

Saddam Hussein rose to rule Iraq in succession to a cousin from the Takriti clans, and depended upon cousins and near relatives to consolidate his hold on power. Iraq's heritage has been at least as much shaped by Ottoman rule as Romania's, but equally Saddam and the Iraqi Ba'ath Party modelled their organization and secret police methods on those of the Soviet Communist Party and its little brothers. Perhaps, one day soon, we will discover that in the most secretive Communist state of all, Kim Il Sung's Hermit Kingdom of North Korea, the Party was still more nepotic and clannish than in the Balkans or in Iraq. But, until Pyongyang opens up (and the suppression of a plot against the 'blood-line of the Party' in February 1991, suggests not everyone welcomes the prospect of Kim Jong Il taking over),[6] it seems safe to say that Romania under Ceauşescu (like Iraq under Saddam) had one of the most inbred political élites in the modern world.

In Romania, in addition to the blood relatives of both Nicolae and Elena Ceauşescu, they both relied on people from a similar background and frequently from the same part of the country. What the district around Takrit was to Saddam, Oltenia has been to the Ceauşescus. In Romania, 'Socialism in One Family' meant rule by the Ceauşescus and Petrescus plus lesser client-families who attached themselves to the dynasty. Equally, it meant that rivals were judged not only personally but in their relatives too. Whole families rose and fell together.

In the 1930s, both Nicolae Ceauşescu and Elena Petrescu seem to have been introduced to the Communist Party by relatives who had already made their way to Bucharest from the country. This no doubt guaranteed their trustworthiness to their new comrades and may well have persuaded them that if communism was for their brothers then it would do for them too. In his rise to absolute power, neither Nicolae Ceauşescu's brothers and sisters nor his in-laws played any significant role. However, once at the pinnacle of his ambition, his only aim could be to preserve his complete control of the Romanian Party and State, and to pass it on to his own chosen successor. Whereas in his rise to power, Nicolae Ceauşescu had needed to make deals and alliances with other, equally ambitious, apparatchiks, once at the summit, he needed to dispose of them to preserve his position and to protect it from intrigue. He needed an able team of allies during his rise, but they became the greatest threat to his predominance after the mid-1970s. His brothers deserved to share in his success – family obligation could not be neglected – but they could also serve a useful purpose by occupying positions which blocked access to real power by other people from outside the clan. That at least was the rationale behind the nepotism, though in practice Nicolae Ceauşescu's brothers were as little use to him in the final analysis as Napoleon's brothers were to the beleaguered emperor.

Relying on brothers and cousins to help administer the family's good fortune – in this case, the Romanian state

– was not at all unusual, but to promote the career of a wife was a remarkable innovation. In so far as women had played a prominent part in Romanian politics, the precedents were not happy. Magda Lupescu was held to have been an avaricious and pernicious influence on Carol II. Ana Pauker was commonly regarded as a brutal Stalinist. (In fact, Stalin, who shared many Romanian peasants' anti-Semitic distaste for Pauker's origins, supported her purging at the end of his life.)[7] Most Communists, despite their theoretical commitment to sexual equality, looked askance at any woman who aspired to be more than a tractor driver or street-sweeper. The elevation of their leaders' wives to positions of political power in their own right happened more and more often by the 1970s, but it was not well regarded even in countries where the wife was not like Elena Ceauşescu in combining arrogance, brutality, stupidity and self-confidence.[8]

Elena's promotion over the heads of more senior comrades with much greater political or administrative experience not only humiliated them, it also antagonized their wives. Many of the politburo members had married good bourgeois ladies or fashionable actresses. They regarded the General-Secretary's wife as uncouth and comic in her attempts to ape the styles of the more chic among the Communist élite. Elena Ceauşescu later became infamous for her lavish wardrobe. Certainly, it surpassed in bulk and cost anything yet seen in Romania and was on a scale approaching Imelda Marcos's spendthrift acquisitions. However, it should not be forgotten that Nicolae Ceauşescu's colleagues and their wives had quickly learnt to reward themselves for the hardships of their long struggle for power. Under Dej, the once affluent bourgeois residents of Herastau, the attractive northern suburb of Bucharest, were evicted and their houses occupied by the new élite. Even today, Ion Maurer and the surviving leaders of the old regime live in fine turn-of-the-century houses, surrounded by high walls, with guards at the gate. Ceauşescu's family and favourites have gone, but their places have generally been taken by the prominent figures of the new regime – some of whom have not had to move far.

It was not only in Communist Romania that the leaders of the Party quickly adapted their lifestyles to their capacity to exploit the state. Every country in Eastern Europe has been rocked by scandalous revelations about the special privileges of their former rulers. In this, as in much else, the fallen Communist leaders could plead that all they were doing was imitating Lenin. After all, from the very first weeks after the first seizure of power by a Communist Party back in November 1917, special rations, housing and other privileges had been the order of the day. The people who were devoting their lives to transforming society into an egalitarian paradise could not be expected to live like other people who had nothing better on their minds than scratching a living. From Lenin's use of an 'expropriated' Rolls-Royce and 'socialized' imperial palaces and capitalist villas onwards, the People's representatives had found it necessary to insulate themselves from the daily difficulties of ordinary life.[9]

Apart from Elena's promotion, two of Nicolae's brothers were most important in this respect: the military-historian, Ilie, and the younger Nicolae Andruţa. Both were given positions near the centre of power, unlike their other brothers and sisters, who were installed in basically honorific positions, with the partial exception of the eldest of the siblings, Marin. Marin Ceauşescu's position at the Romanian Foreign Trade Mission in Vienna made him the provider of the family's needs when it came to everyday items from razor blades to video films. Regular sums of hard currency were put at his disposal so that he or his aides could buy whatever the residents of the Palaţul Primaverii wished. In fact, with the exception of the occasional exotic demand, such as orchids from Singapore for Elena, Marin's job was little different from the agents of the other communist élites placed in Western Europe to provide the videotape recorders and other appurtenances of power for the *nomenklatura* from East Berlin to Moscow and beyond.[10]

In 1989, both Nicolae Andruţa and Ilie Ceauşescu were deputy ministers in their respective departments: Nicolae Andruţa at the Interior and Ilie at Defence. Both were supposed to supervise appointments inside their ministry to exclude anyone capable of disloyalty to their brother. Events do not suggest that they were very efficient as watchdogs of Nicolae's interests. In the moment of crisis, Nicolae Andruţa at least made a show of coming to his brother's aid and brought the cadets from the Securitate training school at Baneasa into the centre of Bucharest. Ilie by contrast seems to have panicked and tried to run away. It is said that he was found out by one of the groups of civilian vigilantes who sprang up spontaneously on 22 December: apparently he had disguised himself in ordinary working clothes and was driving a Dacia 1300 when stopped, but suspicion was aroused when a search of his car revealed citrus fruits, like oranges and pineapples, in the boot – no ordinary Romanian had access to them!

At the time of the revolution there was a great deal of speculation about the Ceauşescus' wealth which, it was often claimed, had been stashed away in Swiss banks. No evidence of huge deposits has come to light despite the Swiss authorities recent willingness to assist foreign governments in pursuit of funds embezzled by fallen dictators. The Marcoses may have stashed away well over a billion dollars plus other Philippino assets, in the USA, Switzerland and elsewhere, but neither Nicolae nor Elena Ceauşescu felt under any compulsion to insure themselves against a rainy day. They were confident that they were on the winning side of history and did not need to take precautions against exile in the autumn of their lives. A few million dollars were kept abroad to provide for the family's regular needs from videos and colour television sets through to Nicolae Ceauşescu's preferred Gillette razors.

By the time the threat to their system became suddenly

apparent in the summer of 1989, it was too late to shift the sort of fabulous amounts rumoured at Christmas 1989 into foreign accounts. Romania simply did not have billions of dollars for the Ceauşescus to purloin. In any case, the pair had no intention of renouncing power and going into graceful retirement. Their chaotic flight on 22 December revealed their complete lack of serious contingency plans for the eventuality of a *coup*, let alone a popular revolution.[11]

Until very late in the day, the possibility of their downfall does not seem to have occurred to Nicolae and Elena Ceauşescu, any more than it had to Zhivkov or Honecker. Their regimes seemed insulated against instability. Dollars and Western valuables were not hoarded against a rainy day in the manner of Latin American dictators. History appeared irrevocably on the side of the ageing generation of Communists who had come to maturity in the era of the great depression and Hitler. The possession of Western consumer goods of all kinds, from plastic carrier-bags via bottles of Johnnie Walker to sophisticated high-tech household items like hi-fi systems was vital to the status of high Party officials throughout the Communist world. Not only did Japanese stereos or Italian fridges add to the comfort of life, they were badges of rank, proof of one's standing in the hierarchy of power. Lesser mortals would be overawed by them. Subordinates with the right to travel to the West knew that when they returned, a suitable gift, whether a silk-tie or a pornographic video, would be expected by their immediate superior. Naturally, the Ceauşescu clan had to possess more consumer goods than anyone else in order to assert their authority.

When the crowds stormed the Palaţul Primaverii on 22 December, they were astonished by what they found: The lavish – if ugly – real and imitation Louis-Quinze furniture; the use of marble and gold for everyday objects; and, most striking of all, was the presence of a large Philips colour television and videotape recorder in every room. Throughout the Communist world, the videotape recorder was the greatest status symbol because it implied ready access to a constant supply of Western videotapes. Nobody, least of all a Party boss, could be expected to watch, still more record, domestic television output! Ironically, in the West, the sale of video-tape recorders has often seemed to grow in step with indus-trial unemployment. Perhaps it is a reflection on the economic failure of communism that its greatest status symbol should have been the most precious household item of the unemployed in the West.

The fact that the Ceauşescus had countless colour tele-visions added to the perverse aspect of their superabundance since ordinary Romanians had to put up with only a couple of hours of black-and-white television each day – and that largely devoted to the doings of the residents of the Palaţul Primaverii. But, apart from that, the Ceauşescus' collection of television sets, indeed their domestic arrangements as a whole, were not so far out of line with what any politburo member in the Bloc would have regarded as normal. Take Boris Yeltsin's description of the official dacha he was treated to on joining the Soviet politburo in 1985:

> I was met at the door by the commander of the bodyguard, who introduced me to the domestic staff – the cooks, the maids, the rest of the bodyguard and the gardener. Then began the inspection of the house. Even from the outside I had been overwhelmed by the size of the place. I went into a hall . . . with an enormous fireplace, marble panel-ling, a parquet floor, large carpets, chandeliers and luxuri-ous furniture. We went on passing through first one room, then a second, a third, a fourth, *in each one of which was a television set* . . . I lost count of the number of bathrooms and lavatories . . . And everywhere there was crystal, antique and modern chandeliers, oak parquet floors *ad infinitum* . . .

This dacha had belonged to Mikhail Gorbachev before he moved on to bigger and better things.

Ceauşescu's Balkan neighbour, Todor Zhivkov, maintained a fairly dynastic system, also with a bizarre, pseudo-academic angle – at least until the death of his favourite daughter, Ludmilla. Her interests in the paranormal were unorthodox for a Communist but not unusual among the post-religious élite in Brezhnev's Europe. (Ludmilla's intellectual ambitions were posthumously immortalized by her father's generous establishment of a research fellowship named after her at Oxford University.) His son, a Bulgarian double of Nicu Ceauşescu, became deputy minister of culture, while his illegitimate son, Petko Danchev was deputy premier at the time of Zhivkov's fall. But there were also a few marked differences.

Although the number of his palatial residences and hunting lodges – twenty-two – rivalled his Romanian neighbour's collection, unlike Ceauşescu, Zhivkov had fairly good taste. On visits to Romania, the curators of Ceauşescu's residences, the state guest-houses and museums, noted that Zhivkov only stole or requested as presents the most exquisite items. Ceauşescu casually approved these, either as a generous host or because he did not recognize the value of rococo or recherché items. Ceauşescu's sensitivities in matters of art were hardly developed: as he was to show later in the planning of the enormous House of the People (see chapter VIII below), he knew what he liked but had difficulty envisaging it, and tended to change his mind. If he lacked Zhivkov's taste, Ceauşescu showed greater consistency of purpose: Zhivkov survived his fall and lived long enough to explain that he had not really been a Communist after all; Ceauşescu never gave his judges the satisfaction of hearing him renounce his beliefs.

Nicolae Ceauşescu devolved a considerable amount of the routine authority and privileges of a general-secretary on to his wife. Elena shared some of Zhivkov's perquisites of power. The most important was the monopoly on the re-sale of valuable Western goods, especially cars, within the country. Elena received a fee for permission to purchase what was by Romanian standards a luxurious limousine, even if in the

West the car might have been only a family saloon. Elena's greed was resented by the privileged few who could both afford the fees and knew who to approach to get permission. Not satisfied with her cut from the sale of foreign cars, Elena also asserted her prerogative with regard to the distribution of the standard Romanian car, the Dacia 1300, making Party officials pay up for getting a car ahead of others in the queue (which, as usual in Romania, seemed to grow ceaselessly).[13]

By the late 1970s, Elena had come to share most of her husband's prerogatives and was almost his co-ruler. Ambitious as ever for more recognition than was either possible or reasonable, she was no longer satisfied with receiving honours worthy of a spouse, or even a 'world-ranking scientist' in her own right. Travelling abroad, in defiance of all customary diplomatic niceties, the Romanian couple began to demand that the First Deputy Prime Minister receive the same awards as her husband. Hours of wrangling over the protocol of such matters was squandered during both the preparation and the course of the pair's ceaseless round of state visits to ever more obscure countries. In 1984, Ceauşescu almost went home in a huff from Greece when even Andreas Papandreou's government balked at awarding the highest honours twice over.

Romanian propaganda could not entirely disguise the fact that it was somewhat unusual for the wife of the president to hold high office herself. In the official English-language biography of Nicolae Ceauşescu, published in 1983, the subject was broached and settled in the following inimitable way: '"I would like to ask you," a journalist from abroad [in fact *Le Figaro*] asked the Romanian Head of State, "what is the role of Madame Elena Ceauşescu, who is not only your wife, but also a person with a political function: she is First Deputy Prime Minister?"'

The First Deputy Prime Minister's husband replied in his standard way, larding his lengthy answer with the typical verbiage of the *langue de bois*: 'I will answer you starting with a more general presentation of the mechanism of societal government,' he began, before launching himself on about ten minutes' worth of the following: 'A principle of collective leadership operates in the Romanian socialist society . . . All work in a collective manner; make collective decisions on all problems. The government operates on the principle of collective leadership . . . In this framework – the Comrade concluded his exposition – 'Elena Ceauşescu contributes to solving the questions of our society's development.'[14]

Although Ceauşescu kept open the question of who would succeed him as both Party leader and head of state, by the 1980s there were only two candidates whom he would tolerate in the necessary launching-pad positions around him. Like his father, Nicu Ceauşescu had gone to the top of the Communist Youth League at an early age. This post had often served as a launching-pad for a future general-secretary as the careers of both Erich Honecker and Egon Krenz in East Germany show. Then Nicu had been sent to the country's second city, Sibiu, as leader of its Communist Party and *de facto* head of the local administration. Away from Bucharest and the constant oversight of his parents, Nicu perhaps developed some critical ideas about the realities of life in Romania for people outside the Communist élite.[15]

Elena Ceauşescu was not without her own ambitions and may well have agreed to the (temporary) sidelining of Nicu after he made some mild protests about the state of the food supply in Sibiu. Ceauşescu's typical response was to improve the distribution of food to his son's county so that people would see the benefits of Nicu's administration and quieten down. The fact that the supplies to Sibiu were simply deducted from another area's quota apparently did not cause anyone to lose sleep. What mattered was that things should appear to function well in Sibiu, because Nicu's presence there had to cast credit on the family. At least, the image of a good situation should be preserved for the rulers if not their subjects.

Nicu's political career owed everything to his father's

power. Clearly Elena's advancement into the inner sanctum of the Romanian Communist Party's decision-making bodies depended on her husband's prestige and influence. But her other, 'scientific' career was also in reality an expression of Nicolae Ceauşescu's power. Step by step, Elena advanced up the academic tree in pace with Nicolae's progress up the hierarchy of the Communist Party.

Why Elena latched onto chemistry as the science which she would master is not clear. Her choice seems almost eccentric, certainly bizarre in a woman otherwise monotonously crude in her ambitions for power, comfort, and status on behalf of herself, her husband and her family. Perhaps the very unintelligibility of her final subject matter, 'the stereospecific polymerization of isoprene' appealed to her. Certainly, if her husband was increasingly the master of 'scientific socialism', she became the mistress of the natural sciences in Romania.

The application of the wife of a politburo member to study at a research institute would never have been easy to reject. Leaving aside the fact that already under Dej the standing of a student's relatives in the Party hierarchy already counted for a great deal when it came to handing out exam results, connections with the very summit of political power could offer useful patronage and protection to scientists and their institute. Already under Dej, Elena was granted higher degrees by the Bucharest Polytechnic, despite the doubts of some scientists both about the quality and authorship of her work. But once she took over the directorship of the Institute for Chemical Research in Bucharest (ICECHIM), she began to purge those scientists who had been foolish enough to cast doubt on her credentials or to refuse to 'co-operate' with her research.[16]

There is very little evidence for Elena's scientific activity in the ten years after 1955 when she took up her 'studies' before becoming director of the Institute. What is clear is that she rapidly took in hand the Communist Party cells in the various academic bodies to which she was attached. The secretary of each level of the Party had quasi-absolute power over the members below him, and Elena had a double advantage: not only was she the Party secretary able to veto or grant small privileges for her colleagues, her husband was much of the time the Second Secretary in the Party at large, controlling the day-to-day business of the Romanian Communists under Dej's supervision. Co-operating with Elena had its rewards and falling out with her could be catastrophic.

Unfortunately, Elena knew no happy medium: her approach to her better-qualified colleagues was parasitical. Professor Murgulescu, the original head of her field, was subordinated to her and witnessed her takeover of his institute which she amalgamated with her own operations to obliterate any trace of professional independence. Stories abound of Elena's ignorance. Her approach to academic seminars would seem to confirm some of the claims that she was totally out of her depth when it came to discussing the new discoveries which she had allegedly made. Like her brother-in-law, Ilie, the historian, when faced with foreigners who could not be simply forbidden to ask questions, Elena graciously used to encourage her colleagues to show their mettle by contributing to the discussion. (No doubt, a future feminist biographer will revise our verdict on Elena Ceauşescu's contributions to macro-molecular chemistry and maintain that far from plagiarizing Murgulescu and his colleagues, they tried to deny to a peasant woman the credit for *her* discoveries.)

Had she not treated her subordinates with vindictiveness and meanness, Elena's desire to cut a figure as 'a world-ranking scientist' would have a comical charm. To be as fair to her as is possible, it can at least be said that the work which she had plagiarized on her behalf (since she had neither the time nor the inclination to copy it herself) was generally of good standard. Unlike Stalin and Khruschev, Elena did not use her dilettante approach to science to promote a bogus figure like the Soviet agronomist Trofim Lysenko – though it must be admitted that Nicolae Ceauşescu's interventions in agricultural practice often recalled the half-baked interference of Lysenko's patron, Khruschev. It was perhaps evidence of some restraint that Elena did not oblige Romanians to praise her for *her own* inventions, but only those expropriated from others. This was a small mercy for those who fell foul of her and faced ruined careers or worse.

Apart from her scientific achievements, Elena was anxious to be regarded as a woman of taste and refinement. She had suffered at the sharp end of the tongues of some of Dej's more sophisticated barons' wives in the 1950s and Dej's favourite daughter did not respect her. As Pacepa's notes of the foreign minister, Stefan Andrei's, collection of her *faux pas* and *bêtises* suggest, Elena never grew into the *grande dame* she dreamed of becoming. Nonetheless, as the cassettes of a BBC teach-yourself English course found in her bedroom after the fall indicated, Elena never lost her taste for self-improvement.[17]

Elena was also determined that her children should have successful educations. Although Valentin seems to have passed his exams by his own efforts (though no doubt crammed by special tutors) and achieved a respectable degree at Imperial College, London, his sister and brother followed their mother's educational model more closely. Both Zoia and Nicu showed early promise in mathematics and teachers or professors too blind to recognize it were shunted aside. Some even fled the country. Elena fostered Nicu's interest in nuclear physics. He was destined to head Romania's nuclear power and research programme, which was as good a reason to emigrate as any other.

The steady growth of the grip of family members on so many walks of life had a stifling effect on initiative, which had hardly been encouraged before 1965. In Romania from the late 1970s, the ubiquituous portraits of Nicolae Ceauşescu increasingly came to be replaced or to share prominence with pictures of the couple together. The front pages of every publication from the Communist Party's daily newspaper, *Scînteia*, through to obscure literary journals and even the calendar of religious festivals issued by the tame Orthodox Church, always displayed a portrait of Nicolae Ceauşescu or a photograph of the 'most beloved couple'. So much so that the joke went around: 'Why are there no pornographic magazines in Romania?' 'Just imagine which couple would appear on the front cover!'

Jokes about the Ceauşescus abounded from soon after Nicolae became General-Secretary of the Communist Party. They grew more pointed as his rule inflicted growing hardships on the population and the cult surrounding his alleged genius and its successes became more absurd. One typical story recalled the fate of the apocryphal Lupescu, who was the alleged inventor of several scurrilous stories with the Comrade as their butt and who was supposed to supplement his income with hard currency or Western cigarettes given him by his appreciative audience. After being arrested by the Securitate, Lupescu is dragged in chains before Ceauşescu, who demands to know how much he is paid for his jokes.

The trembling Lupescu replies: 'Perhaps two or three dollars for an ordinary joke, but five for a really good one.'

'What!' exclaims Ceauşescu. 'For that pittance, you're willing to sell out the most beloved son of the Romanian people, their greatest leader in history?!'

At which Lupescu collapses in fits of hysterical laughter, and crawls over to Ceauşescu and embraces his knees and kisses his feet, saying, 'Thank you, Comrade, for a joke like that, I could get ten dollars!'[18]

Well before the revolution, Valentin Ceauşescu had a good reputation among Romanians – unlike his younger brother and sister. They were regarded as at best degenerate and self-indulgent, and at worst as vicious. Stories circulated in Romania reflecting Valentin's reputation as a quiet sceptic about his parents' policies. A standard rumour was that someone the story-teller knew personally had been hitching a lift one dark night. A Dacia 1300 picked up the friend-of-a-friend and the driver and his passenger fell to talking and telling jokes. Eventually, the passenger felt confident enough of his new friend in the driving seat to tell him jokes about

the regime, culminating in obscene calumnies of Elena Ceauşescu. When they reach their destination, the driver stops
the car beneath a rare working streetlamp and his passenger
feels a tremor of recognition, but is reassured by Valentin
that he has heard all the jokes before and he won't be passing
them on to his mother.

In practice, very few Romanians would have recognized
Valentin Ceauşescu before his family was exposed to public
denunciation after his parents' fall. By 1989 even his brother
Nicu was rarely given publicity. Sometimes he appeared
unidentified alongside his parents in photographs which were
invariably captioned with Nicolae and Elena's superfluous
titles. Listing the offices held by the pair was not done for
information purposes – every five-year-old knew who they
were – but to assert their authority. The very anonymity of
everybody else in their entourage was part of making clear
who was in charge. It emphasized that there was no alterna-
tive to their rule. Even if Nicu was intended to be their
ultimate successor, he was not allowed to appear as dauphin,
particularly not after making the critical remarks to his
father about the economic problems and social conditions
in Sibiu.

Valentin fell foul of his parents much earlier. He showed
no interest in politics, certainly not in his own advancement.
Although not a particularly gifted student, he preferred to
pursue scientific interests and his involvement in the Party's
youth wing was blatantly perfunctory. However, it was his
decision to marry the daughter of one of his father's political
rivals, and a defeated one at that, which brought into the
open his unreliability from the clan's point of view. He married Iordana Borila, whose father Petre Borila had opposed
the break with Moscow in 1962. Like many of Nicolae Ceauşescu's critics within the Romanian Communist Party, Borila
had been an émigré from Romania during the 1930s. Like
Valter Roman, he fought in the Spanish Civil War, and had
good contacts with the Soviet advisers from Stalin's secret
police, the NKVD. Also like Roman, Borila was of Jewish

origin, something which neither of his daughter's prospective in-laws looked upon favourably.[19]

Valentin has been discreet about his upbringing. It was widely rumoured that he was adopted by the Ceauşescus in 1946. At this time the Party especially urged its officials to set an example to the country by rescuing orphaned or abandoned children who were destitute as a result of war and, in Moldavia, famine. Other tongues suggested that Valentin was Elena's illegitimate child by another man, but the chronology of his gestation and birth seems to rule that out as malicious gossip. Whether these rumours reached his impressionable ears as a child must also be doubted. If they did, they do not seem to have affected his psychological balance or his relations with his parents. On the other hand, he must have been a disappointment to his dynastically inclined father and mother since he never showed any aspirations for political office despite their encouragement. Unlike his younger brother, Nicu, Valentin would have preferred a life of anonymity. Of course, he could not escape from his parents' ambitions. At the last Congress of the Romanian Communist Party in November 1989, they added Valentin to the Party's Central Committee where he joined his brother and uncles, but even in the heat of the revolution a month later, no one thought to use his promotion as a serious charge against Valentin Ceauşescu. He had been added to confirm his father's hold on power: if the Congress would passively accept such a nomination then there could be no threat to Nicolae Ceauşescu's authority from within, or so it must have seemed.

Whatever expectations his parents had of him, Valentin grew up the best-balanced and the least ambitious of their children. Certainly, the sort of rumours and gossip which were common about his sister and brother were not attached to him. (Even so, Valentin's marriage did not survive and it is difficult to avoid the conclusion that its atmosphere must have been far from normal. It cannot have been easy for his wife to have Nicolae and Elena Ceauşescu as in-laws.) Although it was common gossip that Zoia's private life was deeply and messily unhappy, and that alcohol was a frequent source of consolation, and of course the stories about Nicu's debauchery and coarseness were unparalleled, Valentin's public reputation (which is to say, the cautious whispers between friends about him) was positive. Unlike both his younger brother and sister, who clearly suffered from an inability to form stable ties with other people and seemed to depend on the bottle to bolster their self-assurance, Valentin's reputation was almost that of a good prince in a fairy-tale.[20]

Nicu Ceauşescu swaggered around Bucharest from his early teens onwards. Stories abounded of his drunkenness and adventures with women, including attempted rapes, even before he was legally an adult. Both his parents indulged him, particularly his mother. Whereas Nicolae preferred to turn a blind eye to his son's misdemeanours, which were so unlike his own abstemious and dedicated youth, Elena seemed almost to prefer Nicu's bad behaviour to Valentin's modest and retiring example. Of course, younger sons often enjoy their mothers' particular favour, but most do not have a mother like Elena to indulge them.[21]

Not all the stories about Nicu's uncontrollable and violent lusts were true. Many Romanians took a prurient pleasure in whispering news of the latest outrage, but many of the alleged crimes of the 'Crown Prince' were invented by the fertile imagination of his parents' subjects. People wanted to believe that rulers who were denying their people every small pleasure were engaged in orgies of Neronic excess. Many of the grisliest stories about Nicu's alleged brutal debauchery were attached to the gymnast, Nadia Comanecj, whom rumour had it that he claimed was 'state property' and that he even ripped out her nails for refusing his attentions. Comanecj's dramatic flight to America just weeks before the revolution robbed Romania of one of its few remaining internationally known citizens and further encouraged the stories about Nicu's behaviour.[22]

Zoia retreated into a world of pets blurred by the bottle. She showed little understanding. Like Nicu she studied nuclear physics, but unlike Valentin, she was never considered suitable for study abroad. Her written work and exams in mathematics and physics were prepared by professors, who preferred a quiet life to academic suicide.

Unlike their children, Nicolae and Elena Ceauşescu were not the subject of much trivial gossip. Even their discontented subjects could not imagine routine vices. Those acquainted with them, like Sergiu Celac, who acted as interpreter for so many meetings with English-speaking heads of government and heads of state, sometimes thought that they detected vestiges of their changing sexual relationship. According to Celac, Elena came to dominate her husband as he grew older, though he attributes her authority as much to her marginally more elevated social origins as to her sex.[23] Given Nicolae's peculiar lack of empathy with other people, it may be that all his human emotions were concentrated on her, and on getting and keeping power of course. Even his children found him strangely distant and impersonal.

The daily life of the couple at the height of their power was marked by a contrast between their frankly *petit bourgeois* devotion to each other and the grandiose back-drops to their carefully analysed and tasted diets or their regular watching of junk videos and films. They had no aspirations to be patrons of the arts and to regale themselves like proletarian Ludwig IIs with grand opera or private performances of the classics. An American detective film sufficed. Like most Romanians, who were not in a position to exercise any discretion in the matter, the couple had an almost slavish regard for the most commercialized features of capitalist culture. For ordinary people in undernourished Bucharest to regard the trinkets of capitalism as the symbols of liberty as well as the rewards of prosperity is understandable, but to have the wealth of twenty-three million Romanians to squander at one's will and to choose to watch *Kojak* or to sit on the sort of lumpish gilt furniture that Western department stores export to their Arab allies would not have suited Caligula.

The oil sheikhs at least have the excuse that it is their countries' natural wealth that they are frittering away, not the fruits of the toil of their peoples. Their appetites are limited to the exorbitant enjoyment of expensive and clashing furnishings.

Tucholsky once remarked that there were people who thought that staying in an elegant hotel made them elegant themselves. Casting one's eyes over the palaces and lodges in which they lived, it is difficult to avoid the conclusion that Nicolae and Elena had stayed in one over-decorated and garish hotel too many. Even their private quarters, presumably the scenes of touching fidelity, were equipped to make the lobbies of Gulf hotels seem intimate. They could not distinguish public splendour to dazzle and impress their people and foreigners alike (if that is the effect their trappings achieved) from the conveniences of private life.

Romania was not only dotted with scarcely visited residences, each filled with furniture in gilded styles that the reigns of twenty more Louis XIV's could not have conjured up. There was also a presidential yacht which cost more than three hundred million lei and whose very occasional guests included the French Communist Party leader, Georges Marchais, in 1984. By December 1989, even French Communists were embarrassed by that sort of holiday.[24] If the presidential yacht was under-used, the special train built for the couple was never put into service. It sat in sidings, waiting for the revolution, as it turned out, so that foreign tourists with more money than taste could buy a night-ride in the bed in which Nicolae and Elena had never slept.

After the revolution, Romanians sat in their flats lit by a maximum of two 40-watt bulbs by order, usually wearing winter coats as they had become accustomed to years of sudden power cuts, and watched television pictures of their late rulers perusing menus to decide what to eat. The commentators told people used to queuing for a bare minimum that the General-Secretary and the First Deputy Prime Minister had a choice of six different menus. Their food was grown

94

on special farms, when not imported exclusively for their consumption. Anything they did not eat went to waste: nothing was recycled or left for the servants, though Nicolae's beloved dogs got scraps, if they tired of their imported frozen meat. By all accounts, Elena was the architect of this meanness: it could hardly be called peasant hoarding, since she would not keep leftovers, but certainly discouraged even her husband from rare bouts of generosity to the staff.

Some of the stories about the Ceauşescus' wastefulness were exaggerated, but were hardly malicious given the truth. Pacepa says that Ceauşescu was afraid of poisoning after the CIA's attempt to murder Fidel Castro by impregnating his clothes with potions to make his beard fall out, and so he ordered the Securitate department which provided all his personal needs free of charge to arrange for the manufacture of a new set of clothes for every day of his life. In fact, he seems to have contented himself with only forty new suits per annum and an unlimited supply of underwear and shirts. On the other hand, as much as assassination attempts, Ceauşescu feared infection with common contagious diseases. His regular hand-washing using alcohol as a disinfectant was reported by foreign hosts as well as witnessed (off camera) at public events in Romania. Hitler had a hand-washing fetish too. Stalin seems to have been more relaxed about human contact.

Ceauşescu's distancing himself from his fellow countrymen, whether for reasons of security or hygiene, meant that his daily life involved him in regular contact with relatively few people. He chose to spend his moments of relaxation with his political cronies, though none of them could be said to have enjoyed his full confidence. Long-term associates on the politburo, like Ilie Verdeţ or Manea Manescu, made up regular members of the 'family'. So closely was Ceauşescu identified with the policy of nepotism that local people and foreign observers often presumed that men like Verdeţ or Manescu were intermarried with the clan.

Ceauşescu's 'family' included the coterie of long-time sycophants and aides who lived in the villas around the presidential palace in northern Bucharest and who were on call to
attend upon the Comrade should he feel the need for advice,
flattery or entertainment. Access to the ear of the General-
Secretary was a sign of power. So long as an apparatchik
continued to be invited to join the Ceauşescus at play, even
the ceaseless rotation of offices could not disguise his continuing status as one of the leaders. But when it became known
that someone ostensibly in the top echelon of the regime was
no longer seen at the Ceauşescus' palace at the nightly film
shows or for chess, then whatever the victim's ostensible rank,
his own hangers-on would begin to look for another patron.

By the late 1980s, Ceauşescu's suspicions and caprices had
whittled down the numbers of his long-term favourites. Long
gone from the family circle was Ion Iliescu, who once was
photographed playing hoopla with Nicolae and Elena in
1976, and who was one of the Comrade's partners for chess
at one of his many elaborately decorated boards. Ceauşescu
liked to win at chess: the result of the game asserted his
supremacy over his opponent in politics as much as the skills
of the game itself – few risked beating the Comrade. Similarly, while he was still fit enough, Ceauşescu inflicted games
of volley-ball on his colleagues: his team was made up of
bodyguards and young relatives, the opponents were politburo members or deskbound apparatchiks of one sort or
another.

One of Ceauşescu's most gifted loyalists was Stefan Andrei
who was also from Oltenia. A cynical nihilist, Andrei
expected a sticky end (if only at the hands of his master and
mistress) and wanted to live well before it came. In the last
discussions of the Communist élite as Ceauşescu struggled to
preserve his hold on power, it was Andrei, rather than the
more completely self-abasing types, who urged tough action
against the demonstrators, and who showed no qualms about
shooting down the crowds. Better to hold on to power for a
few days or hours longer. After the revolution, Andrei's

starlet wife loyally tried to defend her husband by portraying him as an opponent of the Comrade and the victim of persecution, but this unoriginal line of defence is not borne out by the facts, except insofar as all the members of the ruling group lived precariously. So long as they were in favour, they were free to feather their nests, which Andrei did as industriously as anyone else.[25]

The petty corruption of the élite is striking. No doubt, Dej's cronies had enjoyed access to the small pleasures of life which were increasingly denied to their subjects by the impact of their own economic policies, but it is the tawdry nature of men like the Minister of the Interior, Tudor Postelnicu, which is so unattractive. No means of gratifying their trivial desires was too demeaning. Their prosecutors at the trial of the politburo took pleasure in revealing how many cartons of Western cigarettes each of the defendants had possessed at the time of the revolution. To Romanians, every carton of Marlboro represented a week's work.

Ion Pacepa, Ceauşescu's chief intelligence officer who defected in 1978, takes particular pleasure in his memoirs in exposing Stefan Andrei as both corrupt but also as well aware of the absurdity of the Ceauşescus' pretensions, especially Elena's academic titles. Although Andrei may have been more intelligent than his colleagues, his greed was no less than his more stupid comrades such as Postelnicu. Pacepa tells a typical story about Postelnicu's cupidity. When he became Minister of the Interior and thus boss of the Securitate, its various intelligence activities and methods were explained to him. After the idea of a dead-letter drop had been made clear to Postelnicu with some difficulty, the new minister took the intelligence officer to his bathroom and asked if the lavatory's water-cistern could be used as a letter drop. When told it could, Postelnicu made it clear that he expected a regular supply of Scotch to be discreetly deposited there. Any agent worth his salt knew that promotion under Postelnicu depended upon satisfying the minister's whims as much as doing his proper job well.[26]

At his trial at the end of January 1990, Postelnicu blubbed out his guilt in connection with the shootings in Timişoara and the incineration of the forty victims there, but he was anxious to defend himself from charges of cupidity. He managed to blurt out at one stage in the proceedings: 'I didn't have any dollars, no gold, I don't smoke and I earn 3,500 lei a month.' The attorney-general cut off this unlikely tale: 'You had eleven radio-sets, sixty-six cartons of cigarettes, four hundred bars of soap, ten kilos of gold, and two hundred kilos of meat in your deep-freeze.'[27] Postelnicu's life at the top was a sorry story of petty venality. To the Romanian audience for these trials (which were broadcast live on television), the lists of cartons of cigarettes or kilos of refrigerated meat were as fascinating as the tales of the riches of the Sultan in *One Thousand and One Nights*.

Manea Manescu, who counted as the intellectual of the group, tried to explain how 'the road to hell is paved with good intentions', but, despite all the difficulties of his position, he had remained 'faithful to the principles of his youth'. He even claimed to have been reading a book on cybernetics at the time of the revolution, but his scholarly interests did not prevent him from amassing enormous wealth by the standards of his fellow citizens.[28] Ordinary people regularly broke the rules and resorted to bribery if they could get away with it to obtain essentials or medical care, but then their corruption was a sign of independence asserted against the system, whereas Manescu's was typical of a deep inner decay of the system.[29]

Nicolae's sister, Elena Barbulescu, who administered the family's birthplace like a feudal domain, was also a typical representative of this corrupt élite. Her petty tyranny and ruthless exploitation of anyone who fell under her sway was typical of the behaviour of hundreds of local Party bosses in Romania. Her status as sister magnified her authority and the disparity between her limited abilities and her responsibilities, as, among other tasks, inspector of schools. Would she have been a normal and contented woman had she not been Nicolae's sister, or did her willingness to abuse every chance to profiteer from her position and to humiliate those she disliked reflect a deeply unpleasant cast in the Ceauşescu genes?[30]

V

Ceauşescu Between East and West

> Take the case of Ceauşescu. He served you, you in the West, as
> a footbridge into the communist world. You praised his tolerance
> and his modern attitudes. He was your friend until the last few
> months preceding the insurrection in Romania.
>
> Saddam Hussein[1]

1978 marked the apogee of Ceauşescu's acceptability in the
West. In April he had paid an official visit to Washington
along with Elena. Then he paid a call on President Giscard
d'Estaing in France. In mid-June the social climax of the
couple's political ascent was reached when, together with an
entourage of light-fingered bodyguards, chefs and food-
tasters, Nicolae and Elena stayed with Her Majesty the Queen
at Buckingham Palace for three days. (Giscard d'Estaing had
already warned the Palace about the Romanians' insatiable
pilfering during their recent stay in France, but Palace
officials remain discreet about any misdemeanours during the
Ceauşescus' visit.) The British establishment has remained
remarkably reticent about the whole episode, which culminated in Her Majesty the Queen bestowing an honorary
knighthood on Nicolae Ceauşescu, while distinguished academics and scientists joined together to honour their 'colleague', Elena Ceauşescu.

The embarrassment of the British establishment in
December 1989, caused a great deal of well-deserved *Schaden-
freude* among those who had always been sceptical about the

Ceauşescus. There was also a great deal of indignation among ordinary British citizens who discovered for the first time after the massacre in Timişoara that Romania was ruled by a brutal tyrant who enjoyed the privileges of a Knight Grand Cross of the Order of the Bath. Of course, the Bath was not the only order of Christian chivalry into which Ceauşescu had been admitted. The Danes had given him the appropriately named Order of the Elephant. Belgium and the Netherlands had bestowed equal honours. Western republics like Italy, Austria, and West Germany also gave out medals and awards.

Ceauşescu elected to exhibit his trophies in the National History Museum in Bucharest, in salons of 'homage' where his subjects could see the admiration Western democrats felt for their leader. The display of honours was indiscriminate: alongside the insignia of a *commandeur* of the *Légion d'honneur* awarded by Giscard d'Estaing, a certificate of honorary citizenship of Disneyland aroused the admiration of the visitor to the museum. The salons of '*Omagiu*' crammed with foreign honours and gifts contrasted with the rather paltry display of genuinely historical artifacts recording the history of Romania itself. The lavish donation of Western honours helped to reinforce Ceauşescu's propaganda that his period in power represented a completely new epoch in Romanian history. 1965 became the 'year zero'.[2]

The willingness of the Western democracies, led by the USA, to endorse Ceauşescu's rule was based upon the view that his regime was pursuing independence from Moscow and that such a 'nationalist' line must involve domestic reform and liberalization. Despite his claims to originality in his foreign policy, in practice Ceauşescu built on the foundations laid by his predecessor. Romania's growing independence from Moscow had started under Gheorghiu-Dej. Khruschev's half-hearted attempt to oust Dej in 1957 encouraged him to look for allies to counter Soviet influence. De-Stalinization in the Soviet Union threatened Dej but was also disliked by Mao. The Chinese were equally touchy about Soviet predominance in the communist world, and were in a much stronger position than the Romanians to assert themselves.

In April 1964, the Romanian Communist Party under Dej issued its famous Statement asserting its independence from Moscow. There could no longer be a relationship based on Moscow leading, and the Romanians following orders from abroad. The Romanian Statement asserted equality between Communist Parties. It was the beginning of the independent foreign policy which was to become a hallmark of Ceauşescu's rule and reach its zenith in the summer of 1978.[3] Ironically, according to Silviu Brucan, who briefed the Romanian politburo on the implications of such a step, Ceauşescu was the most prominent member of the Romanian politburo who opposed Dej's desire to make clear the limits of Khruschev's influence over Romania. Ceauşescu was already the heir-apparent and perhaps hoped to improve his chances of taking over sooner rather than later by siding with the pro-Soviet lobby. Or perhaps he was merely expressing caution about Romania's chances of escaping from the Soviet orbit. In any case, he recognized the success of Dej's gambit and made it his own after 1964.[4] In fact, when Khruschev was toppled by Brezhnev in the autumn of 1964, three counts in the lengthy criticism of his methods that was levelled at Khruschev by the new Soviet leadership referred to his errors in his dealings with the Romanians.[5]

By the spring of 1967, it seemed that Ceauşescu felt confident enough to reiterate Dej's insistence on Romania's independence from the Soviet Union. For a start, he continued Dej's policy of distancing the Romanian military from the Red Army: he discouraged contacts between Romanian Army officers and their Soviet counterparts, insisting that Romanian soldiers be trained in Romania. Sometimes the public distancing of Romania from its Warsaw Pact allies, especially Big Brother in Moscow, was done in a quite insulting fashion: Ceauşescu could even implicitly put the Kremlin in the same category as the White House: 'The small and medium-sized states refuse to play the role of pawn in the service of the interests of big imperialist powers any longer.' Instead, Romania, like other middle-ranking states, intended to pursue an independent foreign policy. But it went further than that: Ceauşescu was anxious to assert Romania's claim to be among the leaders of the underdeveloped countries. He insisted that 'by vigorously defending their legitimate interests', the Third World countries 'can play an outstanding part in international life'. A country like Romania could 'considerably influence the course of events'.[6]

This rhetoric was intended to make Ceauşescu new friends outside the Soviet bloc, particularly in the West. Despite his words suggesting solidarity with the Third World, Ceauşescu's initial actions as maker of Romania's foreign policy were designed to build bridges to the West. He opened diplomatic relations with West Germany, to the fury of the Communist rulers in East Berlin. Then in June 1967, Romania failed to break off diplomatic relations with Israel after the outbreak of the Six Day War. There seems little reason to doubt Ion Pacepa's insistence on Ceauşescu's evaluation of the importance of the Jewish lobby in US politics. Whatever the reality on Capitol Hill, Ceauşescu undoubtedly believed the pro-Israeli gestures would win Romania influence in Washington and would perhaps lead them to accept his differentiation of Romanian foreign policy from the Kremlin's at face-value.[7]

Ceauşescu liberalized the regulations restricting emigration from Romania by Jews. He probably guessed instinctively that the West would confuse the granting of special privileges to individuals with the extension of human rights. Ceauşescu was right: a few years later, the US Congress made freeing trade with the Soviet Union dependent on it permitting emigration, particularly of Soviet Jews. Little thought was given to the conditions in which people who had no desire to leave the country of their birth had to live.

Ceauşescu made the granting of exit visas into a profitable business, first with Israel and the USA (which paid the bills), then with West Germany too. The West Germans were prepared to pay handsomely for the right to emigrate of hundreds of thousands of German-speaking Romanian citizens whose ancestors had lived in the country for centuries. Ceauşescu's policy killed two birds with one stone: on the one hand, he began the process of ridding Romania of what he considered troublesome alien minorities and earned hard currency from their new countries for the privilege; and at the same time, he gained a reputation in the West as a 'good' communist, a man to do business with – in this case, by bartering for human beings. No wonder he liked to joke that 'oil, Jews, and Germans' were 'Romania's best exports'.[8]

Liberalizing emigration was just part of Ceauşescu's strategy to gain acceptance in the West and thereby access to its storehouses of wealth, technology and industrial secrets. As far back as Lenin, Communists had recognized what he called the 'objective contradictions' of capitalism. The capitalists hated the idea of the abolition of private property, but they liked to do deals; the Communist state, by virtue of its total control of an individual economy, was in a position to do business unhindered by ethical or trade union considerations. Rich pickings were available to those willing to swallow their ideological prejudices. What Lenin did not abandon in return was his fundamental antipathy to capitalism. Individual capitalists could serve his cause, even making a personal profit on the way, but they were also selling the rope with which they and their class were going to be hanged. It never quite worked out as Lenin planned, but his strategy was inherited by Communists after him. Ceauşescu knew that greed and gullibility often went hand in hand. His genuine differences with Moscow about where authority in the communist movement should lie could be exploited to give the impression of a total break with the ideology itself.[9]

In their efforts to impress the United States, the Romanians went so far as to compare their position *vis-à-vis* the Kremlin with Cuba's in relation to Washington. It says a lot about the quality of US diplomatic thinking that the Americans were flattered to be put on the same level as the Soviet rulers. Equidistance was the key theme of Ceauşescu's foreign policy. He wanted other states to see Romania as part of neither bloc. Yet at the same time, he needed each superpower to see Bucharest as a natural place for influencing the views of the other one and other players in the international game. Ceauşescu was anxious to be the broker. It was a part which he played well. But he was never an honest broker.

When Ceauşescu's chief intelligence adviser, Ion Pacepa, defected to the United States in 1978, he claimed that Ceauşescu had been engaged in a long-term strategic plan codenamed 'Red Horizon'. Its aim was to deceive the West and to obtain key political, military and technological secrets which he intended to share with the Soviet Union. Pacepa argued that Ceauşescu was hand-in-glove with Brezhnev and that the split between Romania and the Soviet Union was a deception agreed by both parties to cheat the West. Pacepa was not the first defector from the world of Soviet bloc secret services to make such a claim. At the very least, it says a great deal about the conspiratorial mentality which the leaders of the Communist system have created that so many defectors tend to see deception at work everywhere.[10] The truth is probably that Ceauşescu cheated on everyone, and that Pacepa, involved on the pro-Russian side, was unaware of the extent to which Ceauşescu was also double-crossing Moscow.

Western academic Sovietologists have gravitated to the opposite pole: they have been unwilling to question the professions of good faith repeatedly made by Communist leaders. Despite the evidence of more than seventy years of clandestine activities by communists, many Western 'experts' seem psychologically unable to enter into the minds of Communist leaders. They have preferred to regard them as basically sharing the mentality of their Western counterparts. At worst, Western politicians, and some academic and journalistic commentators, have shared the mentality of the apparatchiks, but most have remained attached to their illusions that differences between East and West were based on misunderstandings rather than fundamental disagreements.

Even a cynical American politician like Richard Nixon did not approach the habitual level of 'doublethink' which an ideologically motivated communist like Ceauşescu regarded as natural. Since the revolution in 1989, it has been revealed that not only was Romania passing on *some* of the Western secrets obtained in the long honeymoon with the West to Moscow, but that Ceauşescu's brother, Ilie, the Deputy Defence Minister, was passing Soviet military secrets and technology to the Americans. How valuable this Romanian channel of military information was to the Pentagon may be doubted, but it is revealing of the extent of Ceauşescu's duplicity.[11]

In the summer of 1967, Richard Nixon was received with the honours usually reserved for heads of state when he arrived in Bucharest. Nixon was less than eighteen months from becoming President of the United States, but when he was received by Ceauşescu he was very much a political has-been. He was the Republicans' defeated presidential candidate in 1960, and the man who had stomped out of a press conference in 1962 when he failed to win the governorship of California, telling the reporters that they wouldn't 'have Nixon to kick around any more'.

This proud, but humiliated, most complicated of politicians was not averse to flattery. Ceauşescu's treatment of Nixon paid off handsomely. Henry Kissinger recognized that Romanian co-operation could be useful to the United States in its efforts to get out of the Vietnam War and to open up relations with Mao's China. He also saw that by inviting Nixon when he was out of office with few prospects of getting back into it, Ceauşescu struck a chord with the future US President, who would remain loyal to his friend in need. According to Kissinger, 'Nixon never forgot courtesies of this kind . . .' They met several times more up to 1985, but seem to have remained in touch until the last few months of Ceauşescu's rule.[12]

Oddly enough, Ceauşescu was always a shrewder judge of the likely choice for the highest offices of democratic electorates than of who would come out on top of the Soviet politburo. He anticipated and insured himself for the re-emergence of Richard Nixon from the political wilderness in 1968, and correctly judged that Ronald Reagan would defeat Jimmy Carter in 1980 (which was not such an inevitable result as the next eight years made it seem). Ceauşescu was, however, confident that Andropov would not succeed Brezhnev – as he told Nixon earlier in 1982. From their meeting after Brezhnev's funeral in November 1982, relations between Ceauşescu and Andropov were understandably poor.[13]

As head of the KGB since 1967, Andropov was well aware of the pluses and minuses of Romania's independent role in the world. He was less tolerant of Romania's cheating the USSR than Brezhnev had been. Brezhnev expected everyone to take his cut at home and abroad (as he himself had done). Andropov wanted to reintroduce discipline among the Soviet Union's allies as well as at home. Andropov died early, but Chernenko's sickly reign in the Kremlin was brief and when Andropov's protégé, Gorbachev, came to power he was even less sympathetic towards Ceauşescu than his patron had been. Apart from any policy clashes between them, Ceauşescu adopted a rather patronizing attitude towards his younger equivalent in the Soviet Union. Ceauşescu's arrogance in presuming not only to treat the Soviet General-Secretary as a person on a par with himself, but also one without the necessary experience to speak with the full authority of a veteran revolutionary like himself undoubtedly aroused a mixture of irritation and amused contempt in Gorbachev. It was the sort of pride which comes before a fall – and it was a fall which Gorbachev became increasingly willing to envisage.

After 1985, the Romanians played up their independence

from Moscow for all it was worth. Gorbachev's talk of *perestroika* was met by Ceauşescu's insistence that he was 'perfecting' the functioning of socialism in Romania. But Ceauşescu's continued use of the slogans of independence belied a growing reality: whereas in the 1970s, Romania had diversified its trade away from dependence on the Soviet bloc, by the mid-1980s only Comecon countries were willing to buy each other's low grade products – and Romania's were amongst the lowest. Just as he wanted to assert Romanian sovereignty, Ceauşescu found his economy increasingly intertwined with Gorbachev's.[14]

Even before 1985, Pacepa's defection and still more the growing criticism of Ceauşescu's human rights record in Congress made the United States government distance itself from him. Once Gorbachev was entrenched in the Kremlin and wooing Ronald Reagan directly, Ceauşescu's value as an intermediary between East and West waned rapidly. Even when Andropov and Chernenko ruled in Moscow, Reagan had sent his Vice-President, George Bush, and his Secretaries of State, Alexander Haig and George Shultz, to pay court in Bucharest. After Reagan had forged direct personal links with Gorbachev in Geneva in the autumn of 1985, Ceauşescu's role quickly disappeared. He soon discovered how fickle capitalist affections can be.

The Soviet government continued to honour Ceauşescu as one of its fraternal allies. If anything as Ceauşescu's international position weakened the men in the Kremlin bestowed more medals on him, as if to mark each step in his growing dependence on them. Receiving the Order of Lenin from Gorbachev's men must have been almost a humiliation for Ceauşescu on his seventieth birthday in 1988. The fact that Gorbachev sent the old Stalinist Andrei Gromyko to perform the pinning on of the award must have been scant compensation for what Ceauşescu probably saw as a badge of his growing servitude to Moscow. It was one thing to act as the go-between in the 1970s and to be a successful defrauder of the Americans and other Western states. It was quite another to see his 'independence' from Moscow discounted by the gullible Western leaders, especially when they fell for Gorbachev's 'revisionist' charms. Ceauşescu could trust himself to play the liberal, but he could not be certain of Gorbachev's real intentions.[15]

After 1985 the Americans were increasingly happy to forget about their affair with Ceauşescu, but for almost twenty years it was a important plank of their foreign policy.[16] The Romanians had played it for all it was worth. At times Ceauşescu almost seemed to suggest that Romania might become an informal ally of the United States. In fact, cruel strategic reality, as well as Ceauşescu's commitment to communism, meant that Romania could never become to the United States what Cuba was to the USSR. The main value of Romania was as a conduit for undercover contacts between the United States and other Communist countries, especially Red China.

Of course, both the Americans and the Chinese knew that there were clear limits to Romania's autonomy. Even before Pacepa revealed the extent of Ceauşescu's double-crossing of them, the Americans recognized that Romania's geo-political position made it very vulnerable to Soviet pressure and limited its freedom of movement. The Chinese even suggested to Kissinger during the years of backdoor diplomacy before Nixon's visit to Peking in 1971 that his channel to Peking via Bucharest was far from secure: Ceauşescu kept Brezhnev informed. Of course, it was useful to both Romania and China to let Moscow know how deeply involved they were with the Americans, because such knowledge could deter Moscow from interfering in their internal affairs. Whether Ceauşescu's leaks to Brezhnev about Nixon and Kissinger's assignations with Mao and Zhou Enlai helped US-Soviet relations is less obvious.[17]

Ceauşescu served Brezhnev well by promoting the idea of what became the Helsinki Conference in 1975. The Soviet leadership had long hoped to persuade the West to accept the division of Europe as the price of *détente*. At last, the capitalist leaders were prepared to treat Brezhnev *et al.* as their political and moral equals by signing an agreement which committed them all to the same values. This was utter nonsense from a communist point of view and neither Ceauşescu nor Brezhnev had any intention of abiding by the terms of the Helsinki agreement, but its value to them lay in its public announcement to the peoples of Eastern Europe and the Soviet Union that the West had abandoned them to their fate.[18]

The smug foolishness of the Western leaders was typified by the British participants. Harold Wilson announced that a conference graced by statesmen like himself and Gerald Ford (who rarely knew which country he was in, let alone what its politics were) made the Congress of Vienna in 1815 look like an 'overdressed tea-party'. Even after Ceauşescu's death, Lord Callaghan, who had been Foreign Secretary in 1975, recalled generously that Ceauşescu was 'always a rogue elephant in the Warsaw Pact' and had 'helped us' in drafting the Helsinki accords and as a go-between with Moscow.

Of course, it was during James Callaghan's premiership that Nicolae Ceauşescu received his knighthood. At the state banquet in Buckingham Palace, the British Prime Minister was too busy negotiating a deal with a fellow guest, the Liberal leader David Steel, to prop up his minority government, to pay much attention to Romanian affairs. (Steel was an old acquaintance of the Ceauşescus' and once gave Nicolae a dog. Later he inquired of the 'elderly autocrat' how it was getting on. Since it was fed with steaks served in gold-plated bowls, the creature presumably regarded a dog's life in Romania as greatly preferable to its existence in Britain.)[19]

Ceauşescu's first contact with British statesmanship was through the interest that he had in obtaining British technology and the up-and-coming Antony Wedgwood-Benn had in selling it. In June 1968, at their first meeting, Ceauşescu shrewdly let a twenty minute courtesy call run on for a flattering two and a quarter hours. Benn came to the conclusion that 'Ceauşescu . . . is modest mannered, very penetrating in his ability . . . I liked him.'[20]

Benn had already met Ilie Verdeţ, then First Deputy Premier, in January 1968 in London. He noted condescendingly in his diary that the wily Verdeţ was 'a most agreeable person who had never been outside a Communist country in his life . . . I took him to the Savoy Hotel. We got on very well and he has an excellent sense of humour.'[21] It helped that Verdeţ had been a miner. A genuine working class origin must have impressed the former Viscount Stansgate.[22] (It cut less ice with Romanian miners in 1977, for which see chapter VI below.) In Bucharest, six months later, Benn 'told a few jokes. They had a great sense of humour . . . We sat at a special table and just told jokes about the Russians, the Americans, and ourselves.' Benn joked to Ceauşescu that he should stand for the general-secretaryship of the Labour Party too! Ceauşescu must have amused his colleagues with his remarks 'strongly in favour of the acceptance of free will' and his thought that 'the withering away of the State would be very welcome though he didn't quite see the withering away of the [Communist] Party!'[23]

Ceauşescu played with Benn. He assured Benn that the French were not going to let themselves be tied by COCOM: 'Frankly, the French do promise integrated circuits and the dates and deliveries are laid down.' De Gaulle had told Ceauşescu 'embargoes were made to be broken'. Benn's patriotism knew no bounds when confronted by the assertion that the French were more conciliatory than the British. 'So I answered, "Well, anything they can offer we can offer too and I can offer it now subject to the same conditions."'[24]

Benn's willingness to encourage the Romanians to believe that a way could be found to sell high technology to a Warsaw Pact state was ardent indeed. At a reception for Benn at the British Embassy, several of the Romanian ministers turned up including 'Dragonescu, the Minister of Electricity, who is also a great computer king, a tall, angular, intellectual man. I took him around the garden and told him simply, in the hope that it would feed through to the Romanian government, that we were making the most enormous efforts to try to break this COCOM problem. I think he understood.'[25] Presumably, Mr Dragonescu resisted the temptation to say that Romania and all the other allies of Moscow 'were making the most enormous efforts to try to break this COCOM problem' too.

In 1968, Benn's desire to sell Romania sophisticated jet-engines was frustrated 'despite the fact that Ceauşescu made a courageous speech attacking the invasion of Czechoslovakia.' At that point, Benn had to admit, 'my aims to encourage further trade with Russia [as well as Romania] and to break through this whole strategic nonsense have come unstuck.' Along with a few other consequences, the Soviet occupation of Czechoslovakia 'means my Russian visit is affected'.[26]

Benn was so impressed with Ceauşescu's Romania that he found nothing odd in the following suggestion from Bruno Pittermann, the former chairman of Kreisky's Austrian Socialist Party: 'Pittermann said he would like to see parliamentary links with Romania, Poland and Yugoslavia, and to study their election process and procedure. He thought we had a lot to learn from that and it would encourage them . . . I found this highly intelligent.'[27]

Self-important democratic politicians who have been themselves well-treated by tyrants of all stripes come dangerously close to the stance of classic fellow-travellers like George Bernard Shaw – in Shaw's words, as seven million starved to death in Russia in 1932, 'I have never eaten so well.' The professional political apparatchiks of the West too often found themselves among kindred spirits in the East. Their response reminds one of Ribbentrop's description of the Kremlin banquet with Stalin, held to celebrate the Nazi-Soviet Pact in 1939: 'It was just like being with old party comrades.'

It was not only left-wing politicians who were taken in.

With the publication of his diaries in 1989, Benn has been disarmingly open about his dealings with Ceauşescu. Figures such as Margaret Thatcher and Edward Heath, on the other hand, have remained remarkably quiet, although the idea of the state visit and some signal honour went back to 1970–4.[28] Even the most crusty of Tory right-wingers were not immune to Ceauşescu's charms. Perhaps they lacked the ideological baggage, or even the intellectual equipment, to recognize the type of mentality which lay behind the smiles and jokes.

One Tory MP, an aristocrat of impeccable right-wing views, who helped renegotiate some of Romania's debts at the beginning of the hard years in the 1980s, also enjoyed joking with Ceauşescu. He once told the *Conducator* the old (apocryphal) story about Churchill's meeting with Stalin in October 1944. The two war-leaders had a good dinner alone together, and then a heavy drinking bout, typical of inter-Allied summit meetings of that period. Afterwards Churchill is supposed to have sent a note to the Marshal, thanking him for his hospitality and reminding him of the details of their verbal agreements of the night before the morning after. According to legend, Stalin replied that he too had greatly enjoyed himself, but had completely forgotten the contents of any agreement between the two and had, unfortunately, in the meantime, had the interpreter shot! Ceauşescu was amused by this story, particularly by his own interpreter's stuttering as he came to translate the punchline. At the end of the interview, Ceauşescu neatly added his own twist to the story. As his English guest turned at the door of his study to bow to the Romanian head of state before leaving his presence, he saw that Ceauşescu was holding out his fingers in the shape of a gun pointing at the head of his own interpreter!

The catalogue of Ceauşescu's British admirers would not be complete without a mention of the former Bishop of Southwark, Mervyn Stockwood. At first sight, his praise of the Romanian regime seemed to put him in the same class as the 'Red Dean', Hewlett Johnson.[29] Stockwood wrote an article,

'The Big Improvements', welcoming the state visit to Britain by the Ceauşescus in *The Times*. 'Each year I have noticed a higher standard of living', the bishop wrote in his eulogy of this 'brave man', whose 'exceedingly generous' treatment of the churches in Romania was something of which 'we in Britain might well be envious'.

After the outbreak of the revolution in December 1989, the press thought that they had caught an even bigger fellow-travelling fish than the old Dean of Canterbury. At first, Stockwood seemed to prevaricate when journalists asked pointed questions about his admiration for Ceauşescu: his praise, he said, referred to Ceauşescu before he went off the rails. The Red Bishop seemed hooked. But then, a few days later, Mervyn Stockwood revealed that he had all the time in fact been helping dissident priests in a variety of clandestine ways, still too secret to be fully detailed: not so much a Red Bishop as a clerical Scarlet Pimpernel.[30]

British academic institutions which had been involved in satisfying Elena Ceauşescu's desire for recognition by her colleagues handled their embarrassment with little aplomb after Christmas 1989. Even before the outbreak of the Romanian revolution, there had been a growing scandal about Elena's academic acceptability. The evident plagiarism which underlay her 'prodigious' contributions to polymer science was too obvious to require special demonstration except to the inquiring scientific minds of the committee of the Royal Society of Chemistry which elected Elena Ceauşescu to its membership. According to Sir Richard Norman, the President of the Society, Elena Ceauşescu was a 'distinguished scientist' whose work on the 'stereospecific polymerization of isoprene, on the stabilization of synthetic rubbers, and on copolymerization . . . [had] the dual merit of increasing our effectiveness in exploiting chemistry for the benefit of mankind.' A picture of Nicolae Ceauşescu looked down over these proceedings, which were graced by the presence of the Nobel Prize winner Dorothy Hodgkin, Mrs Thatcher's former chemistry tutor at Oxford (though she had no sympathy for 'that woman') who had contributed an introduction to an English translation of one of Elena's works.[31]

In an exchange of letters with lay critics of the Royal Society of Chemistry's award of a fellowship to the 'world-ranking scientist and academician', J. S. Gow, the Society's Secretary-General, had tried to distance it from the Romanian laureate. He gave a perfect demonstration of how egg on the face leads a pompous body still further into the mire. It was not true to say the Society had honoured Madame Ceauşescu, Mr Gow argued. All it had done was grant her professional membership 'on the same basis as everybody else – i.e., specifically on her qualifications and experience as a chemist'! Presumably, the other professional members were not supposed to feel dishonoured by this explanation: after all, what had Elena Ceauşescu done other than engage in those everyday academic activities – plagiarism, paying others to write one's work and bullying those unwilling to comply?[32]

After the revolution, B. A. Henman, the Registrar of the Royal Society of Chemistry, explained that Elena Ceauşescu's 'application was supported by a long list of papers *published in her name* . . . There was no talk in 1978, nor has there been (to our ears) until recently . . . about the extent of Elena Ceauşescu's qualifications.' The unfortunate Mr Henman concluded cautiously, 'If, in the final analysis, it turns out that the qualifications were deficient . . .' then it would be a matter of 'hindsight'. In any case, lest anyone think the Royal Society of Chemistry had pandered to Elena Ceauşescu's vanity, he assured the public that 'the fellowship was presented at a ceremony no grander than would have been arranged for any other spouse of a head of state.'[33]

The Central London Polytechnic gave an honorary professorship, but wisely refrained from public defence of its decision. A portrait of Elena Ceauşescu graced the Polytechnic's building in Central London until it disappeared during the Christmas vacation at the end of 1989. The honorary professorship was a pitiful affair. More prestigious universities, showing a surer touch than the Royal Society of Chemistry, had refused to get involved with Elena, but the Romanian Embassy pointed out that she would have taken the Central London Poly for a much grander institution than it really was. As in Paris, so in Bucharest, the Polytechnic ranked amongst the most prestigious academic bodies. Elena would regard anything called the *Central* London *Polytechnic* as an institution of the same rank, and therefore worthy of her. Of course, the staff at the Poly could only be flattered to take part in a state visit. So it was arranged.[34]

The bizarre story of British academic institutions' flattery of the Ceaușescus could be repeated many times over in other impeccably democratic countries. The relations between Romania's ruling couple and the leaders and universities of the Third World is a more straightforward story. It is not surprising that the University of Manila felt obliged to honour the Romanian guests of the flagrantly corrupt and nepotic Ferdinand and Imelda Marcos. Nor should Juan and Isabellita Peron's promotion of the couple seem out of place – though Elena found little to admire in Peron's second wife, an ageing and broadening nightclub hostess, compared with the legendary Evita.

Even the encouragement given to the Ceaușescus' globe-trotting by Robert Mugabe was pretty much a case of like endorsing like. Both the Zimbabwean President and his wife Sally, the Mother of the Nation, seem to have taken to Nicolae and Elena. Mugabe gave the Comrade the opportunity to fulfil one of his long-held ambitions as Romania's Great White Hunter – to shoot one of Zimbabwe's increasingly rare elephants and to take the tusks home as a trophy. Even as late as June 1990, the Zimbabwean President publicly expressed his disbelief at what the ungrateful Romanians had done at Christmas 1989 to his former honoured guests – but then he was still bent on making his country into a one-party state according to the tried and trusted recipe. The world and its leaders reacted very differently to the news of Ceauşescu's fall: Westerners, even those who had flattered him, rejoiced, but the rulers of Third World or Communist states mourned him – not only for his own violent end, but also because they saw it as a premonition of their own impending fates.[35]

Despite Romanian support for the Emperor Bokassa, the Central African Empire was one of the few African states which the Ceauşescus failed to visit. Their devotion to African and Asian states was surprising in view of their dislike of humidity, and Nicolae's aversion to mosquitoes, as well as their well-developed sense of superiority to those they still thought of as negroes. Large quantities of Western insecticides as well as elaborate pest-proof bedding had to be transported for their regular journeys into the Dark Continent. The quest for international recognition, almost regardless as to the importance of the state bestowing it, took on an almost manic quality by the later 1980s. The fewer Western states wished to receive the *Conducator*, the more he had to fill his diary with visits to other self-proclaimed National Heroes and Liberators of the People. Another African host, the late President Samuel Doe of Liberia, had much in common with Elena: he aspired to study at Cambridge University. It was because the rebels believed that he had stashed away rather more cash abroad than might be necessary to pay his tuition fees that Doe met an end still more grisly than that of his Romanian guests.

Whereas his state visits to Washington, London or Bonn had given Ceauşescu enormous status even within Romania, his tireless travelling around the Third World helped to undermine respect for him at home. It was one thing to have turned his own country into an 'underdeveloping' society, but to seek out the company of the other basket-cases of the world economy was to add gratuitous insult to already grave injury in the minds of most Romanians.

Although the endless state visits to Harare or Mauretania always climaxed with the publication of pompous declarations and assertions that trade was going to increase by generous percentages within a few years, the consequences of these visits were negligible apart from providing a few more exhibits for the trophy rooms in Bucharest. However, the buttering-up of Western politicians was not wasted. Its object was to get access to modern technology as cheaply as possible and as much effort was put into charming Western bankers and businessmen as their political leaders. As good students of Lenin, the Romanian leaders needed no reminding of the short-sighted lust for profit of many capitalists and their lack of concern for the public interest, in their own countries or abroad. Ceauşescu and his intelligence advisers recognized the corruptibility of many Western businessmen, but even more, they knew how to play upon on Western wishful thinking and self-deception.

If Romania was to get cheap credits and access to high-tech goods it needed to prove its credit-worthiness to the prestigious foreign institutions which specialized in economic analysis. Some institutions like the World Bank employed many economics 'experts' who were thoroughly sympathetic to the claims made for the efficiency of planned economies, regardless of the empirical evidence. In 1979, the World Bank published a glowing report, *Romania: Industrialization under Socialist Planning*, which claimed, on the basis of official Romanian government figures, that in the quarter century between 1950 and 1975, the Romanian economy had grown at an average compound annual rate of over 9%. Few countries in the world – certainly not economic sloths like Japan or West Germany – came near such a rate of progress. Clearly Romania was well on its way to becoming an economic super-success and anyone with funds to spare was well advised to lend them to Ceauşescu.

The sceptical economist Peter Bauer did a simple calculation, reversing the World Bank's growth-rate. Bauer asked himself: what was the economic level of Romania in 1950 and what was the average annual income of Romanians then? De-compounding the dramatic 9% growth-rate revealed that in 1950, the Romanian economy would have been too small to sustain human life on the income available.[36] In other words, the World Bank's figures were bogus, but what mattered was that they provided welcome fodder to those who were already convinced of the value of Ceaușescu's friendship and wished to promote further deals with his regime.

Ceaușescu's double-game of continuing to recognize Israel while courting the Arab states paid dividends in his relations with the Western democracies. They saw him as the 'honest broker' who might help negotiate a resolution of the Middle East's problems. Ceaușescu fondly imagined the day when the Nobel Peace Prize would be added to his trophy cabinet. At the same time, he was anxious to foster Romania's influence in the region as a supplier of arms and the provider of a safe haven for the training of Palestinian terrorists, among others. The officially published diaries of Ceaușescu's engagements reveal that Yasser Arafat was his most frequent guest: on average they met six times a year and saw each other for the last time only a month before the revolution. During the Christmas revolution, it was claimed that Arab guerrillas in training camps formed the core of the last defenders of Ceaușescu's regime. This was one of several useful myths propagated by the men who overthrew Ceaușescu, but was widely believed by Romanians, who knew from experience that Romania housed thousands of young, unattached Arab 'students'.

Ceaușescu was an important intermediary between Egypt and Israel in the lead up to Anwar Sadat's dramatic visit to Jerusalem in 1977. He met both Israeli leaders and Sadat beforehand. It was Ceaușescu who reassured Sadat with positive answers to his key questions: Could he trust Menachem Begin and could Begin deliver on any promises he might make to Egypt? Of course, Jimmy Carter's support for the negotiations was vital to their success: the USA could both reassure Israel and reward Egypt with economic and military aid. But without Ceaușescu's discretion – Bucharest was not as leaky a diplomatic centre as Washington – the American President would not have been able to achieve the one great success of his presidency, the Camp David Agreement between Israel and Egypt. This debt helps to explain Carter's willingness to receive Ceauşescu in April 1978.[37]

In retrospect, Ceauşescu's first important meeting with a Western head of state on equal terms took place in circumstances which made it a curious anticipation of his own downfall. In May 1968, Charles de Gaulle paid a state visit to Romania, the first by a Western leader. De Gaulle had made of France's relations with the United States and the rest of NATO, what Ceauşescu seemed to do for Romania over the next decade within the Warsaw Pact. The visit should have been a great success for both the tall and the short mavericks of the respective alliances. Unfortunately, the students of Paris saw to it that the French President had to beat an undignified and premature retreat from Bucharest. For a brief moment, it seemed that it was not only the presidents of newly independent Third World countries who had to take special precautions before departing on state visits. On 18 December 1989, Nicolae Ceauşescu arrived in Teheran for the last of countless travels abroad. He laid a wreath at the tomb of the Ayatollah Khomeini. After all the drama of '68, de Gaulle, of course, simply went querulously into retirement in 1969 after the students had gone back to their studies and the French electorate felt it was safe to dispense with his services. Within a week of going to Iran, Ceauşescu was dead.

VI

Challenges to the Clan's Power

Let them hate so long as they fear.
                                        Caligula

On 4 August 1977, the Romanian Communist Party's daily
newspaper, *Scînteia*, carried a report of 'Comrade Nicolae
Ceauşescu's working visit to the Jiu Valley'. The bland
account, superficially no different from hundreds of others
carried every day, continued: 'in the course of his visit, Comrade Nicolae Ceauşescu met with representatives of the miners
of Lupeni.' During this meeting Ceauşescu noted 'some shortcomings in the organization of the mines, some abuses in the
application of laws, and some deficiencies in the leadership of
the mines'.[1] Behind the bland terms of *Scînteia's* unimposing
announcement lay the greatest challenge to Ceauşescu's
power, in fact to communism's control of Romania, to date.
A few days earlier, the 40,000 miners of the Jiu Valley
towns of Lupeni, Vulcan and Petrosani, in the foothills of the
Carpathians two hundred and fifty miles to the north-west of
Bucharest, had done the unimaginable in a communist state:
they had gone on strike. They occupied the pitheads, and
even took the government's emissaries hostage, demanding
that the Comrade himself come and hear their grievances
about changes in their output quotas, wages, and pension
rates, as well as about poor housing and worse food.

In 1972, the miners of the Jiu Valley had already shown that they were not the reliable toadies who could be expected to applaud the Comrade without comment on his 'working visits'. Even the Party daily, *Scînteia* had noted during one of Ceauşescu's endless round of 'meet the workers' visits, that some of the miners 'did not hesitate' to put their 'point of view' to the General-Secretary. It was one of those uncomfortable collisions with discontent about housing and the quality of food which Ceauşescu's aides were supposed to keep out of his itinerary. Despite evident irritation, the *Conducator* blamed the local officials and issued firm instructions to resolve matters, in the hearing of the miners. Such dressings-down of the local bosses were naturally popular with the ordinary people and for a while at least they helped to foster the paternalist image of the General-Secretary. In many absolutist states the myth that if only the Tsar or the Führer knew about the people's grievances he would act to resolve them was carefully fostered by state propaganda and even more so in Romania by the Securitate's rumour machine.[2]

Like their peers elsewhere in Eastern Europe and the Soviet Union, the Communist rulers of Romania were shrewd enough to know that not even village idiots believed the official media. What Radio Bucharest announced was what people had to believe in public, in other words the formulas that they needed to repeat to prove their loyalty and conformity to the regime. What people actually believed about their country and the world around it was derived either from foreign radio stations, which enjoyed greater credibility the less their news coincided with the local stations, or from rumours. Whereas people throughout the communist world were inclined to believe the opposite of what their masters told them (e.g. Pinochet was a good democrat – why else would 'They' abuse him?), very often their scepticism collapsed in the face of an unsubstantiated rumour. The Securitate had a department devoted to analysing the rumours in circulation and putting out its own to promote the regime's purposes, which often could not be publicly stated.

The news in August 1977 of the strike of thousands of coal-miners in the Jiu Valley was the realization of the waking-nightmare of all Communist regimes. That the working class in whose name the Party bosses ruled from East Berlin to Vladivostok should suddenly denounce its leaders and abuse them as a 'red bourgeoisie' was the greatest trauma of the *nomenklatura*. Ceauşescu responded to the threat by sending the ever-reliable Ilie Verdeţ and the Minister of Mining, Constantin Babalu, to negotiate with the strikers. They were instructed to fob them off with promises in order to get them back to work as quickly as possible.

To the embarrassment of Verdeţ, it became clear that the strikers at Lupeni would settle for nothing less than meeting the Comrade face to face and putting their demands to him. Verdeţ was pushed into the porter's cabin at the entrance to the mine and obliged to telephone Communist Party headquarters in Bucharest with the miners' message. To reinforce it, several miners crammed into the little wooden hut with Verdeţ, adding the odour of their own sweaty bodies to the air of tension. Ceauşescu was unwilling to come to the phone and Verdeţ had difficulty controlling the mood inside the cabin. He could only imagine the impatience of the thousands waiting in the late summer sun outside. The officials of the Central Committee who first dealt with Verdeţ were not entirely certain of the situation in the Jiu Valley. They left Verdeţ unsure about how Ceauşescu would react to the miners' insistence that he himself should come.[3]

While they waited to hear what the leadership in Bucharest would decide, the miners held the high-ranking emissaries as hostages in cramped conditions at the pithead. To pass the time, they told Verdeţ what his fate would be if the government resorted to violence to suppress the strike or to try and rescue them. They also insisted that they would blow up the mines if Ceauşescu tried to force them back to work. Quite correctly, they reckoned that ministers and central committee secretaries might be expendable to their Boss, but coal-mines were something he could not afford to lose.

Eventually, after three days, Ceauşescu came in person. When he appeared before a great crowd of miners and their families in the primitive football stadium at Lupeni, he was greeted with catcalls about the 'red bourgeoisie'. However, he had taken several precautions to distance his own image from that of the *nomenklatura* as a whole. He came in an open-necked shirt and walked to the makeshift podium without a very obvious security presence. Some elderly miners, veteran communists, were supposed to have guaranteed his safety. When he spoke, Ceauşescu emphasized his own working-class origins as well as his recognition of the hard and dangerous life of the miners. He reminded them that shortly after he became General-Secretary in 1965, he had revised plan targets for coal output in order to put less strain on the miners and to reduce the risk of accidents at work.

Ceauşescu agreed to reverse the pay cuts that the men in effect faced because they could not cut enough coal to meet the Five Year Plan's targets. The pension arrangements of miners had been changed earlier in the year: instead of receiving a set pension, retired miners were to be paid pensions based on their average earnings in any five of their last ten years at work. Since older miners were usually no longer fit to work at the coal-face and did less well-remunerated jobs on or near the surface, this meant that in old age – if they reached it – their pensions were to be a calculated on the basis of their more poorly paid years at work! These obnoxious changes to their pension arrangements were also reversed. Their other demands were met, or at least Ceauşescu promised to satisfy them. Any cheers that met his statement – which was not heard in silence – were not for the General-Secretary but for his concessions.[4]

Ceauşescu knew that he could not both meet the miners' demands and achieve his economic targets. He made it clear to Verdeţ that some way around his promises would have to be found, but one which would not simply revive the workers' militancy. During his stay, he set to work himself on the principle *divide et impera*. The only positive aspect of the strike from the Party's point of view was that the miners had only formulated demands about their conditions of work and life. They had not taken the step of demanding political change to make the decisions which affected their lives a matter of debate and consent before they were taken.

The miners' representatives had not even pressed for a free trade union, though they had demanded the removal of trade union officials whom they did not like or trust. Ceauşescu was happy to meet this condition: for him, as for any true follower of Lenin, a trade union was 'a transmission belt of authority'; if the union officials could not get the workers to meet their targets, failed to anticipate strikes, and then did not resolve them at once, what use were they to the regime?

The chief spokesman of the strikers was Costica Dobre. He had been catapulted into the awesome role of negotiator with his country's ruler more by chance than anything else. Life had not prepared him for the task, and it soon became clear that he lacked the natural shrewdness and strength of character that a Gdansk plumber was to show the Polish bosses three years later. If Costica Dobre was no Lech Walesa, nor was Ceauşescu a fool like Eduard Gierek. Taking Dobre aside, Ceauşescu made it clear to him that his talents were wasted down a mine. A man of his abilities should go far in the Party. The chance to escape from the daily drudgery in the pits must have been more than attractive. Shortly after the end of the strike, Dobre left the valley to go and study at the Communist Party's university in Bucharest, the Academy Stefan Gheorghe. There he met and came under the influence of one of the instructors, Professor Virgil Magureanu, who was to be one of the judges at the trial of Nicolae and Elena Ceauşescu, thirteen years later. No one would then have anticipated Magureanu's distinguished future. In the early 1980s he was put in charge of Securitate activities in Western Europe. He survived the revolution to become head of the Romanian Information Service – that is to say, the Securitate under its new name. Magureanu was not able to help Dobre settle down in his new calling as an apparatchik in the service of Ceauşescu, though he kept a 'paternal' eye on the erstwhile rebel over the next decade.[5]

Over the next year or so after August 1977, the concessions granted to the miners were gradually revoked. As the miners and millions of other Romanians came to rue with each passing year until December 1989, the greatest chance to change the leadership had been missed. Ceauşescu did not mean to let it come again. The mines were flooded with thousands of new workers. A decade later 7,000 soldiers were working alongside civilian miners. Many of these civilians were brought in from other mining areas in Romania. Just as in his rotation of Party officials to areas with which they had no connection and where they would have difficulty building up a power-base, so now Ceauşescu was transferring people into new places of work, forcing them to move from their old homes. He knew very well that fear of Securitate informers was as effective a way of hamstringing opposition as actually deploying agents in the field. Of course, Ceauşescu was not a man to leave things to chance. At the end of 1977, to confirm the Securitate's control over the pits, the Party secretary in charge of security matters, Vasile Patilineţ, was appointed the new Minister of Mines.[6]

Ceauşescu knew Lenin's dictum, 'trust is good but control is better', and ordered the Securitate to send in new informers and to recruit more from among the existing workforce as well. As ever, rank-and-file Party members and local trades union officials provided the core of the listening web which was supposed to embrace all citizens of Romania from cradle to grave.

Ion Pacepa has described how scientists working for the Securitate designed a telephone which could be used to bug both phone conversations and any talk in the room where the apparatus was located. How many of these telephones were installed remains unknown, but after the revolution many Romanians who had telephones (a small minority of the population, of course) ripped open their own apparatus to find the hidden microphones. Needless to say, given the universal inefficiency of the Socialist Republic of Romania, relatively few listening-devices were found, at least by do-it-yourself de-buggers. What enthusiastic amateurs often managed to do after the revolution was to disable their telephones by removing components which looked suspicious, but were innocent and vital to the functioning of the machine.[7]

In some ways, the broadcasting by Radio Free Europe of extracts from Pacepa's *Red Horizons* served the regime well. From the Securitate's point of view, belief in the omnipresence of its surveillance was often as important as the actual capacity to intercept everybody's telephone calls. As George Orwell noted in *1984*, the fear that the thought-police might monitor everybody at all times was enough to keep Big Brother's subjects in a state of paralysed terror.

A perverse testimony to the feeling that most Romanians had of being constantly under the scrutiny of an all-embracing network of human and electronic observers were published by an official Romanian journal in the summer of 1988. A twelve-year-old schoolgirl had written a science fiction story, 'The White City', which read like a thinly veiled satire on Romanian reality:

> Liliana Cojacaru creates a huge urban settlement, which initiates mankind's good and peaceful actions, a kind of general headquarters of quiet and security. Extra-sensitive radars are continually detecting not only tensions among countries and peoples anywhere on Earth, *but also the smallest disputes among friends, or even among parents and children*.[8]

Despite the well-founded fear of the Securitate, for most of the period of Communist rule in Romania, the secret police was not in the front-line of control over the population. Ten years after the Jiu Valley miners' strike, a protest demonstration erupted in Braşov on 15 November 1987, the day of local elections. The crowd which stormed the local Party headquarters and found stocks of fresh citrus fruits in store there, were soon suppressed by special troops.[9] In the aftermath of the events in Braşov, Silviu Brucan became the first old Communist apparatchik to break ranks with Ceauşescu and publicly criticize his policies. It is also striking how far he took issue with Western critics of Ceauşescu's Romania who saw it as a police-state pure and simple. In his statement smuggled to the *Independent* in London, Brucan said: 'I must take issue with a misconception prevailing in the West that this regime owes its survival to the repressive organs of the State. Surely this could not explain more than two decades of political stability. In fact, *the main instrument of power has been the Communist Party*, with the security forces playing only a marginal role and dealing with especially deviant cases.'[10]

'Kill one, frighten ten thousand' was Mao's dictum about the use of force. Of course, in practice, the Great Helmsman acted on the principle: 'Kill ten thousand, frighten a billion', and not just once. But Ceauşescu preferred to terrify his opponents into silence and conformity rather than to kill them. A few ringleaders of trouble like the miners who failed to follow Dobre's example in 1977 were 'disappeared'. Similarly in Braşov, the Securitate used photographs of the crowd taken from an armoured car which had swept through it on 15 November to identify 'especially deviant cases'. They were then 'dealt with' over the next eighteen months. When faced by demonstrations or strikes, Ceauşescu's regime generally avoided head-on clashes. They preferred to isolate the area of discontent, reduce any crowd to its hard-core and then to move, or even wait until after people had dispersed before taking action. So long as it could prevent news of discontent travelling from one region to another and igniting a bush-fire of revolt, the Party was able to restore its control relatively quickly and with little loss of life.

On 1 March 1989, a group of British skiers were horrified to see a man set fire to himself on the ski-slopes outside Braşov. He left a plea behind him: 'Stop the killings in Braşov.' But at the time his name was unknown. It was testimony to the effectiveness of the terror inspired by the Securitate that unlike Jan Palach in Prague in 1969, the dead man's suicidal gesture of protest remained anonymous. It was only after the revolution that Liviu Babes was named as the martyr. Ironically, at the same time as Babes was killing himself in protest against Ceauşescu's tyranny, the BBC ran a holiday programme detailing the pleasures of skiing around Braşov and suggesting that viewers go to Romania for a glimpse of *glasnost*.[11] Despite the repression which drove Babes to suicide. Ceauşescu was not after all Pol Pot, though in his last hours on earth perhaps he wished that he had been. Pol Pot lives to fight another day despite butchering millions of his people. In the end, Ceauşescu fell because he degraded most Romanians without destroying them. He taught them hatred and fear, but when at last their fear waned, their hatred devoured him.

It was not long after the autumn of 1977, that things began to look very bleak for the Romanians. The future promised only worse to come. Towards the end of the Shah's reign, Ceauşescu made a deal that was supposed to earn Communist Romania a fortune in hard currency from the capitalist West. Romania would import Iranian oil via its port of Constanza and then process it in refineries specially built for the purpose. It would then sell on the finished product to the West for dollars, which would in turn fund other high-tech developments.

Using money borrowed from Western banks, Ceauşescu embarked on building an oil-refining capacity three times greater than Romania's domestic production of oil. (He also borrowed heavily to fund other projects: a vast aluminium-smelting complex at Slatina, for instance, that threatened to consume as much electricity as the domestic consumers of Romania!) Then the Shah fell. His old friends were no longer welcome with the Ayatollah. Not only did the deal fall through, but the Iranian Revolution, and then the Iran-Iraq War which followed it, drove up the price of oil in the West. Ceauşescu could not profit from this because he had none to sell. Worse still, interest rates shot up and Romania had to pay more and more to the Western banks simply to service the debt. Capitalism had always been baffling to Ceauşescu, now his involvement with it was a curse. In Poland, Gierek's regime plunged into crisis in the face of its mountain of debt. Ceauşescu's colleagues watched the rise of Solidarity with anxiety. Some Romanians, however, saw the emergence of General Jaruzelski and his apparently successful suppression of Solidarity after 13 December 1981, as a good omen: perhaps, the local incompetent might be replaced by a reliable general and perhaps the Soviet Union would not mind either.

Meanwhile Ceauşescu became convinced, in common with other East European states in hock to Western bankers, that credit was being used as a political weapon and that Reagan intended to finance his rearmament through the interest due on their loans. Only Ceauşescu came to the 'obvious' conclusion: the debt should not be rescheduled, it should be paid off as quickly as possible. From 1982 onwards, Romania's Western creditors found themselves faced by a baffling response from Bucharest to their offers of further credit. It was unwanted. The Western banks regarded Romania as a good risk: cynically, they judged that Ceauşescu would keep the lid on the pot in Romania in a way that Gierek had manifestly failed to do in Poland. Whatever his faults from the perspective of Amnesty International, those very same blots on his reputation were what made Romania much more credit-worthy than many less brutal regimes. But independence is indivisible, so Ceauşescu thought, he should not have let Romania become dependent on Western credit any more than he had let it fall under Soviet political control. By 1989, he was publicly proclaiming his intention of imitating Albania and anchoring a ban on foreign loans in the constitution, which was clearly going to be more binding on his successors than himself.[12]

Paying off the debt meant cutting consumption at home of the few things which were imported and almost anything which might be exported. Ceauşescu set the target: $10 billion had to be repaid by the end of the decade. Rationing was introduced on most food items – not to share the burden equally but to reduce consumption so that more foodstuffs could be exported. Romanian meat went in every direction. Even the US Army in West Germany was fed on beef and pork from Romania in the early 1980s. Only unappetizing parts of animal carcasses remained for the domestic market. Romanians called pigs' trotters 'patriots' because they were the only bits of the pig allowed to remain in the country. In a typical joke a teacher tells her pupils to draw a pig. They diligently draw its head, trotters and tail. 'But where is the body?' asks the teacher. 'You didn't say to draw an export pig!' chorus the children in reply. Jokes about their own plight and sarcasms aimed at 'Them' at the top went the rounds as the standard of living fell steadily throughout Romania in the 1980s. Outbreaks of popular discontent became more frequent, but were no more effective than the great strike of 1977.[13]

In October 1981, Ceauşescu repeated his direct intervention when the miners of Motru rioted and attacked the local Party HQ. However, he recognized that the days when he could play the benign ruler, satisfying the grievances of his subjects and punishing guilty lesser officials, were waning – even if he had nothing more positive to put in its place. In 1982, he sacked on the spot several high-ranking officials for failing to maintain an adequate food supply to the main market in Bucharest – as if it was their fault that there was nothing to show the General-Secretary when he put in a surprise inspection visit. Everybody knew that they lived in a 'planned economy' and they also knew who, in the final analysis, drew up the plan. But such Machiavellian gestures on the part of a benevolent ruler increasingly cut less ice with the people. After 1981, the Securitate and other security forces were used as the prime means of settling industrial disputes and demonstrations.[14]

It was not surprising that even within the upper reaches of the Party discontent began to come into the open, or at least to be expressed clearly behind closed doors at meetings of the Central Committee or Council of Ministers. By 1981, Virgil Trofin had been downgraded, like so many former protégés, and was now Minister of Mines and Petroleum. Suddenly, at the Central Committee meeting in November, he failed to respond to the criticisms levelled at his ministry for failure to meet plan targets in the standard manner, neither would he take the blame for the strike at Motru. Instead of criticizing himself, begging for forgiveness, and promising to follow the example of Comrade Ceauşescu more closely in the future, Trofin launched into a tirade against the absurdity of Ceauşescu's methods of planning. He described the impossibility of extracting high-grade coking coal from the worn-out mines under his control, particularly if investment in modern machinery was cut. The heresy was heard out, but then the heretic was expelled from all his posts and finally the Party itself. As in the rest of Romanian society, even in the Party leadership, no one could rely on anyone else with confidence.[15]

A year later, Virgil Trofin died. At the time it was rumoured that he had been murdered or committed suicide. In fact, it seems he had a stroke, but that the doctors were discouraged from treating him quickly by the Securitate. Although Trofin had been an ally of Ceauşescu against the old guard in the mid-1960s, in an act of rare solidarity, perhaps even comradeship, Draghici, Bârladeanu, Brucan, Corneliu Manescu, and others turned out to mourn him at his funeral. At the time, it seemed that nothing could break Ceauşescu's hold over a servile and cowardly Party élite. A couple of years later, Ion Iliescu followed Trofin into the wilderness. He apparently remarked in his capacity as Minister of Water Affairs that not even socialism 'could make water run uphill' during a discussion of Ceauşescu's favourite project to complete the long-abandoned canal linking Bucharest to the Black Sea. Unlike Trofin, Iliescu did not raise his voice against Ceauşescu, but remained a simple member of the Communist Party and waited for times to change.[16]

*

Disputes within the Communist Parties of Eastern Europe were veiled from public view and the West knew little about them. In fact, most Western interest in the slim possibilities of reform in the East tended to focus on the academic and intellectual dissidents in Eastern Europe rather than either disgraced apparatchiks or those stubborn, principled ordinary people without contacts abroad who defied the system in anonymity just because they would not bend any further. The fate of the common person who refused to conform and voted 'No' in the bogus elections beloved of Communist rulers rarely attracted attention in the West. How could it? But at a day-to-day level, the resistance of ordinary people was reflected by the 'silent strike', the carelessness and indifference people paid to their work. Even quite senior figures in the system just went through the motions of working and fulfilling the crazy plan laid down from a great height without taking local conditions into account.

Georgi Markov, the Bulgarian dissident writer, recalled the first speech given by a new factory director which could have been given by any Romanian middle-ranking cynical conformist when put in charge of an operation by an arbitrary decision from the top. The director told his new subordinates:

> Frankly, I don't know why I am here. I've no idea what you're doing, how you are doing it, and what it all adds up to. However, as They've sent me here, I'm going to stay. But I don't want us to tread on each other's toes. I shall be the director but you will work in the way you're used to and as you think fit. Don't ask me questions because I can't tell you anything.[17]

It was that sort of genial incompetent who plagued the management of Ceauşescu's industry, but what else were ill-trained bureaucrats to do when orders rained down on them which could not be obeyed even with the best will in the world. Ceauşescu himself knew the cynical and cringing apologetics of those managers who were caught out for gross failure to follow the Plan. In 1988, he complained, 'I must say that I have the impression that there is a certain mentality with some activists. "I will be criticized again, I will once again admit my mistakes, I will make some more pledges; and that will be all."'[18] That was exactly what the average person called on to make self-criticism thought: all that mattered was getting through the ritual humiliation, and then going for a drink. Such people were the most irreducible problem for the Communist system everywhere and perhaps its ultimate downfall.

Of course, Nicolae and Elena Ceauşescu did not deal personally with every village dissident or industrial worker who spoke his mind. Perhaps pressure from his local boss or Party secretary would revise the awkward customer's views in an acceptable direction. If not the Securitate, with the help of its 'special measures', or even psychiatrists with their drugs, would change the victim's mind once and for all.[19]

The better-known intellectual dissidents risked incurring the wrath of the Comrades at the top. The name of the writer Paul Goma, for instance, was enough to make both of them spit with rage. Like most other people in Romania the Ceauşescus were fascinated by Radio Free Europe's reporting on the country and were always anxious to hear its latest news. The ruling couple preferred, however, to receive RFE's news at second hand from a minion, who all too often had the thankless task of retailing the unflattering commentary or the contents of a critical letter smuggled out to the Munich-based radio station by one of their subjects. Elena particularly suffered from a painful fascination with the appalling contents of radio broadcasts. According to Pacepa, it was her obsession with the scurrilous anonymous letters sent to RFE that led to the establishment of the national handwriting archive, as well as the decree requiring all typewriters to be registered with the authorities and a regular sample of the typeface to be provided.

In early February 1977, Romanian listeners heard the text of an Open Letter to their president from the novelist, Paul

Goma. A month before, Goma had been the first Romanian to try to imitate the initiative of the dissidents of Czechoslovakia. Led by Pavel Kohout, Vaclav Havel and other Czechs and Slovaks who would not buckle under to the regime imposed on Czechoslovakia by Brezhnev's tanks in 1968, the first permanent group of dissidents in Eastern Europe issued their statement of inalienable human rights at the start of the year – *Charter* 77. Goma signed up to support *Charter* 77, but very few other Romanians, and certainly fewer still of his fellow intellectuals, took the risk of publicly associating themselves with the critics of the fraternal Communist regime in Czechoslovakia. Undeterred by the understandable timidity of his acquaintances, Goma hit upon a masterstroke of irony.

The Open Letter broadcast by RFE in February 1977 was addressed to the President of the Socialist Republic of Romania 'at the Royal Palace'. Goma appealed to the man who denounced the Soviet invasion of Czechoslovakia in August 1968 to stand up and be counted, and so give an example to his fellow citizens to persuade them to overcome their reticence about signing the *Charter*:

> I turn to you in despair. You are my last hope . . . Ever since *Charter* 77 was published . . . I can find no rest, and, I am sure of it, neither can you . . . I try to convince my acquaintances to join in the action of the Czechs and Slovaks, but I fail . . . The Romanians fear the security forces . . . It seems that only two persons in the country do not fear them: Your Excellency and myself . . . An entirely different situation would be brought about should Your Excellency send a declaration of support to *Charter* 77. I am profoundly convinced that millions of Romanians would follow you.[20]

Naturally, Ceauşescu had no intention of engaging in a debate with Goma. Subtle word-play had never been the *Conducator's* forte. Instead, he chose to reply to Goma's letter in his own direct way. The former champion boxer of Romania, Horst Stumpf, now a captain in the militia, was sent round to Goma's home to teach him his manners. It was not the first time Stumpf's skills had been put to such use. Like the other athletes of the Interior Ministry's Dinamo Sports Club, he was in the service of the state at all times. Goma still showed signs of his beating when he was allowed to emigrate to France shortly afterwards.[21]

Goma did not show the gratitude towards the Comrade expected from someone given the privilege of leaving Romania and he continued to agitate against the regime from Paris. It was decided to teach him the final lesson, which would also warn off other émigrés who thought that they were secure in the West and could say what they liked about Ceaușescu. The Romanian secret agent, Matei Pavel Haiducu, who was based in France to pursue industrial espionage, was instructed to silence both Paul Goma and another troublesome dissident, Virgil Tanase. He was equipped with a special poison designed by Soviet specialists to kill the victim through cardiac arrest without leaving evidence of his murder. Haiducu not only failed to assassinate Goma and Tanase, but handed himself over to the French authorities with his weapon.[22]

Not all of the émigrés from Eastern Europe were so fortunate as Goma and Tanase, who lived with the constant threat of assassination at least until Christmas 1989. At about the same time, as Haiducu abandoned his mission, the Bulgarian exile, Georgi Markov, whose revelations of the corruption of Zhivkov's cronies infuriated Ceaușescu's Bulgarian counterpart, was murdered by an unknown agent of the Bulgarian secret police in London. Another Bulgarian 'traitor' survived a similar stab from an umbrella in Paris. The Romanian section of Radio Free Europe in Munich was repeatedly the object of attempts by the Romanian secret service to penetrate it and to harm its staff members. The Romanian section's staff had an alarming tendency to die from cancer. After his defection to the United States, Pacepa claimed that Eastern

Bloc scientists had developed a method, known as RADU, of irradiating an enemy and inducing cancerous tumors. This was Ceauşescu's preferred weapon in dealing with his critics at home and abroad, when the case was not urgent and when the very length of the victim's sufferings might add to the satisfaction of his elimination.[23]

The Securitate was also anxious to make sure that any suffering on the part of a non-conformist at home was made known to the dissident's contacts in the West. In the summer of 1988, Doina Cornea, the former lecturer in French literature at Cluj University, smuggled a letter to the BBC and RFE attacking Ceauşescu's plan to demolish thousands of villages as part of 'systematization'. Her friends in the West were told that she would be beaten until they stopped publicizing her case.

To the thin-skinned Ceauşescus, the broadcasts of Radio Free Europe and the BBC were intolerable, but they recognized that the émigré broadcasters had little or no influence in the West. When Haiducu defected he named, among others, the Romanian Ambassador to France as one of those involved in plots like the one to murder Goma and Tanase. The Quai d'Orsay (the French foreign ministry) said that it did not consult with the French secret service before accepting the credentials of East European diplomats, and apparently had no intention of instituting such an undiplomatic practice. It would take a great deal more than flagrant attempts to assassinate people in Western capitals and the hardly less obvious espionage of the Directorate of External Intelligence to make Nicolae Ceauşescu *persona non grata* in the West.

VII

The Cult of Personality

Somoza Unveils the Statue of Somoza in Somoza Stadium

Not that I believe the people raised this statue to me,
I know as well as you that I commissioned it.
Nor that I thereby hope for immortality:
I know the people will one day destroy it.
Nor that I wished to give myself in life
The monument you will not raise when I am dead:
But that I raised it knowing you hate it.

Ernesto Cardenal[1]

In April 1968, the reformer Ceauşescu told his Central Committee, 'We don't need any idols . . . Marxism-Leninism rejected and rejects any such concepts, which have nothing in common with the ideology of the working-class.'[2] Less than a dozen years later, television, radio, newspapers, posters and placards proclaimed the same slogans extolling life in the 'age of Ceauşescu'. 'Epocha Ceauşescu', became the shorthand both in official propaganda to justify every acclaimed new success in building a multi-laterally developed socialist society and in ordinary people's bitter sarcasm when confronted by another breakdown in supplies of energy or food. Even foreign tourists who had not yet caught on to the realities of life in Romania and perhaps were over-insistent in demanding from a minor bureaucrat of the tourist office why some essential and prepaid feature of their holiday had failed to materialize would be confronted by a shrug of the shoulders and the muttered words, 'Epocha Ceauşescu' as the only explanation.

Comparisons between twentieth-century dictators and the classical tyrants of Ancient Rome are alluring but misleading. Of course, Roman emperors deified themselves, made their horses consuls and existed in a state of terrifying paranoia which eventually provoked genuine plots and assassinations, but in retrospect the gross crimes of a Caligula or Nero lacked the all-pervading hypocrisy of the modern tyrants. Caligula was degenerate but, by all accounts, did not deign to hide the fact. Ceauşescu's vices were mundane, but probably more damaging to his people as a whole than a debauched emperor's capricious treatment of Ancient Rome's élite.

From the time of Stalin, at least, modesty and megalomania have gone hand in hand. Stalin's humility was put on record in the official history of the Soviet Communist Party — at his own suggestion. Countless twentieth-century dictators have been defended from their detractors by pointing out the asceticism of their private lives. If the propaganda portrait of Hitler reached the pinnacle of self-denial, showing him virtually celibate, certainly teetotal, non-smoking, vegetarian and animal-loving, the other would-be saviours/butchers of humanity such as Pol Pot have all conformed, at least publicly, to type. Some of the worst tyrants have in fact been without private vices: as Bertrand de Jouvenel once noted, 'power is the most perfect form of self-indulgence'. (Henry Kissinger, practical as ever, called power 'the ultimate aphrodisiac'.)

Nicolae and Elena Ceauşescu's devotion to each other was unaffected by their complete power. Unlike Nicolae's sister, Elena Barbulescu, Elena Ceauşescu was never tempted by her power to stray from fidelity to her husband. Although Elena possessed the powers and ambitions of a Messalina, she had the domestic virtues of a good bourgeois, but then so did her husband. Of course, their domestic tastes were more grandiose than most contented couples, and Elena played her part in promoting the over-decoration of their apartments in the various palaces they used, and even in those they never visited. But though, at the revolution, Romanians were shocked by stories about the pictures of the luxurious excesses of the Ceauşescus' lifestyle – which until then had remained private – they had to whisper about their children, especially Nicu, if they wanted gossip of a Neronian quality.

Until 22 December 1989, the General-Secretary and his wife were presented to the Romanian people (despite Elena's highly visible furs and cashmere clothing) as a hard-working, abstemious couple with only one thought – the well-being of 'The People'. Both Nicolae and Elena constantly emphasized in their speeches that they had sprung from the common people and therefore shared their hopes and sufferings. Of course, rumours abounded about what went on behind the barriers which prevented the common people from entering the districts where the Communist élite lived, but no one knew for sure. Naturally, the building of the huge Palace of the People could not be hidden from public view, but the actual details its plans or internal designs were never discussed or published in the media. The ignorance of ordinary people sometimes led to exaggerations of the self-indulgence of the Ceauşescus after the revolution. Quite often features of their palaces would be described as made of solid gold, which were in fact merely brass. Perhaps the Ceauşescus were themselves sometimes cheated and knew no better.

The Palace of the People was, of course, a massive exercise in doublethink. Although clearly designed to the specifications laid down by Ceauşescu so that it would be a suitable monument to his glory as well as a home and office for the remainder of his working life, the colossal building was always officially described as the Civic Centre. This name suggested that the capital's citizens might make some use of it. In fact, only the square in front of the eastern face of the building was intended for their use: up to 250,000 could assemble there to cheer the *Conducator*. The Civic Centre complex with the Palace of the People (later renamed Palace of the Republic) at its heart was designed to function as the

main shrine and nerve-centre of the cult of Nicolae
Ceauşescu.[3]

From about 1967 the praise of the General-Secretary pouring out from all the media took on more and more extreme
forms. At the IX Party Congress that year, both Ion Maurer
and Alexandru Bârladeanu emphasized in their speeches to
the delegates how much they owed to Nicolae Ceauşescu's
inspiration. After 1968, genuine approval of his anti-Soviet
stance gave a boost to the incipient cult and by 1974 it had
already reached its high-point, from which it never subsided,
but simply spread to a suffocating extent into all areas of
public life.[4]

The year 1974 saw both Ceauşescu's 'election' as President
of the Socialist Republic of Romania at a ceremony in which
he bestowed on himself not only a sash of office but a sceptre
too. It was the first overt addition to the rituals of Communist
adulation. The 'self-coronation' of Ceauşescu was a gesture in
imitation of Napoleon's crowning of himself in 1804. At the
XII Party Congress in the same year, Ceauşescu was compared
with great men and monarchs of the world's past. Many of
them were difficult to reconcile with orthodox Marxism, but
on the other hand, the Soviet Communist Party, for instance,
had long since annexed the great Russians of the past to grace
the progress towards Stalin or Khruschev or Brezhnev (or
whoever reigned in the Kremlin), Ceauşescu's hagiographers
chose Alexander the Great, Napoleon, Julius Caesar and
Abraham Lincoln (among others) to compare with Romania's
new president – in fact, he combined in himself all of their
virtues. Like the latter two, he was to die a violent death,
but that was not in the mind of his flatterers at that time.
Fifteen more years would be needed. From Augustus to Peter
the Great, the history books were ransacked to find suitable
comparisons.[5]

By 1967 Ceauşescu had already staged several historical
pageants at which he met the heroes of the Romanian past
and of his own childhood games. Actors played the parts of
the giants of Romania's chequered history, like Stephen the

Great, and gave a kind of historical blessing to the new General-Secretary. It was a sign that Ceauşescu intended to go much further than Dej in rehabilitating the Romanian past and distancing the Communist regime from the original Soviet model, at least so far as public presentation went.

In his early years, Ceauşescu liked to cock a snook at Brezhnev by making visits to the districts bordering the territories Romania lost to the Soviet Union in 1940. Once in the Southern Bukovina, a beautiful hilly land, he raised his glass to toast 'the Bukovina', implying Romania's right to the whole territory including the northern half now inside the Soviet Union. Such gestures appealed to many Romanians, as they did to Western observers anxious to see Ceauşescu as a 'patriot' and reformer. Of course, these gestures cost him little, but the gains in public opinion in Romania and the West were worthwhile.

The homage and cynical words of approval from foreign heads of state and politicians were ceaselessly recycled inside Romania to impress upon ordinary people how famous and how much admired their president had become. Ceauşescu's fame was supposed to compensate the ordinary Romanian (who could not travel) for life's temporary difficulties. They were expected to think to themselves as they rose before dawn to struggle off through bitter winter colds to join a pre-shift milk or bread queue: things may not be perfect but at least Ceauşescu has put Romania on the map! Those who could not console themselves with the thought of world-wide respect for their domestically heartily despised ruler were at least supposed to despair when they heard Western statesmen pour flattery over Ceauşescu. Many Romanians did despair. Others were baffled, not able to believe that free people, famous and rich too, could say what they saw printed or heard on Romanian television or radio. But then the BBC or Radio Free Europe would confirm the incomprehensible that this president or that queen had honoured Ceauşescu. Worst of all for the morale of ordinary Romanians was the ceremony in June 1978, when *the* Queen knighted Him.

Queen Elizabeth II had words of praise put into her mouth by Dr Owen's Foreign Office, which the Ceauşescu propaganda machine recycled endlessly. This culminated in their gaffe on the Comrade's birthday in 1989 when *Scînteia* carried a telegram of birthday greetings from the Queen which was promptly denied by the British Government. Although Ceauşescu continued to receive a daily deluge of congratulatory telegrams from tinpot rulers the world over until the last days of his rule, the reprinting of old praise from the Queen shows how desperate he was to present his people with evidence that he was acceptable to the West.[6]

Praise from Western quarters was used to reinforce Ceauşescu's standing at home. No one in Romania was allowed to forget the honours and flatteries which Western governments poured onto their maverick ruler. As time passed, Elena too became the subject of such gestures of endorsement from the West which were duly recorded for the benefit of Romanians, lest they forget by just how an extraordinary couple they were ruled. Books and newspaper articles were published in the West, often with a large subsidy from the local Romanian embassy. They were frequently on paper of a quality – and had typesetting of an eccentricity – that suggested they had actually been printed in Romania itself. Such books, and even genuinely spontaneous expressions of foreign admiration, soon found their way into displays in Romanian libraries and bookshops. After the revolution, those authors who were not simply names to fill space on the badly produced jacket were usually sufficiently embarrassed to try to explain away their participation in the cult of Ceauşescu and thereby in lengthening his rule.

Every European country seems to have had a student of the Ceauşescu legend. Britain's leading exponent of this minor publishing phenomenon was Stan Newens, the Labour MEP for London North-Central. At meetings of the European Parliament's Human Rights Committee (at which even the French Communists stayed silent), Newens compared Ceauşescu's plan to demolish half the villages in Romania and to relocate millions of people into standardized concrete blocks with the effects of redevelopment around Kings Cross on his own constituents. Some of the Romanian émigrés and ex-political-prisoners present as witnesses at the hearing were shocked that a Western politician could express such views. Newens's views were perhaps influenced by his contacts with Ceauşescu and he had written or edited at least three books about Ceauşescu: *Nicolae Ceauşescu – the Man, His Ideas and the Achievements on the Road to Socialism* (which appeared in at least three editions between 1972 and 1978 to satisfy popular demand), *Talking with Nicolae Ceauşescu*, and *Nicolae Ceauşescu – The Effort to Create a Modern Romania*.

Newens caused some unintentional hilarity when he commented on the policies of the Ceauşescu regime towards its Hungarian and German minorities. Far from being persecuted, their language and culture was promoted, according to Newens. He could testify to seeing many books on display in Romania in foreign languages including German and Hungarian. It was not clear whether he caught the aside from one witness that Nicolae and Elena's speeches and writings were translated into many more languages than that. Perhaps even some of his own words about Ceauşescu had been translated into the languages spoken in Romania for the edification of Ceauşescu's subjects. Such examples of foreign respect and admiration for the Comrade and his wife were displayed throughout Romania in every museum and library.[7]

The National History Museum on the Calea Victoriei in Bucharest had a floor devoted to 'homage' to the Comrade and his wife. The salons were filled with honours, medals, awards, degrees from all corners of the earth, set out in cabinets according to the continent of origin. They were displayed with an almost subversive indifference to the impression made upon the spectator. Towards the end of the era, in fact, the attendants in the salons of homage became alert to the fact that among their few Western visitors, the majority were not as in awe of the *Conducator* as they might be and photographing the exhibits or taking notes of the sycophantic citations attached to the awards by their Western donors was discouraged.[8]

As in so much else, the 'Omagiu' in the National History Museum and its lesser imitators in every other museum and exhibition hall in the country, were Stalinist in inspiration. Tito, Ceauşescu's role-model as a 'new type of patriotic communist', had long ago immortalized his universal popularity in his own lifetime by establishing the Memorial Centre to Josip Broz Tito at Dedinje, outside Belgrade. Stalin had had his birthplace at Gori in Georgia converted into a shrine and much the same was done for Ceauşescu's home village at Scorniceşti. His parents' cottage was restored to make it a suitable birthplace for such a great man. Other places associated with Ceauşescu's career, like the prisons at Doftana or Caransebes, were made into shrines to his onward march through life and became regular centres of his cult. Ceauşescu may have learnt this technique from Kim Il Sung who has pock-marked North Korea with memorials to his every stage of development.[9] In addition to memorials marking the places associated with his career, the great dates – his birthday; from the mid-1970s her birthday too; the anniversary of the overthrow of Antonescu on 23 August – were marked by ceremonies, parades and shows in honour of Ceauşescu. Schoolchildren could spend days or weeks drilling for athletic and balletic diplays in his honour. Some were even chosen to meet him and offer him flowers, but only after careful screening for infectious diseases, and vaccination. Their god was mortal and had to be protected from germs.

Ceauşescu told *Newsweek* in the autumn of his life that the cult was not his doing. He was lucky to be so popular. In fact, he would like more people to enjoy his level of popularity: 'If this is a cult of personality, then I should like all the poorly developed countries to enjoy such personalities capable of ensuring a rising standard of living for the people.'[10] Ceauşescu knew very well from his travels to so many poor countries (including some getting poorer even more rapidly than his own) that he was not alone in promoting a cult of himself.

But the Romanian model of glorification went beyond the norms seen in Sub-Saharan Africa – not even Emperor Bokassa was able to make the cult of himself pervade every aspect of life in his country, as Ceauşescu did.

Elena's cult was if anything more bizarre than her husband's; the claims made on her behalf were even less credible than the praise lavished on Nicolae. The humiliation involved in asserting and lauding Elena's scientific accomplishments was bitter for the country's intellectuals, in fact for anyone with common sense. By the mid-1980s, Elena's birthday, though not her age, was celebrated with all the effusions associated with her husband's. In January 1986, the readers of *Luceafarul* were assured that the anniversary of Elena's birth was 'a crucial date in Romanian history, by which the nation, glorifying its chosen ones, is glorifying itself . . .' At the same time another journalist reminded his readers that Elena Ceauşescu was 'the perfect personification of the traditional values of the Romanian people' with her secure place 'in the golden gallery of the great personalities of national history'. Ilie Purcaru described Elena as, 'The woman who today, side by side with the man at the country's helm, is taking upon her shoulders – fragile as any woman's shoulders but strong and unswerving through her strong and unwavering beliefs – overwhelming missions and responsibilities, serving the nation with a devotion that none of our women has attained before . . .'

This idea of Elena as the colleague in leadership of Nicolae Ceauşescu led the poet, Ion Gheorghe, to conjure up a mystical vision of Elena as part of a 'trinity', whose 'three dimensions' were Nicolae Ceauşescu, herself and the fatherland, of which she was mother. Another poet, Virgil Teodorescu, combined his enthusiasm for both birthday celebrants, claiming they were 'the historical couple whose existence merges with the country's destiny.' If once Romania was Ceauşescu, now it became the couple. As one eulogist put it, 'two communist hearts [beat as one] under the Romanian flag.'[11]

The origins of the double-cult lay in the trip to China in

1971. That trip must have revived Nicolae's memories of his time in Stalin's Moscow, but the frenzied adulation of Mao surpassed anything that Ceauşescu could have witnessed in the Soviet Union. In his last years, Stalin lived almost entirely secluded from the public gaze. The constant outpourings of devotion from the Soviet people reached him through the media. He preferred to remain aloof, an invisible presence worshipped from afar. Mao, on the other hand, actually presided over gatherings of a million crying and cheering devotees, before bodily and mental decline made personal enjoyment of ecstatic Red Guards screeching their devotion impossible.

At Mao's side during that visit was his ever more prominent wife, Jiang Qing. If Elena wished to be a great scientist, then Jiang Qing was already a great actress and by the early 1970s a great creative artist, too; as well as being the voice of Chairman Mao on most issues. The role of Jiang Qing was bitterly resented by Mao's male political colleagues, not least by Deng Xiaoping. Undoubtedly, she was hated by countless millions of ordinary Chinese. Jiang Qing could always be counted on to use her influence and pronounce in favour of the most extreme and disruptive policies. For the elderly Mao, she was perhaps a useful alibi: anything which the government did which proved too unpopular was likely to be attributed to her doing. After Mao's death and Jiang Qing's fall, the 'moderate' regime of Deng accused Madame Mao and her associates in the Gang of Four of being the cause of all China's woes, thereby sparing the late Chairman from the most bitter criticisms.

The rapid rise of Jiang Qing – rather than her still more sudden and catastrophic fall – were clearly lessons to Elena. The experience of other ambitious wives of presidents might offer some material for reflection, but, with the possible exception of Eva Peron, none was an obvious model. Elena knew instinctively that by building up a separate cult of herself – in many ways more spurious and grotesque than anything created for her husband – she was laying the foundations for her own take-over in the event of Nicolae's death. Both came from peasant stock of considerable longevity, but the presence of Nicolae's mother-in-law in her late nineties was evidence that Elena Ceauşescu could expect to live well into the twenty-first century – and she certainly had plans to be in charge then too.[12]

Assertion of her supremacy over the other members of the politburo was an essential step to confirming her position as heir-apparent. When foreign journalists were occasionally bold enough to ask Ceauşescu whether he intended Nicu to be his successor he gave non-committal answers. This was partly because both he and Elena saw that it would require a great deal more experience and self-discipline to make Nicu fit for the role, and also because he did not want to rule out Elena. Nicu shared all the vices of Kim Il Sung's designated successor, his son Kim Jong Il, except a megalomaniacal drive for power. He was something of a disappointment to his parents. Perhaps Elena thought that if she was in sole charge she could make a proper tyrant out of him. In the meantime, she worked on demeaning the members of the politburo.[13]

On her birthday on 7 January 1986, the members of the Political Executive Committee, the highest political authority in the country, assured Elena,

> The entire country highly appreciates the outstanding activity you carry out in the field of science and technology . . . Your valuable work – crowned by the high distinctions and titles awarded you by some prestigious scientific, cultural, and educational institutions from various countries of the world represents, much to the pride of all our people, a greatly important contribution to ensure the flourishing of the national and universal science and culture, as a brilliant example of revolutionary abnegation and deep concern with the cause of Socialist Romania's flourishing and the cause of all the nation's progress and civilization.[14]

On her last birthday, the same rituals of praise were ground through. The members of the Political Executive Committee abased themselves once more. The press carried idealized pictures of Elena as a goddess of fecundity and plenty. Florentin Popescu's poem, 'In Simple Words', expressed the whole people's love for the 'woman as scholar' whose 'name we say when we use simple words: water, sun and bread'.[15] Spontaneous demonstrations throughout the country marked its affectionate tribute to Elena as they would a few days later, around 26 January, pour out their loyalty and love to the Comrade on his birthday — for the last time.

The constant repetition of an untruth did not make anyone believe, but it could batter the brain into unthinking apathy. If every day, absurd lies — not even clever ones — are pumped into the atmosphere by radio, television, and newspapers, the mind becomes numbed. After a while you can no longer be revolted every time you hear the slogans or your eyes glaze over while skimming through *Scînteia*. The object of this sort of propaganda was to produce a Pavlovian state of dumb obedience. All the rhetoric about redoubling efforts to fulfil the plan or striding confidently towards the future in imitation of the Great Leader was intended in practice to pacify the people rather than to stimulate them. Everybody from the politburo downwards should know what slogans to repeat in any given situation.

The other purpose of the unrelenting propaganda in praise of the Ceauşescus was to humiliate and degrade its own proponents. How could a Prime Minister who gave voice to such sentiments be regarded as a political figure in his own right? The members of the politburo who queued up to pronounce convoluted and mendacious encomiums upon the 'hero among the nation's heroes' or his 'world-ranking scientist' wife were proving their status as political eunuchs. They served the Ceauşescus just as their emasculated predecessors had served the sultans. Everybody was humiliated by the regular acts of worship staged to glorify the 'Couple' on birthdays and meaningless anniversaries. Everybody was obliged to take part and to applaud longest and loudest the most self-demeaning speaker. It is difficult to decide whether the audience or the speaker was more degraded by participation in these 'homage-giving' events.

Doublethink had entered so completely into Ceauşescu's soul by the 1980s that he could genuinely bask in what he took to be sincere affection at the same time as he knew how stage-managed the whole event was. At his trial, Nicolae Ceauşescu simply switched into the public half of the doublethink which he had imbibed for five decades. He insisted, and appeared to believe, that he was loved by the people and was simply the victim of a *coup*. The force of his sincerity convinced many Western observers at the time that he was simply mad, deluded by his own propaganda. What they missed was that his response was a perfectly normal product of constant exposure to Stalinist thinking.

Enver Hoxha's memoirs are filled with analogous examples. The Albanian leader could express his shock at the gangsterish methods of Gheorghiu-Dej in the late 1940s without for one moment admitting to himself, let alone to his readers, that he was even remotely hypocritical given his own tendency to resort to 'rubbing out' rivals personally (including shooting his prime minister and long-term comrade-in-arms, Mehmet Shehu, in 1981). Self-righteousness becomes second nature to any properly indoctrinated communist. Milovan Djilas, who observed both Stalin and Tito at close quarters, has made the point that self-abasement too is necessary to the system: everyone is loyal to the leader, owes everything to his inspiration, is worthless without him, until someone else is leader: that someone suddenly loses his modesty.[17]

Orwell saw the fundamental insincerity which lurked beneath the loud assertions of pure motives which Stalin and his like repeated *ad nauseam*. Many of their contemporaries, however, thought so much noise must betoken some serious intent; later, others dismissed the noise as meaningless, and looked for different motives. The essence of doublethink was to hold absolutely to the given motive but also simultaneously to its contradiction: that is after all what dialectical thinking is all about. The hunt for other reasons to explain the behaviour of a Ceauşescu misses the point: he was not 'really' a patriot or 'at heart' a reformer, though when he proclaimed that he was at any given moment one thing, he was that but at the same time was the opposite. Although theoretically the benevolent side of the dialectic was as likely to manifest itself as the malevolent, it is the nature of this sort of thinking that Mr Hyde always predominates over Dr Jekyll and lurks behind his actions like a puppeteer. A lie is not simply as good as the truth: it is better, because unlike the truth, lies are completely malleable and creatures of their maker.

At the same time as Stalin had appeared to fulfil the potential of Lenin's thinking by achieving the subordination of humanity to a single will, the uncertain capacity of the system to eternalize its Great Leader of the moment was also evident. As people had long joked: the future under communism was always certain, but the past was constantly changing. Just as Stalin had created a myth of himself which was universally repeated from East Berlin to the Bering Straits, so any successor could rewrite history to suit his convenience.

Stalin had seemed immortal, but within three years of his death Khruschev had begun to demolish his myth. Seven years later he was removed from his place in Lenin's mausoleum. Mao's reputation had fared a little better, but even the Great Helmsman had had to endure the indignity of being retrospectively marked by his former protégés: he was allowed 60% correctness, 40% error in his actions. Other lesser communist leaders, with whom in the privacy of his own thought Ceauşescu perhaps more modestly compared himself, had done even worse. The Czechoslovak Communist leader, Klement Gottwald, who had died in the same year as Stalin and was embalmed like him and Lenin, suffered the indignity of springing a leak, loosing fluid, and slowly decomposing. Eventually, as much for hygienic reasons as out of a desire to conform with Moscow's example of de-Stalinization, the

Czechs were forced to give up the battle to keep Gottwald's corpse from going green and bury him instead. Who remembers him now? Books, posters, stamps, even statues might all be transitory no matter how many were produced. Ceauşescu's imagination turned to a project which could not be reversed by his successors, perhaps even by time itself.[18]

VIII

The Architect of Socialism

It is also in the interests of a tyrant to make his subjects poor, so that . . . the people are so occupied with their daily tasks that they have no time for plotting. As [an] example of such measures, all having the same effect – of keeping subjects perpetually at work and in poverty – we may mention the pyramids of Egypt . . .

Aristotle[1]

Only the Pentagon is bigger than the Casa Republicii, Ceauşescu's most visible legacy to his people. The House of the Republic dominates the skyline of Bucharest not so much through its height but its mass. In cubic terms it is seven times the size of Louis XIV's palace at Versailles. Buckingham Palace could fit inside the areas set aside for underground car-parking at the rear, where the old national football stadium has been turned into the modern equivalent of the royal stables. Around it, other concrete dinosaurs lurk. To the south, across a wasteland which might have become a park, is the House of Science. If the palace was 'His' pet project, then this was to be the home of 'Her' hobby. Both buildings, and the rest of the vast complex stood empty, teetering on the brink of completion, when the only purpose of their existence was snuffed out at Christmas 1989.

Pre-war Bucharest was an architectural jewel-box. In fact, in some ways the title, 'Paris of the Balkans'[2], was unjust to the diversity of its buildings. Despite its boulevards in the

153

north, the city was never as monotonous as the centre of Paris after Baron Haussmann had really got down to work on it in the 1860s. When Nicolae Ceauşescu first arrived in the city, Bucharest contained a dazzling array of buildings of all styles: examples of its older Balkan heritage could be found side by side with grandiose business palaces in the style of Central Europe's *Gründerjahre* of the 1870s, with Art Deco and Cubist designs around the corner. After the First World War, more pompous buildings worthy of a victor were put up. Carol II was sympathetic to pseudo-fascist architecture and several of the most brutal pillar-and-concrete buildings in the capital were put up in his reign, though they were smoothly filled by the personnel of the new regime after 1944.

More than anything else he did, it was Nicolae Ceauşescu's decision to demolish much of this splendid city which aroused the concern of public opinion in the West about his regime.[3] It was one thing to impoverish his people and terrorize them, even to assassinate his opponents abroad. It was still perfectly possible to remain on the international cocktail circuit. However, to knock down old buildings was to put himself beyond the pale – not before time perhaps, but hardly for the right reason. Naturally not all the criticism of the massive demolitions in the 1980s was purely aesthetic. To be concerned about the fate of historic buildings when thousands of people were being uprooted was not necessarily to pity the plumage and forget the dying bird. Undoubtedly, the Prince of Wales' unprecedented public denunciation in April 1989 of Ceauşescu's demolitions in Bucharest and his plan to 'systematize' rural Romania represented genuine revulsion at the human consequences of the *Conducator's* policies. Prince Charles's remarks also hit home when they were repeated to Ceauşescu himself.[4]

Ceauşescu's decision to immortalize his rule in stone, or rather concrete and imitation marble, made clear the anachronistic, even archaic nature of his rule. However, he was not alone: at about the same time Saddam Hussein began his project of rebuilding Babylon on its original site. This surpassed Nebuchadnezzar's original in at least one regard — whereas the Babylonian King of Kings thought it necessary to imprint his seal only every third brick used in the giant project, Saddam's name was stamped on each brick laid in the restoration.[5] Forty years earlier, modern architects and town planners in the West would no doubt have made pilgrimages to the demolitions and building sites in Bucharest and around Romania as they had to Stalin's new Moscow. Ceauşescu's plans to standardize the living accommodation of Romanians would have been hailed as the epitome of human progress. He would have been compared favourably with reactionary governments in the West who had barely begun slum clearance. The connection between modern architecture and tyranny awaits its historian, but it is worth reflecting on the mentality of Le Corbusier and his acolytes before being too harsh on the servile Romanian architects who competed for Ceauşescu's favour so that they could take charge of the vast projects he had in mind. When the democratic French governments of the inter-war period ignored Le Corbusier's scheme for demolishing most of Paris in favour of his own grandiose plan of urban renewal, the architect turned his thoughts to how much better his fate would have been under an absolute monarch like Louis XIV: 'Homage to a great town planner. This despot conceived great projects and realized them . . . He was capable of saying "We wish it", or "Such is our pleasure".'[6]

The decision to create a monument to his own glory and that of the system which he had developed, regardless of the costs such an undertaking would involve, was typical of Ceauşescu's arbitrary approach to his subjects. Rather than let them squander the meagre fruits of their labour as they saw fit, their output had to be confiscated by the state for more long-lasting purposes. Ceauşescu was fond of repeating, 'History has kept not what was consumed [by the people], but what was accumulated.'[7] Left to themselves, the Romanians would have done little to immortalize the 'Epoch of Light', but by devoting 30% of the national income to what was imaginatively described as 'investment' – mainly in unproductive prestige projects – Ceauşescu was determined to transform the country into the image of his ideal and leave it irrevocably marked by his rule.

By the time Ceauşescu came to lay the foundation stone of the palace in June 1984, its title had been changed from Casa Poporlui to Casa Republicii (from the 'House of the People' to 'House of the Republic') just in case, the local jokers remarked, the people got it into their heads to move in as well. At the stone-laying ceremony, Ceauşescu spoke in almost Hitlerian terms: 'Today, I have inaugurated the task of building the House of the Republic and the Boulevard of the Victory of Socialism, the grandiose and luminous foundations of this epoch of profound transformations and innovations, of monumental buildings which will persist across the ages.'[8]

Hitler had talked about architecture as 'the word made stone', the concrete realization of ideology in its most imposing form. Together with his court architect, Albert Speer, the Führer had devised 'ruin-theory' which demanded that the great Nazi buildings should be designed to impress the observer even as ruins after thousands of years. Even in decay, Hitler's edifices were intended to recall his past might.[9] Although nobody dared suggest to Ceauşescu that he might be mortal or that the victory of socialism might not be permanent, the new Civic Centre in Bucharest had the air of being constructed as a vast set of archaeological remains, whose scale and purpose would baffle future generations like the lost pyramid-cities of the Guatemalan jungle.

In fact, in August 1988, when the foundations for several more buildings had already been dug (including an opera-house which would dwarf President Mitterrand's concrete folly at the Bastille in Paris)[10], Nicolae and Elena Ceauşescu went through a ceremony designed to immortalize their rule into the millennia to come. The two Comrades put their signatures to a scroll which was then placed in a stainless steel tube and sealed into the concrete foundations of what was intended to become a new conference complex. Under a dome with the modest diameter of 120 metres the complex was to contain various meeting halls with seating for from two to twelve thousand people.[11] The scroll proclaimed for the benefit, and probable puzzlement, of an archaeologist aeons away:

This 19th day of August 1988, in the 2060th year since the making of the centralized and independent Dacian state, the 44th year since the victory of the Romanian people's revolution of social and national liberation, and the 23rd year since the Ninth Congress of the Romanian Communist Party, we have inaugurated the construction works on the Centre of National Councils of Revolutionary Worker Democracy, a new and monumental edifice rounding off the great foundations of this epoch of strong economic, social and cultural blossoming of our socialist homeland.[12]

Modern archaeologists have at least been able to conjecture possible rational motives for the primitive societies to have devoted enormous efforts to building pyramids or stonehenges, such as their use as astronomical or more likely astrological observatories. What possible reason would scholars of the distant future have been able to deduce from that verbiage to explain the consumption of vast resources on the Civic Centre in Bucharest – except the desire to perpetuate domination even from beyond the grave?

Ceauşescu's favoured style of architecture was 1930s fascist-brutalist with a strange, almost Cecil B. De Mille Biblical-Babylonian admixture. His frequent visits to North Korea since 1971 had kept him up to date with the progress of the reconstruction of Pyongyang under the Kims, father and son. Undoubtedly, he was deeply impressed by what they had created on top of the ruins left by the Korean War. As early as 1971, he had spoken with admiration of the Great Meeting

Hall in Pyonyang with capacity to hold up to 40,000 fervent admirers of the Great Leader at any one audience. In his last visit to North Korea, Ceauşescu had been able to see the thirty-storey concrete pyramid in the centre of Pyongyang which had been built under the inspiration of the Dear Leader, Kim Jong Il (albeit from an original idea by George Orwell).[13] Although he found much to admire in the oriental-megalomaniac architecture of Kim's Korea or Mao's China, in his quest for a style suitable for a monumental Bucharest he looked to precedents closer to home. Undoubtedly, the most important influence on Ceauşescu's architectural and visual imagination was the Stalinist architecture of Moscow which he had had every chance to witness under construction during his stay at the Frunze Military Academy thirty years before.

In the utopian euphoria after the success of the Bolshevik revolution in 1917, many Soviet communists wanted to make a clean sweep of the discredited old order. Everything which recalled the past of tsarist Russia should be destroyed and replaced by new Soviet forms. Language was changed, the structure of society altered beyond recognition and of course the architecture of the old regime had to be replaced by one appropriate to the new collectivist order. The Second World War set back Stalin's hopes of completely rebuilding Moscow and replacing it with a new Soviet city, centrally planned and co-ordinated like the economy. Even so, by 1941 considerable progress had been made. The Cathedral of the Assumption on Red Square had been demolished along with other redundant relics of reactionary religion. The famous metro had been built by the trench method involving the demolition of houses which lay in the path of the tracks. By the time Ceauşescu first visited the Soviet capital, the new wedding-cake skyscrapers of the University and the Foreign Ministry, along with less outlandish and more uncomfortable blocks of flats, towered over the ancient heart of Muscovy. Although he did not master the Russian language during his stay at the Frunze Military Academy in the last years of Stalin, thirty years later Ceauşescu revealed a fine grasp of the vocabulary of Stalinist architecture.[14]

Just as the civic buildings in Moscow expressed the confident power of the Communist regime, so the new housing blocks were designed to conform to the new ideals of social life. Stalin's protégé, Andrei Zhdanov, who controlled the arts and still more closely the artists and architects of the Soviet Union, had said that architecture alone 'is able to reflect the grandeur of the period in an objective way. In a society constructing socialism an architect is not only a building engineer and a street engineer, but also *an engineer of human souls*.'[15]

The Stalinist town-planner, L. Sobsovich, emphasized that 'communal life' was to take priority over personal privacy in Soviet architecture: 'The idea of the one-family, isolated house, whose charms may be obvious from the *petit-bourgeois*, individualist point of view, will no longer have the slightest justification in the agglomerations of the socialist type and will consequently no longer be considered . . .' Sobsovich concluded with an idealized vision of Stalinist architecture: 'Most likely the typical habitation . . . will be an immense apartment building equipped with all amenities, electrified and heated by a central thermo-electric plant, fitted out with elevators, mechanical equipment for maintenance and cleaning, [communal] baths and showers, perhaps even exercise facilities and so on.'[16]

Under Stalin, communal life had other purposes hinted at by Zhdanov's euphemism about 'engineering human souls'. People living in the new blocks or sharing overcrowded flats in old buildings throughout the Soviet Union would not find it easy to defy the conformity demanded by the authorities. Who could express dissenting views openly when neighbours he hardly knew let alone trusted could hear every word in the shared kitchen or through thin partitions passing as walls? Fifty years later, an anonymous group of Romanian dissidents smuggled a critique of the new dwellings planned in Romania. They could have been writing under Stalin: 'Life in blocks of apartments . . . means living under the close scrutiny of your neighbours. It represents a new way of life in which the behaviour and requirements of the collective body are present at every moment.' They concluded that by taking people out of their own homes, however modest, they were being removed from conditions which they knew and made them feel secure into 'a new social environment in which priority is given to the collectivity over the individual.' That collectivity was supervised by the secret police and its resident informers.[17] It was said that at any social gathering one person would be an informer. This claim has never been proved and it may have been part of the Securitate's scare tactics.

The decision to transform the capital city of Romania and the housing of the vast majority of the population was taken with political priorities uppermost in mind. The ideological demand that communists should seek to improve the accommodation of the people was subordinate to the aspiration to house them in such a way as to make it easier to supervise them and mould them as the Party saw fit. Egalitarianism was an important principle. In July 1988, Stefan Dactu, one of the Romanian architectural planners, insisted on the uniformity of internal designs for the pre-fabricated blocks in which people were being rehoused throughout the country: 'The designing of [internal] spaces is in keeping with a unitary legislation. The living room, the bedrooms, the bathroom, the rooms' height and other dimensions are therefore the *same in a small or a big town*.'[18] When suitably indoctrinated, they would see the benefits of the new housing, and perhaps even come to pity those unfortunates who did not share their style of life – like the Party leaders, for instance.[19]

The cost of the mammoth rebuilding of Romania's urban centres, already underway by the end of the 1980s, and the still greater projects announced for the near future, was part of the process of social subordination. The hardships that Ceauşescu imposed were not only necessary to provide the funds and material for everything from the House of the People (to which they would be denied access) to canals without traffic and power-stations without fuel, but also formed part of the folk-wisdom of tyrants going back much further in history than Ceauşescu's own model, Stalin. (Stalin drew from archaic models which emphasized the pyramidal tomb [Lenin's] as the centre of a tribal cult based on forced labour punctuated by religious ceremonies [May Day; 7 November].[20]) What Aristotle had seen as the vice of the pharaohs, Cardinal Richelieu raised to a maxim of policy for Louis XIII, whom he advised 'all politicians agree that when the people are too comfortable, it is impossible to keep them within the bounds of their duty . . . They must be compared with mules, which, being used to their burdens, are spoiled more by rest than labour.'[21] Ceauşescu knew that revolutions do not arise from despair but hope. Keeping the 'common people' of Romania down by always increasing the demands put upon them and diminishing their rewards was good policy as well as economically necessary if his ever-more ambitious plans were to be accomplished.

An act of God is usually held to have been the spark which ignited Ceauşescu's ambitions as a town-planner and architect of communism and spurred him to act on them. On 4 March 1977, Bucharest was shaken by a severe earthquake. At least 1,500 people died as a result. Ceauşescu was hunting in Nigeria at the time and insisted on playing down the impact of the earthquake even before he returned. Even though the authorities were unwilling to acknowledge the extent of the disaster, some Western aid was accepted. As is often the case, much of the 'aid' was more or less off-loaded to clear warehouses in the donor country with little thought of its use to the victims of catastrophe. The United States sent millions of cigarettes. According to local legend, this is how Kent cigarettes rather than any other brand became the currency of the black market in Romania. Soon afterwards every valuable item or service – by definition in short supply in Romania – was available at a price calculated in packets or cartons of Kent. The more valuable emergency aid was siphoned off by foreign ministry officials for their own use or re-sale (just as many of the outpourings of Western sympathy for the orphans and destitute of Ceauşescu's Romania were purloined by the same fat-cats in the ministries early in 1990 after the fall of their master). The worst result of the earthquake was that its consequences gave an excuse to the town-planners, not least the great urban visionary himself, to undertake grandiose schemes of urban renewal.

At the end of the 1970s, Ceauşescu was still far from set on any particular scheme. As in other matters, he showed that typical combination of simultaneous indecision and dogmatic self-assertion in his approach to what became the 'Civic Centre' of Bucharest. Different architects and teams of planners produced drawings and even models in the hope of catching his eye and being rewarded with the most prestigious project of their careers. It was even rumoured that Western architects were approached, but that must have been at a subordinate level since early on one clear idea took hold of Ceauşescu's mind: the whole project, from design through the workforce to the materials used, must come from Romania itself. The final scheme would be a tribute to the vision of 'the greatest son of the Romanian people' rendered by their skill and hands and made from the fruits of their native soil.[22]

Town-planning is in fact a misnomer when applied to Ceauşescu's schemes for Bucharest. Despite their evident megalomania, no coherent vision informed them. At first, the plan was quite modest and not even crudely geometric, as it was later to become. The proposed government centre (not yet a palace) was not situated at the end of converging boulevards, but occupied an already partially derelict and vacant site. The ultimate scheme, which emphasized the simplicity of converging lines on a central pivot, symbolizing state power, was of course much more attractive to the head of state. He could sit in his palace like the sun at the nodal point of an array of beams of light. The great boulevards led to him from all directions, bringing the homage of a loyal and overawed population – who could assemble in the oval-shaped square thoughtfully provided for a quarter of a million of them. But such architectural perfection of an ideological imperative was to come later.[23]

Work on planning the Civic Centre began in a haphazard way. Even before the earthquake of 1977 had provided the opportunity and excuse for clearance, various Romanian architects and planners but also potential patrons, from Carol II onwards, had looked on the so-called burnt-palace site as a suitable location for redevelopment. A former royal palace, burnt down in the eighteenth century, it was a place with historic connections but was also impressive: it was the nearest Bucharest had to a hill. At the rear of the area was the Romanian national football stadium, now only one of several large arenas for the sport in the capital.

Various proposals were debated for the Centre: a group of buildings to house different state and party functions, or just one big one. But the hill-top site was to be the limit of the project. Then someone pointed out the inadequate access to the site through the maze of streets. The security aspect was obviously serious: how could the Comrade's convoy of cars approach the planned government buildings at its usual high speed, if it had to turn sharp corners? The risks to his person were already great simply coming down the nearly straight avenues from the Palaţul Primaverii to the Central Committee building, but the imaginary dangers threatening him in the area to the west of the hill were too great to be contemplated. Naturally, a new approach road to the Civic Centre was required. The planners tried to devise one which would do the least damage to the existing street pattern.

At first, Ceauşescu seemed to accept the solution but still needed to be convinced of the details of the route. Since he was not very good at visualizing maps or plans, it was decided that the Comrade should go to the top of the Unirii department store, the tallest building in the area, about a kilometre east of the proposed site of the Civic Centre. From there he could see the route of the proposed avenue. The planners put red and white markers on the house-tops to indicate where it would go. There was a very obvious kink where the avenue made a bend to avoid some particularly valuable eighteenth-century houses. Ceauşescu was not satisfied. His security could still be threatened at the one point left vulnerable. Perhaps he also had an inkling of an altogether more thorough-going solution. In any case, one was soon proposed.

The critics and defeated rivals of Anca Petrescu in the competition for the Comrade's patronage insist that it was her idea to resolve the question of the approach road to the Civic Centre by the most dramatic and destructive means. Until 1981 she was a virtually unknown architect, hardly more than a student. When Ceauşescu had organized a display of different plans and models for the proposed Civic Centre at Neptune, his Black Sea retreat, she had decided to participate. Unlike the other more senior competitors for the approval of the leader, she did not treat him as a fellow professional or even a well-informed client. Instinctively, she understood that Ceauşescu would not want a standard architect's model made from cheap materials with only general hints at the building's style and decoration. Spending her own money lavishly, she employed jewellers and fine craftsmen to build a doll's house, magnificently decorated and well-displayed, and took it down to Neptune with her.

At first neither Ceauşescu's guards and officials nor the older professional participants in the display wanted to let the young woman take part, but she did nothing to banish any assumption that her surname indicated a relationship with the First Lady. Wisely, if not gracefully, the opposition to Anca Petrescu's taking part in the display of models died away. As in a fairy-story, when the great man entered the room where the models were displayed, his eyes fell immediately on the glittering and finely crafted work of the youngest and least known of the competitors. How the more distinguished men must have gnashed their teeth at the trivial basis upon which great decisions are made — but how delighted they must be today not to be branded with the title of court architect!

Anca Petrescu's model was of a palace which would stand at the heart of a new city. Instead of the relatively modest array of administrative buildings originally conceived for the Civic Centre, she had the imagination to propose a grandiose solution fit to commemorate the rule of Nicolae Ceauşescu. Naturally, a great palace required a suitable environment. Everything around it, from the trees and lawns to other buildings and streets leading to it, had to contribute to its glory. It was obvious that not just a few houses, but whole districts including churches, monasteries, and other monuments to past glories would have to be swept aside to allow for the full appreciation of the splendour of the glorious new order.

A straight, imposing avenue was required to link the palace with the north-south axis of roads which had been Bucharest's traditional main line of communication. This simple solution to the problem of access had the merit of combining a secure approach with a clear vista of the proposed 'House of the People'. Rather like Mussolini's 'improvement' of the approach to Saint Peter's in the 1930s, the *Conducator* wanted the full glory of the building to be evident from a distance. The political pilgrim should not stumble through backstreets and alleys with only glimpses of his goal, then suddenly at the last moment find all revealed; rather he should approach it in awe, aware of its enormous size from a great distance.[24] This 'Boulevard of the Victory of Socialism' was planned to be wider than the Champs-Élysées by precisely one metre, as Ceauşescu's propagandists constantly reiterated with child-like pride. As time passed it was steadily lengthened towards the eastern horizon, requiring the demolition of house, shops, churches, even workshops in its path.

To the town-planners it was obvious that the new boulevard served no purpose. It led nowhere, but cut across many normal routes of communication within the city. When construction, or rather demolition began, thousands of people had to wend their way through the mud and debris to get from their homes in the south of the city to their work in the north or to the shops and market. Nobody went east to west along the axis of the new boulevard. Of course, the more that old buildings were demolished along the east-west line, the fewer people were left to make use of it. The project began to generate a momentum of demolition of its own. If the existing layout of the city contradicted the logic of the new centre, then the rest of the city would have to be changed to bring it into conformity.

Suddenly, other districts of the city began to experience the arrival of the bulldozers. It was not easy to relate them to any obvious scheme. Soon it became apparent that they were part of a general but secret plan for the whole city – which was being destroyed piecemeal. Early on the authorities responsible for displacing the people in the Uranus area realized that if the inhabitants of a particular street got warning of the intention to do away with their homes they might try to organize protests or even resistance. Increasingly, surprise was the weapon of the destroyers. By 1988, people were often given only six hours' notice – sometimes less – of the imminence of their removal to new homes and the destruction of their old ones. Apart from any sentimental reasons, the short-notice drove many to despair. Cases of suicide are well-documented, and there was at least one instance when several people barricaded themselves into a flat and refused to leave. When efforts to persuade them to go proved fruitless, the building began to be demolished around their heads. Naturally, transport for the evacuation was inadequate for the needs of the displaced people. How could people pack and prepare a lifetime's possessions, even with six days' notice? They went to ill-prepared, unfinished blocks, often without furniture or bedding.[25]

More than forty thousand people were moved from the old city centre to make way for the new buildings, but even though stereotyped blocks of flats were put up around the site of the palace and were in many cases completed by the spring of 1988, they remained empty until after the revolution. It was rumoured that the Ceauşescu pair were personally scrutinizing the Securitate files on those considered possibly worthy to live within sight of their own residence. In fact, this was quite normal procedure by now in Romania, since they also determined the holiday plans of their senior colleagues, down to the destination, length of stay as well as with whom they spent their vacation. Naturally, no one could move into any of the new flats until the presidential apartments in the palace were fit for the top comrades, so the Boulevard of the Victory of Socialism took on a ghostly lifeless quality with its empty layer of flats and its vacant shops on the ground floor.

Delays in the determination of the final form and decoration of the palace constantly put back the date for the grand house-warming party. Ceauşescu's interference with features of the design wore down the patience of the architects and their staff. His obsessive need to interfere and assert his taste added enormously to the cost. Even Elena's advice could be unwelcome when it interfered with his contemplation of the project. One of the few occasions for sharp words between them, in public at any rate, occurred when Elena disagreed about internal decorations with him. Perhaps he had a sense that he would not survive its completion. Tentatively, 23 August 1990 was marked down as the official day of opening, when Ceauşescu would address a quarter of a million loyal subjects from the balcony on the second floor.[26]

Unable to visualize plans or even to judge the success of a design from a scale model, Ceauşescu demanded larger and larger mock-ups. In the mid-1980s, architects and interior designers became accustomed to building models or preparing illustrations on a scale of 1:1. Warehouses were used to accommodate full-scale models of rooms. Ceauşescu would climb inside to study the details. Every visit required further changes. The most extraordinary aspect of this unrelenting interference was that Ceauşescu obviously had no clear picture of what he wanted in his mind. The final shape of the building had not been determined before the project got under way. Even the height of it had to be lowered by two storeys when Ceauşescu decided thirteen storeys would be quite enough (unlike Elena he was not superstitious), and no one pointed out that they were already on the fifteenth floor. But the most grotesque moment came when the frame of the building was surmounted by a wooden dome. Ceauşescu viewed this proposed conclusion from all angles, even went inside the palace, when some of the frustrated architects and workers hoped that their flimsy mock-up might collapse.

The dome was rejected. Too religious, perhaps? No explanation was given, least of all to the thousands of workers living in converted railway wagons around the site. Instead finally, by the spring of 1989, the flat-topped, tiered approach was adopted. The building was 84 metres high, though because it was situated on a hill, with five storeys below ground, it looks shorter than it is. It seems squat because it covers more than 265,000 square metres. The whole vast edifice was surmounted by the tallest, and fattest, flag-pole in the country, carrying the largest tricolour in the world. The weight of the material of the flag, which was thirty metres long and sixteen wide, threatened to wreck the pole despite its reinforcements. Several revisions of its design were required.

The exterior decorations on the synthetic white-stone face underwent repeated changes. Columns were raised, shortened, and narrowed. Sometimes one set of sculptors would be finishing an already countermanded set before the news of yet more changes reached them. The desire to teach the experts a lesson took on manic proportions. Designers quickly learnt that nothing could be satisfactory on first viewing. No amount of excessive decoration was sufficient to satisfy Ceauşescu's taste. One of the interior decorators was an admirer of Salvador Dali and found to his secret delight that he could indulge his flights of fancy and still fail to meet the needs of Ceauşescu's imagination. If he surpassed himself with a full-scale mock-up of the ceiling for the Salla Romana with a snake-pit of interwoven flowers and exuberant garlands, he could be sure that a cursory glance by Ceauşescu would be followed by the demand, 'More flowers, more gold leaf.' Good taste to the General-Secretary was a matter of going further than any artist dreamed, and then when the mere craftsman of his vision had caught up with it, going further still.[27]

Only once was the *Conducator's* arbitrary revision of a design previously imposed by him challenged. Running down the centre of the Boulevard of the Victory of Socialism, there were rows of ornate street lights. Their design had been changed several times before they were finally erected. On the day the lights were at last put up, Ceauşescu appeared and showed his displeasure with the design. The trunk of the lights should have been marginally taller, the spread of their branches carrying the individual bulbs broader. They were to be taken down and appropriate changes made. Suddenly, the unthinkable happened: the engineer in charge of putting up the lights, spoke up. In his view, the lights and their trunks were just right. There was silence as the General-Secretary's entourage and the assembled workers awaited an explosion. Instead, after a pause, and looking at the man quizzically, Ceauşescu remarked, 'Have it your way then', and walked off.

Not all the ceaseless changes to designs were due to Ceauşescu's indecision and interference on aesthetic grounds. The air-conditioning of the Palace was designed and installed as a single system. At the time, Ceauşescu was preoccupied with matters of taste rather than safety. Too late, someone in the security department which oversaw all aspects of the planning and construction realized the possibly fatal consequences of the integrated design of the air-conditioning system. The problem was that it was theoretically possible for someone to introduce poison gas into a remote and perhaps unguarded part of the system and for the noxious fumes to be carried through to the General-Secretary's apartments or office. Worse still, a determined, if diminutive, assassin might find his way through the system in order to attack the *Conducator*.

When one of the security men raised the subject tentatively, Ceauşescu grasped the point at once. Whenever it came to matters of personal security, suggestions for improving it were welcome from any quarter. The air-conditioning ducts serving his quarters and bureaux as well as the politburo's chamber and other appropriate parts of the building were ripped out in a most difficult, complicated exercise. An entirely new and separate system, proof against poison and midget assassins, was laboriously constructed inside the massive building. Since it was designed to be earthquake proof and to resist cannon fire, the installation of the revised air-conditioning system was a remarkable feat as well as a test of the building. Deep-down below ground level was an elaborate series of lead-lined bunkers to house the clan in event of nuclear war, or even perhaps an accident at the Cernavoda nuclear plant eighty miles away. There were also tunnels with an electric light-railway to whisk the leadership away in the event of danger even here deep below the ground. The politburo meeting room was connected to the bunker by a direct lift hidden behind the panelling.[28]

These sudden changes of plan caused great damage to parts of the building which were completed. Some of the marble floors in the great halls cracked under the weight of machinery moved over them after they had been prematurely laid down. Of course, if the building had been finished, many of these flaws would have been obscured by carpets. Some of these were intended to cover such large areas (150 metres by 60) that they had to be woven *in situ*, since they would have been too long and far too heavy to transport to the building, and certainly could not have been manoeuvred through its maze of passages.

It was a matter of great personal pride to Ceauşescu that every item in the palace and every part of it should be made out of Romanian products only. For years, marble was refused to people wanting it for tombs to provide a supply for the Moloch in Bucharest. The suppliers lost count of the ancient oaks, not to mention the chestnut and cherry trees, cut down to provide panelling for the two grand offices reserved for the couple, but also for hundreds of function rooms and apparatchiks' offices. The enormous table around which the politburo was supposed to meet would have required the members to shout at each other across oak as old as their collective age.[29]

It was often rumoured that Ceauşescu intended the palace to be not only his home and the centre of his power, but also his mausoleum. After all, from Lenin to Mao and Ho Chi Minh, communist leaders have sought to preserve their bodies in the hope that scientific progress would be able to revivify their mortal remains. (This was the purpose of the embalming of Lenin's corpse and the removal of his organs for research.) In fact, Ceauşescu was not so macabre as to plan to live in his own tomb. But his choice of location for his last resting place was not out of character. On the other side of the Strada Stirbei Voda in the west of central Bucharest which has been converted from a charming street into a new boulevard, almost opposite the old and soon to be redundant opera-house, lies the huge shell of the new National Museum of Romanian History. The existing museums had all been converted into celebrations of the life and achievements of Nicolae Ceauşescu so what could be more natural than that the *Conducator's* body should rest in the museum as the culminating exhibit of Romanian national history. After all, Napoleon rests in state under the dome of Les Invalides. Why should not the greatest Romanian in history imitate him?[30]

IX

Systematization

Point 9. Combination of agriculture with manufacturing industries; . . . abolition of the distinction between town and country.
Manifesto of the Communist Party[1]

The cost of the Civic Centre project in Bucharest was enormous but it was not the fundamental cause of the poverty of
Romania. The Casa Republicii was the symbol of Ceauşescu's
indifference to the well-being of the current generation of
Romanians as much as Versailles was the embodiment of
Louis XIV's quest for glory regardless of the sufferings of his
own people. The palace complex was just part of the *Conducator's* plans to transform Romania as a whole. When Albert
Speer reflected on the enormous scale of Hitler's architectural
ambitions, it dawned upon him that Germany alone could
never supply the raw materials for the monuments and new
cities planned by the Führer. Hitler's architectural schemes
required war to provide the booty and raw materials to fund
them, and slave-labour to construct them.[2] Ceauşescu could
not wage war against foreign enemies – his neighbours after
all were his fraternal allies – so he could only provide means
for his ambitious plans by waging economic war against his
own people.

Just as the court at Versailles came to embody all that was
hateful to the French people in 1789, the construction of

172

the Casa Republicii excited popular resentment against the Ceauşescu clan inside Romania. However, the cost of the palace was almost negligible compared with the funds 'invested' in arbitrary economic projects and the rebuilding of all the major cities in Romania, and with what Ceauşescu intended to spend on 'rural systematization' (which involved halving of the number of villages in Romania and constructing 558 'agro-industrial' complexes). No accounts have ever been published – probably none were kept – but figures of around twenty billion lei are bandied about in Bucharest. Yet so much money and effort was poured down so many drains in the 1980s, that the billions of lei and millions of man-hours spent on the Civic Centre can seem almost modest by comparison with the overall waste.

If Stalin's architectural taste was the chief influence on the new buildings going up all over Bucharest, Ceauşescu's still more ambitious scheme to 'systematize' the rural life of Romania, announced in March 1988, owed more to Stalin's successor, Nikita Khruschev, and even to Karl Marx himself. The *Communist Manifesto* published in 1848 had called for communists to make the 'abolition of the distinction between town and country' one of their chief aims. Marx had welcomed the industrialization and urbanization which was transforming traditionally agricultural Europe in his lifetime. Marx despised the peasantry and even found words of praise for the bourgeoisie's destruction of the ancient way of life in the West: 'The bourgeoisie has subjected the country to the rule of the towns. It has created enormous cities . . . and has thus rescued a considerable part of the population from the idiocy of rural life.'[3]

Marx looked confidently forward to a world in which the Industrial Revolution had triumphed completely, bringing in its train a thorough mechanization of life and the concentration of the population in cities. Marx's vision was of a world re-made to suit man; he demanded the 'subjection of nature's forces to man, machinery, [the] application of chemistry to industry and agriculture, steam navigation, railways, electric telegraphs, clearing of whole continents for cultivation, canalization of rivers, whole populations conjured out of the ground . . .'[4] In Romania by the 1980s, this nineteenth-century vision of the abolition of any restraints on man's exploitation of nature and plundering of the environment was put into practice. The population found itself thrust back even further in time in its working and living conditions.

Of course, when communist leaders like Trotsky talked about how, after the revolution, the communist state would move the features of the landscape around like so much furniture in a room, they still stood only on the threshold of the environmental disasters which have ensued throughout the communist world as dams have been built, rivers redirected, forests cut down, and refuse dumped with abandon to meet the requirements of the latest Five Year Plan. The most ambitious of these schemes was proclaimed in 1949 under the modest title 'The Stalin Plan for the Transformation of Nature'. Its chief legacy has been the drying out of the Aral Sea and the desertification of much of Soviet Central Asia. In North Korea by 1946, Kim Il Sung had taken 'the first step in the materialization of the far-reaching plan of remaking the nature of the country'.[5] Bombing by the USA during the Korean War saved a lot of indigenous demolition work. (As his dreams of conquest crashed, Hitler consoled himself with the thought that Allied bombing was only destroying what he had intended to demolish anyway, to make place for his own buildings.)[6]

Like Marx, the first generation of communists after 1917 still believed that this process of relentless industrialization would speed the emergence of a society without want or privilege, based on the maxim, 'From each according to his ability, to each according to his needs.' However, for more than seventy years in the Soviet Union, the process of industrialization and environmental degradation went on unchecked. Marx had expected the communists to come to power in the most developed industrial societies of the West, where there would already be considerable accumulated wealth, scientific knowledge, and industrial capital to provide well-being for all. Instead Russia and then other largely agrarian countries fell under the sway of his ideas. Lenin and then Stalin turned Marx on his head by trying to use their political power to force through the creation of a modern industrial society as quickly as possible. Romania in 1944 was typical of the sort of partially industrialized society which became Communist and then suffered exaggerated, one-sided industrial development as a result.[7]

Ceauşescu had been part of the leadership under Dej which took the decision to press ahead with devoting enormous resources to industrializing Romania against Khruschev's wishes. By the early 1960s, Khruschev wanted a division of labour between the members of Comecon. Each state in the Soviet equivalent of the EEC would specialize in producing certain things for the general good. Romania was allocated the unspectacular and, from the traditional Marxist point of view, demeaning role of agricultural supplier to its more urban and industrial partners. Dej and his colleagues did not want to remain the poor peasant cousins of the other Communist states which were going off along the high road to communism. After all, Khruschev had claimed in 1962 that the present generation in the Soviet Union would live in full communism. By the end of the 1980s, it was confidently expected that people in the Soviet Union would enjoy a super-abundance of goods and the leisure time to appreciate them. The Romanian leaders wanted to share in that utopia as well to prove their independence.[8]

By the late 1980s, the 'golden dream' had lost its appeal to almost everyone in the 'Socialist Commonwealth' except the few elderly leaders from the generation which had entered the Communist Party at the height of Stalin's predominance. The comrades Honecker, Zhivkov, and above all, Ceauşescu himself, still lived in a mental world shaped by both Stalin's dreams and his cynical realism. Only Ceauşescu had the energy left to push on even in his seventies in the hope of fulfilling the dream. In the spring of 1988, the apparently moribund plan for rural systematization which had been heralded as far back as 1968 was suddenly taken up again. Far from being dead, the scheme had been hibernating. Now, Ceauşescu announced, the time was 'ripe' to complete the process of urbanization and industrialization already under way. What was needed was 'to radically wipe out the major differences between towns and villages' in order 'to more powerfully homogenize our socialist society, to create a single worker people'.

Addressing the Central Committee in April 1988, the Comrade explained how this 'homogenization' was to be achieved: 'It is necessary to cut down to almost half the number of villages, establishing those that are to remain and their size; all new buildings shall have to be erected *only* in these localities and we shall have to put other village areas to other purposes.' The few areas which had escaped collectivization because they seemed too poor were now to be brought into line. What Ceauşescu proposed was the 'expansion of the socialist farming system to encompass *all* agriculture . . .' Thus, he would 'achieve . . . the co-operation [as it was called] of the whole peasantry' in the system of 'agro-industrial councils'. Even shepherds, who grazed animals on what was often already common land, were to be included in the new agro-industrial 'co-operatives' – 'I stress it again.'[9]

The rationale behind the scheme was that by 'liberating' land for agricultural purposes through the relocation of the population into sensibly ordered accommodation, instead of their existing traditional homes, more surface would be available to grow crops or to graze animals. The idea that an economic imperative justified the large-scale demolition of people's homes was not unknown elsewhere in Eastern Europe (or the West). Erich Honecker, for instance, continued demolishing villages in East Germany until the end, but only in the relatively rational quest to get at the dirty sulphuric brown coal underneath them to provide inefficient and polluting fuel for his tottering smoke-stack industries. The East Germans were not set on abolishing the distinction between town and country, just perhaps on smothering it in a pall of acidic smoke and rain. In the case of Romania, people suspected that behind the arguments about economies of scale and equalized standards of living lay more sinister purposes.

Ceauşescu talked about 'raising' the rural population's quality of life to that of the towns, but this was a perverse promise. Any Romanian had learnt instinctively to expect the opposite of what the Party assured them the future had to offer. By the late 1980s, the attractions of city life were not what they had once been for the peasants. Food shortages and the lack of heating or lighting in towns, and the time-consuming difficulties of finding ways round them for city-dwellers, meant that for the first time in a century, if not longer, life in the country was not to be despised. Despite all the restrictions put on private food production and the penalties for hoarding or stealing state or co-operative products, the peasants were markedly better fed than most people in towns. The State tried to expropriate the produce even of peasants' gardens, but native cunning – bargaining with, and even bribing, officials of dubious enthusiasm for the Party line – often meant that rural households could escape from the worst deprivations of the towns. The peasants might have even less electricity than the town-dwellers, but they could collect wood for fuel and could find foodstuffs available only on the black market in the urban centres.[10]

Promises of more schools and hospitals were regarded sceptically by peasants whom bitter experience had taught that talk of better times always meant worse. Most of all, they guessed the implications of replacing their cottages with flats in housing-blocks. The privacy and identity that they possessed by living in family homes separated from other families, even when members of co-operatives, would be broken down under the new arrangements. They would be drawn into the system which mulcted them and bullied them more completely than ever. In fact, they would finally be reduced to the level of docile beasts of burden. Under the eyes and ears of strangers, they would have to work for others rather than themselves.[11]

That ideological and political imperatives underlay the plan of systematization cannot be doubted. By concentrating people in new agro-industrial centres or in particular parts of old villages, the distance peasants would have to travel to their work in the fields would be lengthened. At precisely the time that the Party leadership was extolling the horse as a modern and fuel-saving means of transport, it was also planning to increase the journey-times of the rural population and make them more dependent on motor transport – or perhaps to shorten the time they had left to themselves, to sleep, think and so on. 'Systematization' opened up the prospect of complete subordination to the State, the Party or, to be precise, to Ceauşescu.[12]

Although 'systematization' struck many of its critics in the West in 1988–89 as an insane novelty, in fact its roots went back a long way. Not only did it have the broad ideological stamp of approval from Marx and Engels themselves, but the preparation for it within Romania had started already in the late 1960s. Indeed, the process was implicit in the ambitious plans to industrialize the country already drawn up under Dej. Even Ceauşescu's critics inside the Communist Party revealed how strong a hold over them the anti-agricultural ideology of Marxism possessed. In November 1987, Silviu Brucan compared Ceauşescu's rule unfavourably with the 1960s when 'the Party could successfully control the mass of the workers because . . . a turn for the better occurred in the standard of living in almost three million peasants who joined the urban industrial workforce.' Brucan added that 'There was plenty of food, and there was no comparison with the "idiocy of rural life" which they had left behind.'[13]

Brucan's reference to the benefits of abandoning the 'idiocy of rural life' was the typical presumption of a Marxist intellectual that he knew what was best for the benighted peasant. The shoddy tower-blocks and monotonous housing estates into which the ex-peasants were already being herded twenty-five years ago were in fact the first stage of systematically transforming life in the country. In the initial phases, the distorting effects of the processes of collectivization, planned industrialization and urbanization were not yet completely catastrophic for the normal functioning of life, but there was already a steady degeneration in the quality and quantity of food supplies. In August 1989, Ceauşescu told his interviewers in *Newsweek* in reply to a question about 'systematization': 'We are almost close to completing the modernization of the cities and to solving the housing problem. Practically eighty per cent of the town population lives in new houses [i.e. blocks]. Anyone can see the construction in all Romanian towns.'[14]

Most Romanians knew how much more demolition than construction was really going on. Strange to say in all Communist countries, tower-blocks were always being put up but their development never seemed to diminish the housing shortage. Romania was not unique in cramming its citizens into overcrowded tenements which would have attracted the indignation of Dickens, but the process of urban deprivation was pushed much further because by the 1980s, the shortages of food, fuel and almost every kind of consumer good were worse even than in provincial Russia or small-town Poland.

By the outbreak of the revolution in December 1989, only about seventy villages had been directly affected by rural systematization. The congenital apathetic inefficiency bred by the regime as the best way of keeping people down had also delayed the demolition process. Only around Bucharest itself, where veteran drivers of bulldozers operated occasionally under the eye of the *Conducator* himself, was much done. The large village of Otopeni next to the international airport was half-demolished before the collapse of the regime, as were several hamlets nearby. The procedure was quite simple: the inhabitants of any given building were informed of its imminent demise, sometimes by officials, sometimes by the arrival of earth-moving equipment which dug holes next to the cottages large enough to accommodate the rubble after the individual cottages had been bulldozed into them. The topsoil could then be pushed back across the site and to all appearances undisturbed agricultural land was left. No evidence of a family home should remain.[15]

In the country of Giurgiu, to the south of the capital, Ceauşescu himself supervised the first demolitions at the end of July 1988. I remember watching the television report showing him standing over a map in the local Party headquarters, sweeping his hand across it presumably indicating which areas were to disappear from the face of the earth. The local Party loyalists were standing in a line on the other side of the map-table, glumly applauding in the prescribed manner. Even the Romanian press admitted that progress was not universally welcomed when it meant uprooting oneself and family from the home which had sheltered generations, particularly not when it meant moving into a block-house.[16]

By the early 1980s, Ceauşescu recognized the debilitating effects of under-investment in an over-collectivized agriculture combined with rural depopulation due to exaggerating industrialization. He drew the logical conclusion: in order to bring in the harvest, school children, students, and even soldiers should be sent into the fields to collect the fruits of the earth regardless of their lack of agricultural training 'as was customary before'![17] In practice, many school children had already been long integrated into industrial production: the windscreen wipers of the ubiquitous Dacia 1300, for instance, were often assembled by fifteen-year-olds in Transylvanian Sibiu. Despite his frequent boasts about the progress made under his rule, Ceauşescu was turning Romania into a steadily 'under-developing nation' (to use Alec Douglas-Home's felicitous phrase) and taking it backwards. Increasingly he resorted to the crudest measurements of progress and methods of achieving it. A Czech cartoon managed to appear in the years of 'Normalization' with a caption which summed up this perverse process: 'Thanks to the continuous development of socialism, we became a developing country.'[18]

*

The steady degradation of the Romanian standard of living to meet the burden of rapid debt repayment in the 1980s and the decision to remodel rural life according to a model abandoned by then even in the Soviet Union and China may have been primarily Nicolae Ceauşescu's work. Elena, however, added her own peculiar contribution. Despite being the ostensible representative of women's interests in the Party leadership, it was under her auspices that ordinary Romanian women suffered the worst effects of the Communist regime's insatiable intrusiveness. Not only women, but their children paid a heavy price for Elena's concern for them.

Elena's specific role in the nightmarish final decade of the couple's rule in Romania was to flatter the Comrade's love of statistics for their own sake in the most personal and private area of life: childbirth. Just as the quantities of steel produced or wheat harvested had to grow constantly, so too the population of Romania had to be encouraged to reach a size appropriate to the greatness of its rulers. Perhaps had the Ceauşescus ruled over a larger state their megalomania might have been more comfortably contained, but trapped inside little Romania it began to consume the whole nation and to penetrate into every area of life, even its most intimate secrets. On the other hand, neither Stalin nor Mao were moderated by the size of their countries.

Ceauşescu was determined to boost the population from around twenty million to thirty by the end of the century. He was ambitious to nationalize procreation like everything else. Official propaganda proclaimed that 'population growth is no longer a spontaneous phenomenon in Romania.' Ceauşescu himself insisted that a pregnant woman was 'everybody's concern' because family life was a 'socialized private problem'. Naturally, therefore, Ceauşescu insisted that a large family was a sign of loyalty to the regime: 'a house with many children is proof of a good citizen's concern for the nation's future.'[19]

One of the first measures of all communist regimes had been to legalize abortion. In fact, because of the inadequacy of their quality control in production of condoms, and their inability to produce a contraceptive pill, abortion soon became the only normal form of birth-control. From the coming into dominance of Ceauşescu in the later 1960s onwards, the abortion law in Romania became increasingly restrictive. However, in practice not even the Securitate could prevent pregnant women from preferring to resort to illegal abortions rather than bring children into the 'Epoch of Light'. The official statistics revealed that even legal abortions were outstripping live births in the 1980s. For cartons of Kent cigarettes and a few videos, it was always possible to circumvent the regulations limiting abortion to the victims of rape or incest, or life-threatening complications. Even the *securist* in the maternity ward probably lived such a squalid and impoverished life that his price for turning a blind eye to abortion was not very high.[20]

As chairperson of the National Women's Council and of the co-ordinating scientific bodies, Elena Ceauşescu was the dominant organizer of the regime's pro-natalist policies. Despite having borne only three (possibly two) children, Elena was the promoter of the pressure to breed on women whether married or not. In the late 1960s, Ceauşescu himself had called for a strengthening of the traditional family, but when that failed to have the desired effect of boosting the birth-rate, the regime reversed its direction from promoting old-fashioned morality as a stimulus to conception. Just as in Nazi Germany, ideologues like Himmler had tried to encourage unmarried motherhood by castigating old-fashioned, religious prejudices against illegitimacy, so in Romania in the 1980s. Elena's journalists promoted the idea that bastardy should no longer be a matter of shame. Their aim of course was not to improve the standing of unmarried mothers or to make their children happier, just to increase their numbers. Reinforcing the propaganda were the demographic control units which toured factories and other workplaces carrying out gynaecological examinations on all women from sixteen to forty-five. As ever, those with bargaining power could evade the prying into their private lives. It was those at the bottom of the social pile, without contacts or Western goods to deal with, who had to submit to the ordeal.

Today everyone is familiar with the pictures of the orphans produced by this population drive. Pathetic figures housed in orphanages administered by the Ministry of Public Works (like the drains). The unsanitary condition of almost every orphanage or home for the disabled or mental asylum is striking testimony to the distorted priorities of the regime. There is no evidence that the Ministry of Works spent more on the public sewers than on the helpless, but they can scarcely have expended less money or effort on them. If the rumour is true that Ceauşescu recruited his future guards and secret policemen from among these abandoned souls, then their failure to save him in the crisis of his regime is hardly surprising.

The irrationality of forcing undernourished women to bear children ought to have been obvious without the additional disincentives which the regime's economic and social policies created. Ceauşescu's obsession with numbers ought to have been satisfied by the overmanning which already existed in Romanian industry which could not really provide productive employment for the existing population. At the beginning of Ceauşescu's last decade in power, the average Romanian industrial enterprise was already employing 1,480 people. That was twice as many workers as even the average Soviet factory employed and ten times as many as its West German equivalent.[21] Many of the young people who came onto the streets of Bucharest on 21 December 1989, to protest against the Father of the Nation faced a bleak future of under-employment in a poorly planned industry.

The object of all communist regimes, in theory at any rate, was to facilitate the transformation of humankind from its distorted and unhappy capitalist condition into a new type of person, 'the New Man'. Ceauşescu insisted that 'the moulding of the new man' was the central purpose of the Communist Party's rule. Although he talked about how 'we, as communists, essentially intend to work in harmony with nature', he made it clear that this meant 'understanding and controlling the laws of nature . . . to place them at man's service'. This would enable the regime to fulfil its greatest ambition: 'Now we want to improve nature's best creation – man.'[22]

This was, needless to add, easier said than done. Ceauşescu was aware that the 'moulding of the new man, the human prototype of communism, cannot be accomplished within one, or several, five year periods'. It was in fact going to be a 'complex' process, since it would require 'permanent, steady and patient activity to *delete* from people's minds the remains of the past, the obsolete conceptions, mentalities and customs, and to cultivate a new attitude towards work, life and society.'[23] One such obsolete mentality was religion, which scientists sponsored by Elena Ceauşescu had exposed as a delusion caused by neurological disorders, and which could be cured by simple surgical interventions into the brains of believers.[24]

Ceauşescu admitted at the beginning of the 1980s that it was easier to change the economy and society than people themselves: 'As you can see, we have had an easy time constructing factories. But it is incumbent on us to transform man at the same rate so that he will be capable of mastering new techniques and new ways of thinking.'[25] The role of propaganda and indoctrination was essential to reinforce the concrete pressures on Romanians to change their way of life and thought. In 1981, Ceauşescu insisted that 'the Romanian Communist Party and the Romanian State act in such fashion that *all* the cultural and educational means society has at its disposal [i.e. at his disposal] will be used for the moulding of a genuinely new man inspired by the revolutionary conception of our Party.' But propaganda even on the mind-numbing scale practised in Romania was not enough to re-educate the people rapidly enough, nor was large-scale brain-surgery practical. So long as people continued to live in their old houses, surrounded by their old friends and neighbours, and had not broken with a routine of life which perhaps dated back generations, then the re-moulding of mentalities was going to be a frustratingly slow process, particularly for an engineer of human souls who was no longer young.[26]

In retrospect, it is clear that few of the Party's officials really shared Ceauşescu's enthusiasm for the demolition of almost everything that their country's history had produced. There was a great deal of dragging of feet. Ceauşescu complained about it repeatedly.[27] But no amount of passive resistance and bureaucratic delay could halt the process set in train by Ceauşescu in the spring of 1988. Twenty years earlier, it had been his patriotic rhetoric which had briefly rallied the nation around him and done so much to consolidate his grip on absolute power. Now his incantations of the old slogans of national independence and identity sounded more and more hollow.

The planned destruction of so much of Romania's rural heritage seemed to go against the tenor of Ceauşescu's outspoken nationalism. In 1974, visiting the northern region of the Maramureş, one of the districts richest in the everyday survival of peasant customs and dress, Ceauşescu told a group of folk-artists that adhering to traditions was one way of developing a communist country: 'I appreciate . . . these true works of popular art as an expression of your commitment to maintain the dress and customs of [your] ancestors, as well as to weave them tightly with that which is new, . . . because only in this way will we build a strong socialist society.' In fact, the *Conducator* went so far as to command the peasants to 'maintain the customs and dress of our great-great forebears, so that they shall always be in our memory. I beg you not to forget this.'[28]

A few years on, Ceauşescu's nationalism was in full, almost fascistic flood. He insisted on the purity of the Romanian people and their ancient and immemorial attachment to the soil of their native land. He used almost *völkisch* language, claiming that the Romanians (unlike the Hungarian, German and other minorities) were 'auctocthonous': 'They did not come from elsewhere, they did not fall down from the sky; they were born and lived here, in this land, and they defended it with their blood.' Even as he was preparing to uproot millions of peasants and to destroy their homes, Ceauşescu praised their patriotism in terms ringing with irony: 'In the toughest times, their forefathers did not desert the land where they were born, but in brotherhood with it, with the mountains, fields, rivers and great woods, they unflinchingly remained in these parts, defending their being, their right to free existence.'[29]

Fifteen years later, Ceauşescu's emphasis on systematization left little place in Romania for folk-customs and the traditional way of life outside museums. He told a West German reporter that traditions had to be sacrificed when they blocked either economic or social progress. 'Capitalism after all belonged to tradition too.'[30] In the north of Bucharest, there is a fascinating village-museum, started in the 1930s, which has collected examples of the extraordinary variety of styles of peasant architecture found in Romania. Other towns, like Nicu's fief, Sibiu, have similar though smaller museums. The plan of 'systematization' if it had been carried through would have left them the only repositories of folk-culture and architecture, since the threefold slogan 'Systematization – Modernization – Civilization' would have left little of what remained unscarred. For instance, the peasants of the Maramureş to whom Ceauşescu had appealed to preserve their ancient ways had only been able to do so until then because their poor hill-side farms had not yet been collectivized. It was a typical irony of the effects of the communist system that those who had been least affected by it were best off. Hill-farmers in the north of the country, or the famous millionaire shepherds near Sibiu, had been considered too poor to collectivize forty years earlier, and so had been left to themselves, at least as much as anyone was in the Socialist Republic of Romania. By comparison with their fellow citizens who had been integrated into the collective farm system or recruited from the land to work in the cities, they had prospered. Under Ceauşescu, they were subject to ever heavier taxes and requisitioning of their produce, but even so found ways around the worst shortages suffered by those tied into the State system. The very success of such people was an affront to Ceauşescu's 'golden dream of communism', which left no place for individual initiative. Instead, each person had 'full freedom of initiative in implementing the plan' and it was unacceptable to give 'everyone the right to spend money as he likes.'[31]

Originally, the rebuilding of the cities, especially of Bucharest, and the plan to 'systematize' the villages, seemed to involve the destruction of many cultural and religious monuments. Under Lenin and Stalin, many churches in Russia were demolished as part of the Soviet state's anti-religious campaigns. Propaganda films from the first years of the Soviet system show enthusiastic crowds, and sometimes, in the background, weeping elderly women, watching the officially sanctioned looting of churches, which were then demolished or turned into granaries or museums of 'scientific atheism'. Ceauşescu was not able to whip up any evidence of genuine enthusiasm for his destruction of churches.[32]

Despite his pleas to the peasants of the Maramureş to preserve their traditions, Ceauşescu, like for instance Khruschev, had the ex-peasant's contempt for those still stuck in the rural rut. To that he brought a class-conscious antagonism towards the relics and treasures of the old élites. He probably shared Khruschev's contempt for conservationists and the defenders of the national heritage, who stood in the way of progress and tried to suborn Communist officials from their duty to demolish the redundant vestiges of the old order. In 1961, Khruschev told the Soviet Central Committee:

Near Moscow many unnecessary objects of olden times have been put under restoration orders. You will recall, comrades, that people sometimes throw such matters at you, those who want to warm their own hands skilfully coax you. They say something like this: 'Here you are, a cultured person, you know and understand the meaning of this ancient monument. You understand and value the fact that this famous person walked here, here he sat and considered his plans, and here he spat . . .' I do not exaggerate, comrades; *such outrages happen.*[33]

It was the destruction of thirty churches and monasteries in Bucharest to make way for the Civic Centre which aroused Western criticism of Ceauşescu's rule on a grand scale. A hint of what was soon to befall Romania's historic buildings came in 1976 when Ceauşescu withdrew his country from the UNESCO agreement on the preservation of the architectural heritage. But it was only when tourists and journalists began to return from Bucharest in the mid-later 1980s with photographs of the demolitions and stories about their effects on the local people that any organized criticism of the regime got under way in Western Europe. Eventually, even Western governments began to raise their voices. By 1988, the regime was forced to issue public statements denying it intended to destroy any more religious sites. Already it had made great play of how it had saved certain famous churches from its own bulldozers by moving them out of the path of destruction. It was an extraordinary sight to see a seventeenth-century church perched on steel-runners and pulled a few score metres from its original place. The operation resembled a nineteenth-century historical painting of the Israelite slaves of Pharaoh pulling great slabs of stone to his monuments or a similar scene from a Hollywood Biblical epic, except that the raw energy to pull the building was provided by puffing steam- or diesel-engines rather than human slaves.

In February 1988, the Church of the Stork's Nest, on the corner of Stirbei Voda and Strada Berzei, not far from the shell of the new National History Museum, could be seen moving to a new resting place in order to improve the angle of the street. Quickly an apartment block rose six storeys high around it, almost removing it from sight: passers-by could just make it out looking through the unglazed windows of the unfinished ground-floor flats. After the revolution, it became clear that the Church was far from saved: the process of moving it had severely undermined the stability of its fabric. Cracks began to appear – and were plastered over. Much the same happened to the famous monastery Mihai Voda, which was moved, minus some outbuildings, behind the neo-Babylonian blocks along the Boulevard of the Victory of Socialism, so that the inhabitants of the Palace of the Republic would not have their view disturbed by it.

Elena Ceauşescu in particular was surprisingly superstitious for a scientist. Some Romanians claim (not unreasonably though without evidence) that Nicolae and Elena Ceauşescu were diabolists who had arranged for certain black magical and other superstitious figures to be carved in the decorations of the Casa Republicii or hidden in the overall design and visible only to other satanic initiates of the occult. A few rams heads are visible decorating the tops of some of the countless columns in the building, but they seem more pastoral than sinister. However, Christian symbols certainly were not to the taste of Elena. On 14 December 1989, she visited the Casa Republicii for the last time and expressed alarm on seeing that one of the decorative features of the stairways leading to the southern entrance of the palace had the image of a cross when seen from high above. It was a bad omen, she said. There was no more time to redesign that feature of the building.[34]

The relocation of churches and monasteries was a typical Ceauşescu combination of the spectacularly uneconomic and the cosmetic. Although moved only a few score yards, the fabric of the buildings was sorely tested by what was in effect a prolonged minor earthquake. The churches were usually brick built, and even when their walls did not crack and warp under the impact of the process, there remains, according to Romanian architects, the threat that their very bricks could crumble within a few years. Ceauşescu had naturally received expert advice on the process of relocating buildings in this way, and therefore must have known the consequences. It is difficult to avoid the impression that he wanted to still Western protests about the destruction of Romania's heritage with this dramatic act of transferring churches from one site to another, but was also aware that within the foreseeable future the physical structures of the church would crumble into dust.[35]

In the gigantic concrete suburbs around Bucharest and the other major cities, no churches were built to replace the ones in the areas demolished and to provide for the spiritual needs of the relocated populations. Sometimes even the Falcons and the Young Pioneers did not have adequate facilities for their indoctrination in such new districts. Such was the haste to build that the lower ranks of the Party were often not provided for properly. By the late 1980s, Ceauşescu was on course for creating a new type of humanity: people brought up in a squalid spiritual void, learning only outward conformity and inward cynicism. Those who criticize post-revolutionary Romanians for their lack of civic virtue and their insensitivity to the problems of their fellow citizens, particularly the abandoned young, should remember what sort of society they were forced to live in and what sort of values were imposed on them. Romanians are very well aware of how much they have inherited from the Ceauşescu regime and how difficult it is, with the best will in the world, to purge the moral degradation from their souls.

X

The Crisis of the Regime

'Why weren't you at the last Party meeting?'
'If I had known it was the *last* Party meeting, I would certainly
have come.'

                                        Old joke in all Communist countries

Sixty-seven standing ovations punctuated the General-
Secretary's words during the five hours of his opening remarks
to the XIV Party Congress on 20 November 1989. Most of
the eruptions of enthusiastic approval were, as usual, written
into the script of the speech. A few were more or less spontaneous, if a claque can ever really be so. In any case, the
applause and cheers were usually started by the man in the
electronic control room high above the conference hall who
switched on the pre-recorded applause at appropriate points
in the text. It was then played through the loudspeakers at
the back of the hall and amplified by dubbing the actual
applause and chants from the three thousand or so delegates
into the mix. All in all, if the co-ordinated cheers were
added to the ovations, Ceauşescu's speech was interrupted one
hundred and thirty times by his appreciative audience. The
combination of rhythmic clapping and slogans like 'Ceauşescu
– Heroism' never failed to bring a smile of modest, embarrassed pleasure to Ceauşescu's face.

The XIV Party Congress of the Romanian Communist
Party ran according to plan – with the exception of an
unscheduled half-hour-long break during the *Conducator's*

speech when he began to lose his voice and to fear that control over his bladder might be failing. However, even by the standards of previous outbursts of 'monolithic unity' and 'organized spontaneity', the Congress was a wooden affair. More than ever before many of the participants felt that they were going through almost somnambulist motions. Nicolae Ceauşescu himself seemed less confident than usual. Not only was the Congress surrounded by the tightest and most paranoid security yet seen in Bucharest, but even on the platform in the hall, Ceauşescu seemed in more need of reassurance from Elena than ever. Equally, her baleful looks determined the course of the Congress programme with unprecedented clarity. She traditionally determined the length of any outburst of applause; her patience was clearly stretched at times and she stopped clapping remarkably quickly, permitting the next in the hierarchy to rest their chapped hands a few moments later and so on down the line.[1]

Everybody knew the reasons for the tension in the air, but of course none of the delegates gave voice to them. The absence of fraternal delegates of world status – with the exception of the ever-loyal Yasser Arafat, the only 'head of state' personally greeted and embraced by his host[2] – underlined the isolation of the Comrade from the real world outside. But as they applauded Ceauşescu's reiteration of the old certainties of the triumph of scientific socialism, the irrefutable necessity of the dictatorship of the Party, even the absence of poverty in Romania, every delegate knew that the Berlin Wall had been breached two weeks earlier. They had heard that Todor Zhivkov was in custody less than one hundred and fifty miles away and knew that when his pro-Gorbachev successor, Petar Mladenov, denounced him, he had accused Zhivkov of 'eating out of the same trough as the rotten dictator Ceauşescu'.[3] They did not need to be told that at that moment in Prague huge crowds were applauding the collapse of another bastion of the old order. No one in Bucharest needed to hear the Czechs chanting 'Ceauşescu will be next' to know that the regime was facing its most dangerous moments. The hordes of plainclothes policemen surrounding the conference hall made this show of the people's monolithic unity behind their leader even less believable. The ordinary people of Bucharest faced even more inconvenience than usual from the travelling arrangements of the Comrade: each day, three separate routes from the Palaţul Primaverii to the Congress hall were sealed off to all other traffic and pedestrians.

The unanimity of the vote by the Congress re-electing Nicolae Ceauşescu, Elena Ceauşescu and all the rest of the old gang (even adding Valentin Ceauşescu to the Central Committee for the first time) fooled no one. In fact, it proved the isolation of the leadership. A decade earlier in 1979, Ceauşescu's supporters had shouted down the unprecedented dissent expressed by Pîrvulescu at the XII Congress. Then there was still some genuine support in the Party for Ceauşescu, not just naked fear and inane conformism. His grip over it did not dissolve at the first expression of criticism, however shocking, indeed blasphemous, it must have been to the average well-drilled delegate. By November 1989, only a stage-managed ritual could be permitted even with the Party faithful for fear of anything spontaneous. The life had gone out of the cult, and artificial measures could not sustain it much longer. The immense security surrounding the Congress was as much to intimidate the delegates as to protect them from any dissident protests.

Even before the Congress met, voices of protest had made themselves heard. Naturally they were not reported inside Romania but broadcast into Romania from abroad. Then in 1989, suddenly, the letters and statements of protest against Ceauşescu's rule read out over the BBC and Radio Free Europe had famous names signed at the bottom. Instead of obscure academics like Doina Cornea from Cluj, in March 1989, six of the best known former leaders of the Communist Party put their names to a statement denouncing Ceauşescu, his clan and all their works. Ceauşescu knew as well as his subjects that if he had fallen out with some of 'Them', the members of the Communist élite who lived in a manner as remote from the daily deprivations of the average Romanian as any resident of Mayfair from the everyday squalor of 'cardboard city', then perhaps the regime's permanence which had seemed unquestionable until now might after all be in doubt. A month before the Congress, a shadowy organization of opposition came into being. It called on the delegates to reject Ceaușescu's renomination for a further term as General-Secretary of the Party. No one then knew who the members of this anonymous Front for National Salvation were, but soon enough everyone would be able to guess the identity of its leaders.[4]

At the start of the spring 1989, Romania's isolation within the Warsaw Pact became obvious. On 9 March, for the first time, the Soviet Union failed to vote in support of a Warsaw Pact ally when the United Nations' Commission on Human Rights in Geneva decided to establish a commission to investigate the situation inside Romania. (The UN Commission had already decided to investigate Cuba's human rights' record, but Castro forestalled any pro-Gorbachev *coup* against either himself or his brother, Defence Minister Raul Castro, by shooting his most likely rival, General Ochoa, in July 1989.)[5] At the same moment, six elderly former leaders of the Romanian Communist Party published an Open Letter attacking Ceaușescu's rule and calling for him to be replaced. All six were old comrades who lost out to their younger colleague as he had risen to complete dominance over the Party and country. It was, as *Pravda* used to say, 'not by chance' that mutinous voices were raised from within the *nomenklatura* at precisely the same moment that Moscow unequivocally withdrew its imprimatur from Ceaușescu's Romania.

The Six called for an end to the clan's rule, but they couched their argument in terms of true communists criticizing Ceaușescu's deviations from 'the very idea of socialism for which we fought' and which was 'discredited by your policy'. They attacked the systematization and the building of the

Casa Republicii, as well as the laws forbidding contacts with foreigners. But the Six also criticized Ceauşescu for discrediting the Securitate, which they said 'we created to defend the socialist order against exploiting classes', but which he had directed 'against the workers demanding their rights' and 'against old members of the party' like themselves. They ended with an appeal to Ceauşescu to reverse his policy of food exports, to abandon systematization, to renew contacts with Europe, and abide by the Helsinki agreements. 'You have started changing the geography of the countryside, but you cannot remove Romania to Africa.'[6]

The six signatories of the letter all had names which would evoke instant recognition among their fellow countrymen. The oldest of them, Constantin Pîrvulescu, was one of the few surviving founder-members of the Romanian Communist Party. He had fallen foul of Dej in the later 1950s but had been rehabilitated by Ceauşescu after he came to power as part of his campaign to distance himself from his former patron and gain respectability as a reformer. Ceauşescu's action had not won him any loyalty from the irascible old man, as his criticisms of the *Conducator* at the XII Party Congress ten years before the Open Letter had shown. (Pîrvulescu has lived long enough not only to help found the Romanian Communist Party in 1921 and to witness its dissolution in 1989, but also to preside over its rebirth as the Romanian Party of Labour in 1991 – clearly not a man to curry popularity.)

Alexandru Bârladeanu was another veteran communist, who had been a member of the Soviet Communist Party before returning to Romania after the war. He was the architect of central planning in Dej's last years, but fell from favour with Ceauşescu by the late 1960s, and was delegated to control the Romanian Academy of Sciences. Gheorghe Apostol had a similar experience of diagonal demotion after failing to succeed Dej in 1965. He served as Romanian ambassador in Brazil and Argentina, which at least had spared him spending much time in Romania during the years of accelerating decline, but in 1988 Apostol had resigned. As a matter of form, Apostol had to go one last time to see his old comrade from thirty years of struggle and rivalry in order to formally mark the end of his ambassadorial term. The last meeting between the two men was inauspicious: Ceauşescu pretended not to know why Apostol had come to see him, while Apostol was disconcerted by the presence of two large German shepherd dogs who sat at attention on either side of their master's desk.[7]

Unlike the first three signatories, Corneliu Manescu had been one of Ceauşescu's early favourites. As Foreign Minister until 1974, Manescu had been one of the architects of Ceauşescu's foreign policy successes in his first years as General-Secretary. Like Iliescu, Trofin, and so many others of the first generation of Ceauşescu protégés, Corneliu Manescu had fallen foul of his master's growing intolerance of independent initiative or advice in the 1970s. Grigore Raceanu had been among the Ceauşescu acolytes of the early years and his wife, Ileana, had been a favourite of Elena Ceauşescu, but that was long ago by 1989.

The most important signatory of the letter was its drafter, Silviu Brucan. He, too, had been moved from the centre of power in the late 1960s and had since been active as an academic and lecturer, not least on the international circuit. Brucan was by far the most persistent of these opponents of Ceauşescu.

He had been working for the best part of a decade to gain Soviet support for an internal *putsch* against Ceauşescu. In 1984, planning to take advantage of an official visit to West Germany by the ruling couple, Brucan had approached the KGB and Soviet leadership for assistance. His co-conspirators needed special weapons with which their supporters in the military could immobilize the Ceauşescu loyalists in the politburo and their guards. The conspirators wanted guns with silencers which would fire narcotic darts to achieve this end. With Andropov on his death-bed, and Gorbachev still not in position to exercise untrammelled power, the Kremlin was unwilling to get involved. When Andropov died, the sickly Chernenko inherited his mantle and Ceauşescu enjoyed a brief reprieve before his relations with Moscow worsened irretrievably.[8]

In the meantime, Ioniţa, the former Defence Minister and one of Brucan's allies, died, ostensibly of natural causes, but certainly conveniently. Ioniţa's demise undermined the morale of the anti-Ceauşescu camp, particularly as Ceauşescu had moved a loyalist, Olteanu, into his job. In the last year of his rule, Ceauşescu gave the defence portfolio to one of Elena's favourite gossips, the head of the Patriotic Guard, Vasile Milea.[9] Clearly, the full extent of Brucan's plotting was never revealed to Ceauşescu, otherwise he would not have survived to carry on in more favourable circumstances later in the decade. Brucan's extraordinary freedom to travel *after* March 1989 reflects how far important figures in the Securitate, including probably its head, Iulian Vlad himself, were already positioning themselves to ditch Ceauşescu, if not actively plotting to do so.

The appearance of the letter of the Six was an obvious threat to the General-Secretary. At first sight, it looked like a measure of desperation. No one had ever sought to change a Communist Party leader anywhere in the world with public appeals. Backdoor intrigue was the tried and trusted method. The Open Letter, sycophants assured the *Conducator*, was a sign of the bankruptcy of his opponents. They controlled no votes at the forthcoming Party Congress. In fact, they were all old men – the youngest already older than Ceauşescu and the oldest, Pârvulescu, ninety-four. They could not offer a serious challenge to the Comrade.

Ceauşescu was unlikely to be so facile about the Six whatever his sycophants tried to say to dismiss them. If the text of their letter was galling for Ceauşescu, the provenance of its authors was even more alarming. Not only were his critics six of the most senior communists in the country, they were also not unknown in Moscow. Alexandru Bârladeanu had once been a member of the Soviet Communist Party in his youth. Brucan's connections with the Soviet élite were well-documented by the Securitate, though as yet inconclusively, and Ceauşescu himself knew a great deal about his old speech-writer. Ceauşescu had accused Pârvulescu with having spent too much time 'abroad', meaning in the USSR, back in 1979, and had convinced himself of the old General-Secretary's Soviet connections. But even the most suspicious and paranoid mind had difficulty seeing any of the elderly Six as a real challenger for power. The really unsettling feature of the Letter of the Six was the absence of a seventh signature.

Ion Iliescu was the dog who had not barked, but the Securitate knew he was involved with Brucan and Bârladeanu especially. It had also detected in a routine way his meetings with Nicolae Militaru, long disgraced for being all too literally in bed with the Russians.[10] Was Iliescu's failure to sign the letter an indication that he thought that the initiative was premature or even doomed to failure, or did his reluctance to associate himself irrevocably and publicly with Ceauşescu's critics mean that he was holding himself in reserve? In the dying days of his rule, Ceauşescu certainly regarded Iliescu as his real rival, and perhaps as the Soviet Union's favoured candidate to succeed him.[11]

Ceauşescu knew very well that the Six looked to Moscow for support, but he was also aware that they had tried to activate Western sympathy for their cause by sending their Open Letter to Western embassies (first of all, to the US ambassador) and to the Western media. Ceauşescu wanted to destroy them without openly breaking with Moscow, whose hand he saw behind the protest, but whom he could not risk openly denouncing. If he attacked Gorbachev for interfering inside Romania, he might give the Soviet leader a pretext for further clandestine or even open intervention. But he needed to deter his internal opponents from imitating the Six. In the end, he accused them of spying for different countries: 'One is an agent of the Soviet Union, one an agent of the United States, one of Great Britain, one of France. They made deals to act on behalf of those countries. We didn't send them for trial, for they have declared that they regret what they did.'[12]

Using their contacts with the US Embassy as the basis for the charges, the Securitate rounded up the signatories of the letter and began to pressure them to admit to being CIA agents. They also arrested Grigore Raceanu's son, a Romanian diplomat, and accused him of passing State secrets to the Americans. The quiet of the privileged retirement homes of the Six in Herastau was rudely broken. Along with their wives, who were also not as young as they used to be, the signatories were taken by secret policemen from their houses and flats along the tree-lined streets of the old *grand bourgeois* suburb.

There is a scene in Costa-Gavras's film, *The Confession*, when a high-ranking Czech apparatchik realizes that he has lost the confidence of the Party. He emerges from the Central Committee building and calls for his chauffeur-driven limousine: instead of a shiny Tchaika gliding up to receive him, the door-keeper points to a battered two-stroke wreck and says, 'But, comrade, there is your car.' Life is more like a novel than a novel is like life, as the Six discovered. Along with their elderly wives, they were taken from the tree-lined streets of Bucharest's *haut bourgeois* suburb to jerry-built blocks on the outskirts of the city, where there was no running water, an irregular electricity and gas supply, and no special shops or assistants to run errands. They were given a choice: to co-operate and return to their old homes; or to defy the authorities from the modest comforts of their new lodgings as well as facing the prospect of further investigation and probable trial for treason. They could not take any comfort in the bland assurances that they would not be tried that Ceauşescu gave to the Western press.[13]

Only one of the Six cracked: Gheorghe Apostol. Neither he nor his wife could face living in squalor under continuing Securitate observation and harassment. After the revolution, Silviu Brucan was able to see the records of the interrogations: Apostol had signed a sworn testimony implicating Brucan himself as the ringleader of a CIA plot, who tried to recruit the others to work for the Agency. It was a document typical of the demented legalism of the secret police: although the specific charges were clearly only a pretext for a show-trial, they were nonetheless elaborately detailed with references to the paragraphs of the criminal code which had been broken.[14]

But the case never came before the courts. The Big Brother in Moscow made his interest in the fate of the remaining five, and particularly of Brucan, apparent. Each week, the Tass correspondent stationed in Bucharest, Nikolai Morozov, called on the Brucans to ensure their well-being and to advertise the Kremlin's concern. 'Hands off!' was Moscow's message. Around the same time as Ceauşescu celebrated his last triumph at the XIV Party Congress, Silviu Brucan slipped away from Bucharest, although he was officially under house-arrest, and flew to Moscow.[15]

Despite his habitual and well-calculated indiscretion about his own activities inside Romania in the past, Silviu Brucan is unusually quiet with regard to what he did, whom saw, and what was said during his brief stay in the Soviet capital. A year earlier, already in disgrace and under suspicion because of his statement criticizing Ceauşescu after the Braşov riots, Brucan had been allowed out of Romania to visit Britain and the United States. Perhaps the Romanian authorities hoped he would not return, but if they did, he disappointed them. After a stopover in Britain when he lectured at the Royal Military Academy at Sandhurst and to international relations experts in Oxford, he flew on to Moscow before returning to Bucharest. (I remember asking him after his lecture at St Antony's whether he was returning direct to Romania. When he told me that he was going instead to Moscow, the very centre of *glasnost* and *perestroika*, all that Ceauşescu hated and feared, I asked whether this was a popular destination from the point of view of the authorities in Bucharest. 'No,' he said, 'it is not a popular place. But Moscow is a centre of power, and power is always respected.')

*

In a way, the Six were an excellent diversion, to use the Soviet military term. They occupied the time of the Securitate and the attention of the West. They drew the regime's fire from the real threats, making it less likely that they would be detected, but they were not the only dissidents who concerned the West as 1989 went on.

Through the late summer and into the autumn, a strange semi-public clerical dispute in south-western Romania began to surface in the reports of the few Western journalists who took a regular interest in Romanian developments. Until now the regime had preferred to deal silently with the few people brave enough to criticize it. Some disappeared; others, like Doina Cornea, were placed under strict house-arrest, though this was not publicly acknowledged. (At the beginning of 1989, there was a scandal when the British Ambassador to Romania, Hugh Arbuthnot, was prevented from visiting Cluj's most unmentionable resident by the Romanian police. A militiaman even pushed her majesty's representative away from the garden-gate of Doina Cornea's house and grabbed the letter which the ambassador was carrying. Needless to say, this unprecedented insult to an ambassador drew only the most restrained of protests on his behalf from the Foreign Office, always anxious to look to the positive side of any question.)

Romania's complex ethnic composition had helped to divide opposition to Communist rule for years. The Party had of course played upon the suspicions of the Romanian majority that the Hungarians in Transylvania might represent a fifth column if Hungary attempted to reincorporate Transylvania into a Magyar state. By 1989 fear of foreign domination, whether Hungarian or even Soviet, had waned in the minds of most Romanians. The relentless downward pressure on every aspect of their standard of living, caused by Ceauşescu's determination to create an autarkic Romania, had produced a quiet, sullen desperation. By exporting food and anything of value to pay off the country's foreign debts, Ceauşescu was not making Romania self-sufficient but was in practice killing the geese which laid golden eggs (indeed any kind of eggs). The rationing of most items of daily consumption did not spread the burden of shortages evenly but just pushed more people, particularly in the cities, to the edge of despair. It also brought previously mutually suspicious ethnic groups together in a common state of discontent.

The churches in Romania were divided along ethnic lines. This weakened their power to act as a focus of popular opposition to the regime. Unlike in Catholic Poland, no single denomination united the vast majority of Romanians. Furthermore, the Orthodox Church, which was traditionally the church of the vast majority of Romanian-speaking people, had been deeply compromised since 1947. The hierarchy of an Orthodox Church (whether in Byzantium, Tsarist Russia or later-twentieth-century Eastern Europe) had always had a close and subordinate relationship with the State. Under an explicitly Christian ruler, the willingness of the Orthodox Church to preach obedience was understandable, but the continuation of its emphasis on deference to State authority under aggressively atheistic regimes was deeply damaging to the church's standing. Although many ordinary Orthodox clergymen suffered persecution because they resisted the anti-religious pressures from the Party and attacked its human rights record in general, they got negligible support from the hierarchy, which had accommodated itself even to the Ceauşescu regime. Of course, this cosy relationship also reflected the power of the State over church appointments, particularly over the election of the Patriarch and the bishops of the Orthodox Church. By 1989, forty years of carrots-and-sticks had produced a hierarchy which was deeply subservient to Ceauşescu and whose members frequently acted as propagandists for the regime.

The Catholic Church in Romania was numerically weak and its largest component, the Romanian-speaking Uniate Church, which combined an Orthodox liturgy with allegiance to the Pope, was simply illegal. The Orthodox Church had willingly joined in the despoliation of the Uniates after 1948 when they were outlawed following the example of Stalin's policy towards them in the Ukraine. The rivalry between different denominations was fostered by the Party using its standard 'divide and rule' tactics. When it came to splitting the Hungarian-speaking Christians from the rest, it was a relatively easy matter: language and customs, along with historical enmities, divided the generally Protestant Hungarians from their Romanian fellow countrymen. The largest Hungarian denomination was the Reformed Church.

The Reformed Church in Romania is a peculiar creature. Although strictly Calvinist in its teachings, it has bishops to govern it. This was an old institution but it suited the Communist authorities who could control its bishops and therefore the church as easily as they controlled the Orthodox Church to which most Romanians belonged. What made the Reformed Church different was that its members were almost entirely Hungarian-speaking. In the city of Timişoara in the Banat, long a province of Hungary before being joined to Romania in 1918, the most prominent Reformed clergyman was Laszlo Tökes. If ever there was a troublesome priest it was Tökes. He preached the Word vigorously, which was unwelcome enough to the atheist regime, but worse he meddled in politics and denounced abuses of human rights, not least those of the Hungarian minority.[16]

On the other hand, if ever there was a clergyman ideally suited to meet the wishes of a government it was Tökes's superior, the Bishop of Oradea, Laszlo Pap. His Christian duty invariably coincided with the demands of the government. He must often have wished he had three cheeks to turn to prove his loyalty to the powers whom God had set over him. By the summer of 1989, the Securitate and the Party had decided that Tökes had to go from Timişoara. He was completely unsuitable to be pastor: he was becoming a local figure, respected and trusted by people, drawing more people to his church. Pop loyally ordered Tökes to move away to as remote a parish as the Lord had seen fit to create in Romania. Tökes refused to leave Timişoara. His bishop had no other choice but to go to court to have his disobedient subordinate expelled from his parish. The Tökes case came before the courts and sputtered on through October into November. It remains a great mystery why a state machine, which had the power to remove Tökes in minutes, let the issue drag on. Was it really an unimportant case? Then why did the Party pressure Pop to remove Tökes? If it was important to get the agitator out of a big city, why take so long about it? Human rights activists and others were Western observers of Romania already concerned about the pressure on the pastor in the late summer. Inefficiency may be the explanation as in so much else. Or did somebody want to let the affair drag on and become a *cause célèbre*?

At the time of the XIV Party Congress, Pastor Tökes's moment of glory was yet to come. He was still one of a score of dissidents harassed by the police, beaten up by unidentified thugs and worried about his relatives. Unlike the Six and their possible collaborators, he did not feature in Ceauşescu's list of dangers to his power. Lower ranking officials were working in a plodding way on this 'deviant' case, just as they continued to hound the poet Mircea Dinescu who was under house-arrest in Bucharest or Doina Cornea in Cluj.

Until the autumn, 1989 had not seen only bad news for the Ceauşescus. In some ways by mid-summer things were improving. After showing remarkable patience with student protesters, their old friends in Peking had taken firm action. A telegram of congratulations had gone off to the Chinese gerontocrats. Deng Xiaoping had in fact provided the last moment of the sort of international recognition for Ceauşescu which always provided him with so much pleasure. When Gorbachev visited Peking in May, perhaps wishing to rub in China's success at making Moscow bow to all her conditions for a *rapprochement* between the two Communist superpowers, Deng went out of his way to put on record the gratitude of both the Chinese and Soviet leaderships to 'Comrade Nicolae Ceauşescu' for his role as a tireless intermediary between

Moscow and Peking. Gorbachev did not look pleased at this public association with the Romanian leader, particularly as Ceauşescu was doing his best to organize a pro-Chinese alliance between the old men who ruled most of Eastern Europe, against the reformer in the Kremlin.[17]

By the end of August 1989, Ceauşescu's efforts to reverse the tide of reform in Eastern Europe exposed him to ridicule. Twenty-one years after his defiance of Brezhnev over the Soviet invasion of Czechoslovakia, he canvassed his Warsaw Pact allies about the possibility of intervening in Poland to stop Solidarity forming the first non-Communist-led government in the region for more than forty years. However worried they were about developments in Poland, the neighbouring hardliners in East Berlin and Prague preferred to look the other way. The publication of Ceauşescu's note and the lack of response to it made clear his isolation. Very soon Honecker's regime in East Berlin was shattered by the Hungarian decision to open its borders to the West – even to East Germans.

Ceauşescu bore some indirect responsibility for this momentous decision by the Hungarian government to open the Iron Curtain and let scores of thousands of East Germans flood out to the West. Because of his constant pressure on the Hungarian minority in Romania, Ceauşescu had made more than twenty-five thousand Hungarians decide that the risks of fleeing across the border from Romania into Hungary were preferable to remaining for ever in Ceauşescu's grip. The closure of Hungarian-language schools, restrictions on publications in Hungarian and the threat that systematization would destroy their village-based culture convinced many Transylvanian Hungarians that exile in Hungary was their only hope. (Saxons and Swabian Germans had come under similar pressure: some also risked crossing the frontier illegally, but most could hope to be bought by West Germany at the going rate.)

Ceauşescu probably welcomed the exodus, thinking that the fewer Hungarians there were in Romania the better. But the effect on Hungary was profound. The Communist Party there had long since abandoned the effort to control and dictate every aspect of cultural life. Most Hungarians looked across the border to rural Transylvania as the last centre where their traditional culture was still alive in the villages sheltered by the curve of the Carpathian Mountains. With the arrival of destitute refugees from Hungary's Warsaw Pact ally, the Hungarian Communists found themselves increasingly under pressure from their own people to intervene and protest against Ceauşescu's policies. The Hungarian Communists found themselves faced by the recurrent question: were they more Communist than they were Hungarian? Would they let ideological affinity lead them to turn a blind eye to developments in neighbouring Romania?

In May 1988, Janos Kadar's long rule came to an end and he was replaced as General-Secretary of the Hungarian Party by Karoly Grosz. Grosz was hailed in the West as a dynamic, Gorbachev-type of Communist, but he was less wily than old Kadar and his authority slipped rapidly over the next eighteen months. A key event in Grosz's loss of power was his handling of Hungary's relations with Romania.

Kadar and Ceauşescu had not met to discuss their two countries' relationship after 1976. Of course, they had both been present at various Warsaw Pact gatherings together, but they had avoided discussing mutually disagreeable topics. Ceauşescu had always refused to listen to what he regarded as Hungarian interference in Romanian affairs so it came as a great surprise to the Hungarian leaders at the end of August 1988, when they received a telegram from Bucharest offering Grosz the chance to meet Ceauşescu at the border-town of Arad at the end of the month. The Romanian message was couched almost in the terms of an ultimatum, but Grosz decided to go and meet Ceauşescu to discuss the refugee question.

Ceauşescu received Grosz with every outward sign of respect and consideration. At the end of their talks, he even let his visitor speak to a press conference about their talks.

Ceauşescu had vehemently denied that the Hungarian minority was the victim of discrimination and gave Grosz to understand that measures to improve their educational and cultural situation would be adopted. Grosz's positive assessment of the Arad meeting unleashed a storm of criticism of him inside Hungary as Ceauşescu no doubt had intended. The dissidents in Hungary attacked Grosz for naïvely accepting Ceauşescu's assurances.

To rub in Grosz's discomfort, Ceauşescu hardly waited until his guest had returned to Hungary before denouncing 'intolerable' interference in Romania's affairs. The Romanian media obediently took up its tried and trusted chorus that the government in Budapest was now making demands that 'not even the Fascist Horthy had dared to make' in the 1930s. At the time this seemed a skilful manoeuvre: Ceauşescu had turned the Transylvanian issue from a Romanian problem into an issue in internal Hungarian politics, where the nascent opposition attacked Grosz and his allies in the Hungarian Party for an inadequate response.[18]

The fiasco of the Arad meeting was the beginning of Grosz's steady loss of authority in the Hungarian Communist Party to reformers who were more prepared to follow the Gorbachev line of democratization. Ironically, Grosz was far from the great reformer the Western press had hailed him as, and was in fact Ceauşescu's best hope for good relations with Hungary, which might help to insulate Romania from pressure for reform. The new men in Budapest in the spring of 1989 were to push on with internal reform, but also they were sensitive to the plight of people in the orthodox Stalinist states still officially allied to Hungary. Naturally, they were most concerned by the fate of their fellow Magyars in Romania. The Hungarian government's desire to promote the right to freedom of travel for Transylvanians had a corollary: Hungary could hardly demand the right to emigrate from Romania, let alone improvements for those who stayed there, if she was not prepared to abolish her own restrictions on travel.

By 1989, in practice Hungarians could travel freely to the West (if they could scrape together the hard currency to fund a visit), but Hungary still preserved a fierce-looking Iron Curtain on her border with Austria and the Hungarian border guards still enforced the restrictions imposed on travel by the citizens of other Communist countries. The most restrictive state was, of course, the German Democratic Republic. Every year hundreds of thousands of East Germans took their summer holidays in relatively liberal Hungary. Often they met their West German relatives there, but at the end of the holiday, Westerners could pass the border into Austria but East Germans could not – at least not until the summer of 1989.

By the time Ceauşescu visited East Berlin for the fortieth anniversary of the German Democratic Republic on 7 October 1989, Gorbachev's allies in the East German Communist Party were completing their preparations to topple Honecker. His regime had suffered a body-blow when the Hungarian government took down the barbed wire separating the scores of thousands of East Germans from Austria and West Germany beyond. Moscow would not intervene to put the barrier to emigration back in place and rapidly East Germany was being bled dry by the flight of so many of its citizens. The seventy-eight-year-old Honecker's refusal to contemplate reforms and concessions to stem the outflow of people and his resort to the total sealing off of East Germany from all its neighbours was the confession of his regime's bankruptcy.

Honecker's fall was the first in the series in which popular discontent from below, and a well-timed push from Moscow's friends, removed old-timers from the Brezhnev period who neither could nor would adopt the new orthodoxies of *glasnost* and *perestroika*. At the beginning of October, Vladimir Zagladin, the head of the Soviet Communist Party's International Department, reassured French politicians that the reforms in Eastern Europe would continue and even Romania 'would also change'. (Zagladin spoke on 6 October, when Honecker was getting ready to receive both Gorbachev and Ceauşescu in East Berlin to celebrate forty years of the GDR the next day: change had hardly begun.)[19] Soon enough it would become clear that no amount of 'reform' could save the system, but Christmas was already coming by then and it was too late for Moscow to reverse its course. It was to be in Romania (which had seemed for so long the Warsaw Pact country least under Soviet control) that the revolution of 1989 produced the most acceptable regime from the Kremlin's point of view – even though the events of December 1989 seemed to be the most violently anti-Communistic of all that season's East European upheavals.[20]

By late November, Ceauşescu was sure that Gorbachev's hand lay behind his old colleagues' difficulties in the rest of Eastern Europe, however much people in the West were convinced that 'People Power' alone had toppled the Honeckers, Husaks, and Zhivkovs. After the Soviet leader met George Bush at the Malta Summit at the beginning of December, Ceauşescu became convinced that the two superpowers were engaged in a new Yalta-style carve up of the region. Already, at the Party Congress, the Comrade had tried to hit back by sowing dissent inside the borders of the Soviet Union itself.

Even Ceauşescu recognized that appeals to 'socialist principles' alone were not going to stem the tide of reform or deflect the pressure from Gorbachev to change. He reached for his old weapon: nationalism. Even before 1968, in fact before Dej's death in 1965, the Romanian Communist Party had made good use of nationalist propaganda to back up its authority. Playing upon Romanians' natural insecurity about their young country's territorial integrity had proved a valuable weapon in the past. Whether the famous Statement of the Romanian Party in April 1964 declaring 'independence' from Moscow had really given it much genuine legitimacy with the Romanian people must remain a matter of debate, but certainly foreign (especially Western) countries had taken it seriously. Ceauşescu himself had never forgotten the emotional response to his speech against the invasion of Czechoslovakia. Unfortunately for him, most Romanians had come to regard their reaction to that moment of glorious defiance as a matter of shame: the anniversary of the Soviet invasion of Czechoslovakia had become the birthday of their own servitude to Ceauşescu.

Oblivious to how unconvincing his nationalist rhetoric now sounded in the ears of his subjects, Nicolae Ceauşescu chose to raise the long unmentionable subject of the fate of Romanians living abroad, specifically in the Soviet Union itself. In 1940 Stalin had seized the predominantly Romanian-inhabited provinces of Bessarabia and the northern Bukovina. After the Red Army's defeat of Nazi Germany, Romania lost these provinces again, having briefly regained them after 1941. Apart from a few elliptical references to them by Ceauşescu himself in the mid-1960s, no Romanian Communist had mentioned the existence of the more than two million Romanians who lived inside the Soviet Union and were subject to steady Russification. Despite his chauvinistic rhetoric and Romanizing pressure on the ethnic minorities inside Romania, Ceauşescu had abandoned the Romanians to the east silently to their fate.

To the surprise of his listeners at the XIV Party Congress, Ceauşescu departed from his prepared text (and from the rehearsed applause) to denounce the Nazi-Soviet Pact of 1939–41 and to demand the 'liquidation of its consequences'. This could only be taken as a shot across Gorbachev's bows: if the Soviet leader continued to intrigue for reform inside Romania (i.e., Ceauşescu's downfall), then the Romanian leader would whip up Romanian separatism and nationalism in Soviet Moldavia. A year later, Gorbachev would be facing one of his most recalcitrant minorities in the Romanians of the south-western Soviet Union, but so long as Nicolae Ceauşescu lived, the Romanians there were remarkably quiet: what choice did they have? No one really wanted to agitate for incorporation into the 'Epoch of Light'. (In fact, even reunion with Iliescu's Romania has not proved madly popular with the Romanians to the east.)

Ceauşescu's outburst excited no response in Moldavia, but it probably confirmed Gorbachev's determination to rid himself of the embarrassment which an ally like the *Conducator* presented to the image-makers of *glasnost*. The bad publicity which Ceauşescu's 'systematization' and his persecution of dissidents was getting in the West by the autumn of 1989 was also potentially damaging to Gorbachev's reputation with his new-found Western partners. Repeatedly, both Ronald Reagan and George Bush had argued that the Cold War could only be regarded as over, and Gorbachev's sincerity as a reformer be truly proven, if the Soviet leader tore down the Berlin Wall and sent Ceauşescu and his clan into retirement. This was easier said (by Westerners) than done (by the Kremlin), but by the middle of November 1989 the first part of the package had been achieved, albeit with a little spontaneous assistance from the streets of Leipzig and East Berlin. Ceauşescu was a more difficult nut to crack.

It was not just the Soviet leadership's desire to polish the fading image of the Warsaw Pact in the West's eyes that caused their concern about Ceauşescu's maverick regime, though there was a large element of irritation with Ceauşescu's obstinacy at Vienna where he had blocked the updated Helsinki Agreement until the last moment. Moscow had its own reasons for wanting rid of him. In the spring of 1989, Ceauşescu began to drop hints that he would soon be in possession of the technology to make an atomic bomb. Worse still, he told the Central Committee on 14 April, that soon Romania would have the capacity to 'deliver' the Bomb. Ceauşescu's assurances that Romania's peace-loving policies precluded it from going so far as to manufacture atomic weapons and missiles to carry them were not entirely reassuring. Already, at the annual New Year's reception for foreign diplomats, Ceauşescu had endorsed Libya's right to build weapons of mass destruction so long as the United States possessed them, but also announced Romania's unwillingness to abandon its right to them: 'We do not wish to stand at the will of those having nuclear arms. Ultimately, even chemical weapons can be a deterrent for those who have no nuclear arms.'[21] The argument that the threat of chemical and biological weapons might frighten off a nuclear power from attacking a state which possessed them was to be put to the test by Saddam Hussein.

Ceauşescu's attack on the hypocrisy of the superpowers – who, though armed to the teeth, nonetheless preached disarmament for others – was a return to the heyday of his pro-Third World rhetoric. And it was not entirely without reason – though in truth, Washington has always been much more generous in its distribution of weapons of mass destruction than the Kremlin. The United States could trust Britain not to use Trident weapons against her. The Soviet Union could never be certain of the reliability of her allies and was definitely determined to keep a nuclear monopoly within the Warsaw Pact. In the case of Libya, it was West German companies that had supplied Colonel Ghaddafi with factories for making poison gas. Ceauşescu's defence of the Libyans was not purely altruistic.[22]

Ceauşescu had long recognized that Romania was not alone in resenting its second-class status as a military power. His efforts to build up Romania's conventional forces had only produced farcical results – like his bath-tub navy in the Black Sea.[23] In any case, Ceauşescu was suspicious of the loyalty of the Romanian Army and did not want to give it the sort of fire-power which might make it much more effective. After all, the only military threat to Romania came from the 'ever victorious Red Army', so a conventional military build-up made little sense. Instead, following his policy of divide and rule, he had built up the Securitate's para-military so-called anti-terrorist, forces and had promoted the Patriotic Guards, led by Vasile Milea. By the 1980s, the Romanian Army was increasingly deployed in the fields and factories of Romania: the conscript troops were no longer intended to be used as cannon-fodder; instead they found themselves sent down the mines in a futile attempt to boost fuel production or sent out into the countryside to bring in the harvest. Badly trained to be soldiers and hopelessly unskilled as workers or peasants, the soldiers' morale was low. The officers were humiliated by this misuse of them as unskilled labour, but when the issue of a return to proper military functions was apparently raised with Ceauşescu in October 1985, Ceauşescu dashed their hopes of an early return to the barracks: 'In peacetime that will never happen, and I hope there will not be war.'[24] General Stanculescu was one of those present, whose abilities were not satisfactorily used as overseer of Romania's hopelessly inadequate electricity generating industry.

There is considerable evidence that Ceauşescu recognized that conventional forces could not guarantee his regime against intervention by its giant neighbour. Only nuclear weapons would alter the equation of power between Ceauşescu and Gorbachev. Obtaining them, however, was a difficult and time-consuming process, which was even more difficult to keep secret. Soviet awareness or suspicions of Ceauşescu's ambitions would have altered the Kremlin's previous policy of malign neglect.

Whereas Brezhnev had no interest in disturbing the Ceauşescus in their enjoyment of Romania, Gorbachev could not be trusted to keep his 'revisionist' paws out of the place. Brezhnev's spying on his fraternal ally was little more than routine. Gorbachev might be tempted to try to use his influence to change things in Romania. Ceauşescu could remember very well the visit Mikhail and Raisa had paid to Bucharest in May 1987. He had thought that he had taught the Soviet General-Secretary a lesson then, but what Gorbachev had had to say was disquieting nonetheless.

The crowds welcoming the Soviet couple were as well drilled as ever, but they could not be trained to be deaf, so what Gorbachev said at the 'Romanian-Soviet Friendship Rally' on 26 May 1987 was worrying. It had also been heard by millions of other Romanians obliged to follow their leader's participation in such events over live radio. Although Ceauşescu indicated his disdain for Gorbachev's message by glancing at his watch or even yawning whenever the Soviet leader referred to the progress of *glasnost* or *perestroika*, he was infuriated by Gorbachev's comments about Romania's dire economic condition: 'Your concerns are close to us. We know that your country faces a number of difficult problems, that there are difficulties which affect daily life . . .'[25] Such statements could be censored out of the next day's *Scînteia*, but not from the memories of the audience.

Gorbachev implicitly contrasted his policies with those of Ceauşescu. According to the Soviet visitor, *perestroika* 'is not the expression of any one [person's] will'. Gorbachev also added: 'We must not pretend that everything goes smoothly . . . If we are silent about some shortcomings, they will inevitably grow. A half-truth is worse than a lie.' He then reminded his audience, and most of all his host, of 'Lenin's thought that "socialism is not created on orders from above."' Selective quotation from the founder of the Soviet state was always a vital weapon in the armoury of any warrior in an internal party struggle. No one in Romania would have missed Gorbachev's reference to his struggle against nepotism and favouritism in the Soviet Union. But for the Ceauşescus the most sinister point in the speech came at the end when Gorbachev suggested a programme of youth-exchanges to build on Soviet-Romanian friendship and provide 'a human reservoir for future interaction'. In Ceauşescu's eyes this amounted to little more than creating a cadre of Soviet agents out of Romanians who would be corrupted by the 'devationism' rampant in the Soviet Union at that time.

At their meeting in Moscow in 1986, Gorbachev had already riled Ceauşescu by insisting on closer co-operation in an 'internationalist spirit' between the Soviet Union and Romania. The Tass communiqué about their meeting claimed that 'The Soviet and Romanian leaders *reaffirmed* [emphasis added] the unvarying nature of both parties' policy of deepening Soviet-Romanian relations . . . on the principled basis of Marxism-Leninism and *socialist international-ism*', which had unwelcome connotations of the Brezhnev Doctrine for the Romanian side.[26]

From 1967, Ceauşescu had done all he could to cut off 'educational' contacts between Romania and the Soviet Union. He had insisted especially on Romania's sole right to train its own officer corps for its armed forces. He knew from experience how the Soviet Union hoped to influence students at the Frunze Academy into thinking in an 'internationalist' way. The suborning of officers like Nicolae Militaru had convinced him of the dangers of close ties with the Soviet military.[27] It was not only conspiratorial contacts between army officers and the Soviet Union which had long worried Ceauşescu. Again in 1967, long before Gorbachev had disturbed the ideological slumber of Brezhnev's Russia, Ceauşescu had raised the question of 'whether it is admissible for a party member, without the approval, and over the head of the leadership, to establish relations with the representatives of another party [i.e. the Soviet Communist Party].' Needless to say, Ceauşescu answered this question unambiguously: 'The answer can only be: it is inadmissible under any form . . .'[28]

If Brezhnev's Soviet Union had worried Ceauşescu then Gorbachev's was the source of nightmares. Increasingly often, the Comrade in Bucharest took it upon himself to denounce the subversive views of his younger and more powerful neighbour. The Romanian Communist Party was 'not a debating club'. *Glasnost* was out. In fact, at a Comecon meeting in Prague at the beginning of July 1988, Stefan Andrei went so far as to ask for a translation of the word into Romanian when asked by a journalist about the chances of a policy of openness being pursued in Bucharest. The year before, the editorial staff at *Scînteia* had had similar difficulties with the translation of Gorbachev's speech in Bucharest from Russian into Romanian.[29]

Ceauşescu's assumption of his ideological superiority over Gorbachev and his belief that he could teach the Soviet leader a thing or two about Marxism-Leninism recalls the similarly cocksure attitude of the Iron Guard's *Conducator*, Codreanu, towards Hitler. King Carol II's men shot him 'attempting to escape' and thereby saved the Führer from having to teach him a lesson. Gorbachev was certainly irritated by Ceauşescu's gestures of contempt for his ideas and his targeted insistence that the Romanian Communist party was not 'a discussion club: we are a revolutionary party struggling for socialism, for communism.' In spring 1988, Ceauşescu emphasized his role as the guide on the strict and narrow path to true Communism, and took a sideswipe at the reformers in Moscow. 'We must bear in mind the fact that there are deviations – theoretical as well as practical, rightist as well as leftist. Of course, all are equally dangerous. However, in my opinion, it is the rightist deviations that are most dangerous now, for they can greatly harm socialist construction.'[30]

Fear that his regime might be vulnerable to a swift Soviet intervention on the model of Prague in 1968 or Kabul in 1979 grew steadily in Ceauşescu's mind. Already the airports at Otopeni and Baneasa were ringed with anti-aircraft missiles and tanks ready to repel a raid by the Soviet *spetsnatz*. Elena was delicately aware that particularly in the event of her husband's incapacitation through ill-health or worse still of his death, the ruling faction in the Party might face a challenge from outside its ranks. A reformist, pro-Soviet group might act in reverse imitation of the Hungarian and Czech hardliners in 1956 and 1968 and invite in fraternal assistance. Romanian possession of nuclear weapons with a reliable finger on the trigger would make any Soviet revisionist think twice about sending troops into Romania.

Several other pariah states were anxious to obtain nuclear weapons as well as the missile systems to deliver them. The Argentinian military, humiliated in the Falklands War against Britain and oblivious to the democratization of their country, were busy buying and bribing their way into possession of the West German Condor missile as the first step to having a delivery-system for the Bomb. Romanian secret service agents had long been trying to acquire West German military technology and had a well-developed network of German agents in German industry. Norway provided Romania with large consignments of heavy water for the Cernavoda project. By 1989, the Norwegians began to become suspicious that not all the heavy water (12.5 million tonnes) was used in Romania. Rumour had it that Israel was the end user of the Norwegian supplies. Quite possibly that was the case: Ceauşescu was not above dealing with Arabs and Israelis at the same time (just as he had permitted his brother, Ilie, to smuggle Soviet equipment to the Americans in return for a consideration), but by the end of the 1980s, he was deeply involved in joint projects with Arab states who might well have wanted heavy water for their own purposes.

At the end of 1987, Ceauşescu paid his last visit to Egypt, when he promised Hosni Mubarak a credit of US$117 million despite his own determination to repay his foreign debt, and the poverty of Romania. In retrospect his generosity towards Egypt seems to have been linked with his desire to obtain missile technology.[31] Egypt and its then ally against the Islamic Republic of Iran, Saddam's Iraq, had managed to obtain the blueprints for the assembly line of the Condor missile produced by the West German firm Messerschmitt-Bölkow-Blohm (MBB). The Condor missile was suitable for Romanian purposes. It had the range to reach Moscow and could carry a nuclear payload.

The West German government had acted to forbid further exports of Condor technology to Argentina in 1985. However, this was just to satisfy Bonn's American allies, now worried by nuclear proliferation as well as West German firms' involvement in the development of a poison gas plant at Rabta in Libya. In practice, the West German authorities continued to turn a blind eye to MBB's export of material and designs until US and Israeli fears of the consequences of Ghaddafi and Saddam Hussein equipping themselves with German weaponry forced an embarrassing series of admissions of how far West German companies had become intertwined with Israel's self-proclaimed mortal enemies: (It was only after the outbreak of the Gulf War that arrests were made in Germany.)

Egypt acted as the go-between, and not only for the deals between Romania and Iraq. At times Cairo must have been overflowing with Argentinian and West German missile technicians changing planes inconspicuously to travel onwards to Baghdad, where they were admitted without tell-tale visas being stamped in their passports. Their secrets were passed back to Romania via the same route, though Iraq and Romania also co-operated directly and more or less openly by 1989. On 20 April 1989, Ceauşescu's Industry Minister signed a co-operation accord with Saddam Hussein's Minister for Military Industrialization. In a world where the pariah states easily outnumbered the democracies, Ceauşescu was not likely to be short of partners in this business. One at least had even more ambitious and deadly plans than the *Conducator*: but for the Soviet Union at least, Saddam's strategic goals lay in a safe direction. For the men in the Kremlin, Ceauşescu was closer to home and increasingly unpredictable. The more pro-Soviet Romanian Communists conspired against him, the more Ceauşescu actively intrigued against Moscow. If Gorbachev's standing in the world would be enhanced by knocking over his East European dominoes, the fall of Ceauşescu would be the guarantee of the Soviet leadership's commitment to reform.

Although the XIV Party Congress had come to its pre-programmed wooden climax with Nicolae Ceauşescu's unanimous re-election to the general-secretaryship, the calm which followed was tense. Nicolae and Elena Ceauşescu had no allies left in the region. A high-powered delegation from China came to Bucharest in December, but even though it contained the politburo member responsible for directly organizing the massacre in Tiananmen Square five months before, it can have brought little comfort. Zhou Enlai had told Tito a long time before that 'distant water cannot quench local fires'. China could do little to counteract Soviet influence in Eastern Europe. If Ceauşescu was going to be confronted by popular disturbances, all China's octogenarian rulers and their secret policemen could do was to set a bad example.

Kim Il Sung, Ceauşescu's model in so many ways, was even less able to offer any effective support. North Korea was also under pressure from its Soviet sponsor as the Cold War certainties decayed and Moscow looked to trade with booming South Korea rather than the immobile Democratic North. When they had last met in October 1988, in Pyongyang, Kim had laid on the sort of 'popular reception' which only he could stage-manage. Half a million North Koreans had prostrated themselves before their Great Leader and his guests. Kim told Ceauşescu that 'there is no greater joy for a communist than to meet an old comrade.' It was a pleasure never to be repeated.[32]

In Cuba, Castro had perhaps forgotten his contempt for Ceauşescu's attempt to pose as a leader of the Third World when he had sent thousands of Cubans to fight and die for the anti-imperialist cause in Africa while the Romanian had tried to keep in the Yankees' good books. But, now, Castro could no more send 'internationalist' assistance to isolated Romania than could China and North Korea.

Even in the autumn of 1989, Ceauşescu still had many friends and sympathizers in governments around the world, but not where it counted in Moscow or among his near neighbours. In the top leadership of Party and State in Romania itself, Elena's value as the chief of personnel was about to be tested. Since her elevation to the politburo and particularly to the chairmanship of the cadres department of the Party, Elena had effectively been in charge of all promotions and dismissals below her husband. Nicolae's reliance on her judgement was central to his downfall.

Long before Elena formally controlled appointments, Ceauşescu's jealousy and distrust of any subordinate of independent opinions or genuine popularity had led him to purge the upper ranks of the Party of any officials of real calibre. Elena's narrow-minded understanding of what was required of senior Party figures or ministers reinforced her husband's vindictive suspicion of any signs of individuality. Elena confused subservience with loyalty. Initiative, even on behalf of the ruling couple, was discouraged. Elena's attitude was that politburo members should listen to the Comrade and do what they were told. Any difficulties which arose stemmed from the failure to carry out his orders properly. It was a crude mistake: even if Nicolae Ceauşescu's political gifts were extraordinary, his abilities as an economic organizer were hardly equal to the task he had set himself. No one could hope to manage a modern society alone. When he made Elena into his right-hand, Nicolae Ceauşescu set in motion the decay of the system.

By December 1989, the top men knew that they had nailed their colours to Ceauşescu's mast. Cynics like Stefan Andrei knew that a storm was coming and hoped that somehow or other they could cling to the wreckage and still come out with their heads above water. Others like Bobu seem to have been so set on currying favour with their master and mistress that they could not admit even to themselves what the future might hold. Others, less indelibly marked with the brush of loyalty to the Ceauşescus, were less inclined to let past (and continuing) public servility damn them in the future.

While Nicolae Ceauşescu went through the motions of his standard response to crises, therefore, his generals and policemen began to plot a future for themselves. They knew full well that they were not the only plotters. Even as Ceauşescu was sacking ministers for failing to get the supply of food to the markets right and reshuffling others, minds inside his government were thinking through how to react to the likely scenarios of crisis which might very soon arise, just like everywhere else in Eastern Europe.

On 16 December, it began. The authorities in Timişoara at long last decided to enforce a court order obtained by Bishop Pap, expelling Laszlo Tökes from his parish in the city. Instead of acquiescing in his removal, Tökes barricaded himself in his house. When the people's militia turned up to arrest him, a small crowd had gathered. Soon it was joined by scores of people. Events became confused. Crowds gathered elsewhere in the city. Some people broke the windows of bookshops and set fire to the inevitable collection of Ceau-şescu's speeches or Elena's chemistry books which formed the window dressing. Others tore down posters and placards praising the Party Congress for re-electing 'the hero of the nation's heroes'.

From the point of view of Ceauşescu's opponents, this disorder could not have come at a better time. He was due to fly to Iran on 18 December to pay a long-heralded official visit. This was supposed to confirm Ceauşescu's influence in the Middle East as well as enable him to sign a lucrative deal to sell arms to Iran. Despite his co-operation with Iran's rivals, Egypt and Iraq, like almost everyone involved in the Middle East, Ceauşescu was never above dealing with every side simultaneously. In that he was no different from the Saddams, Assads, Mubaraks or Rafsanjanis of the region. Ceauşescu could not cancel his visit to Iran without admitting that a serious threat to his regime had arisen. In turn, such an admission might stimulate disorder elsewhere in Romania. Siren voices in the politburo and government urged him to carry on with his trip. Elena would stay behind and the 'hooligans' would soon be dealt with by the security forces as they had been in Braşov two years earlier.

On 17 December, Ceauşescu held a closed-circuit television conference with all forty leaders of the Communist Party at the county level. He made clear that they were to use whatever means to control public order in their districts. He also decided to close the borders of Romania to travellers from his former East European allies and the Soviet Union. Only Cubans, North Koreans and Chinese were to be let in. Knowledge of this order after the revolution seems to have encouraged conspiracy theories, which even in the atmosphere of plotting were exaggerated. It was said later that the demonstrators in Timişoara had really been KGB agents sent to Romania under the guise of tourists to provoke a riot and then rebellion against Ceauşescu. Unfortunately, there is no evidence that a mysterious group of Soviet tourists (presumably identifiable by the snow on their boots) played any role in the events. The Romanian revolution had much of the quality of a *coup*, but it was a *putsch* precipitated by a spontaneous outburst of discontent by ordinary people, Romanian and Hungarian alike, in Timişoara.[33]

The success of the revolution owed less to the enthusiasm and self-sacrifice of crowds on the streets than seemed to be the case to television viewers at the time. If a single person ensured the downfall of Nicolae Ceauşescu, it was his wife. As ringleader of the committee of three left in charge of the country during her husband's visit to Iran, Elena Ceauşescu mishandled the situation. Whereas the Securitate and Army had acted with restraint in the past to seal off and wear down the resistance of popular protesters, Elena seems to have been determined to crush the protests in Timişoara as quickly as possible and to teach the people a lesson. Although the thousands reported at the time were not killed, at least forty people were shot by the security forces. This violence stirred up more resistance.

More importantly, several of the key figures in charge of the operation to suppress the disorders were not reliable. The simple fact that both Generals Mihai Chiţac and Victor Stanculescu were promoted after the revolution is a persuasive argument that their activities were not directed to saving the skins of Ceauşescu. Stanculescu, in particular, enjoyed the trust of the Ceauşescus, but had spent a long holiday in Hungary of all places earlier in the year. It would have given him the opportunity to discuss the Romanian situation away from the prying eyes and ears of the Securitate, if the Securitate was really still so devoted to the Ceauşescus.

Meanwhile for those Romanians with short-wave radios and the ears to hear, the reports about developments inside their country were coming from unusual sources. The still

Communist-controlled Yugoslav radio and news agency, Tan-jug, gave out graphic descriptions of the brutality of the Romanian security forces in Timişoara. Hungarian radio reported four thousand dead and summary executions. All this seemed to incite further demonstrations. Most strikingly, Radio Moscow condemned the suppression of the opposition and quoted both President Gorbachev and the Foreign Minister, Edvard Shevardnadze, in the same vein. It was obvious that Ceauşescu had no friends outside the country, but also that anyone who helped to overthrow him could look to a friendly reception from Romania's most powerful neighbour.[34]

XI

The End

Treason is a matter of dates.
                    Talleyrand

While the two elderly fugitives wandered the roads of Wallachia hardly fifty miles away, their would-be successors set to work establishing order out of the chaos of their fall. Several competing groups were on hand at the Central Committee building, each claiming to be the rightful representatives of the people. Iliescu's group recognized that the students and other street protesters who had braved the bullets of the army and police were not an immediate threat to them. Such people were too idealistic to think politically until it was too late. However, other ex-communists were about and in fact Ilie Verdeţ tried to form his own government after the flight of the Ceauşescus. That effort was doomed from the start, because the Ceauşescus' generals and police chiefs were unwilling to co-operate. They preferred to ally with Iliescu's group. Without their abandonment of the 'Supreme Commander' who in turn deserted them, the new Front of National Salvation would never have achieved its goal of smoothly stepping into the vacuum of power.

Both the Army Chief of Staff, Stefan Gusa, and the head of the Securitate, Iulian Vlad, were encouraged to think that their co-operation with the Front would spare them any embarrassment in the future. Gusa had already brought the

Army into line with the new government, and Vlad and his staff did their best in the confusion to prevent the Securitate units throughout the country from acting on their contingency plans. These detailed how local forces were to react to a popular revolt. Vlad sent out a general order to all Securitate units and Interior Ministry forces not to fire under any circumstances.[1] Unfortunately, in a few places, detachments of security agents in public buildings, especially hotels, appear not to have received their ceasefire orders – if they were sent – or they panicked and opened fire on the celebrating crowds as in Sibiu and Braşov. Probably, they had local contingency plans for a breakdown of communications with the Securitate HQ in the event of public disorder: if in doubt, shoot into the crowd.

Perhaps we will never know whether the conspirators had a deep-laid plan to revive the fighting after Ceauşescu's fall in order to clear the streets and make it easier to assert their authority. Possibly, the autonomous resistance of a few frightened and desperate *securistii* gave the idea of 'renewing' the struggle to Iliescu and the others. Certainly, when the shooting flared up again, many people who might have been more sceptical about the credentials of some of the anti-Ceauşescu leaders were dissuaded from voicing them at once. If hordes of fanatical 'terrorists' were determined to fight to the bitter end, it was not the time to squabble over what was to follow their 'reign of terror'. A few weeks after the revolution, Brucan praised Stanculescu for putting his skills in psychological warfare at the service of the revolutionaries.[2] Of course, it was not used against the 'terrorists', but to confuse Western journalists and the Romanian people about what was actually happening.

The establishment of a broad coalition of anti-Ceauşescu activists would help to establish the legitimacy and democratic credentials of the plotters, without necessarily forcing them to share power. By no means was everything thoroughly prepared by the conspirators. They were better at seizing the reins of power than at public relations. They had not yet decided what to call the new government or themselves.

While the inner group were discussing how to present themselves to the people and whether to use the name National Salvation Front, the first of several uninvited guests appeared at the door of their conference room in the Central Committee building. Iliescu insisted on admitting Dumitru Maziliu to the room, and formally to the new leadership, recognizing that his reputation as a human rights campaigner under Ceauşescu would bolster the good standing of the new regime with the West. In case of trouble, Maziliu's past as a lecturer at the Securitate's academy could be dredged up to keep him in line or discredit him if he refused to conform (as was the case by the end of January 1990 when he continued to insist that they get rid of all the old communists still in the Front's leadership.)[3]

While Iliescu tried to reach Stanculescu by telephone, the motley crowd debated and shouted at each other in considerable confusion. Even the more experienced conspirators seemed unsure what to do about certain key issues. The most important was clearly to indicate that they alone constituted the new, legal government both to the Romanian people and to foreign states. This would foreclose any chance that the crowd outside the Central Committee building or some of the other politicians within it, like the wily Ilie Verdeţ, might yet set up a rival centre of power. When it came to it, they had not agreed what to call themselves. After a fairly bizarre discussion, they eventually returned to the name which they had operated under for the previous six months, the Front of National Salvation, but they remained unwilling to clear up the mysteries surrounding the Front's existence.

Iliescu had his doubts about the name. It would remind people that the Front had come to life six months earlier as the would-be saviours of communism in Romania, not its pall-bearers, but, as Militaru said, that could not be helped now. Clearly, the crowds in the streets were in no mood to tolerate anything less than the abolition of the old system.

226

Iliescu discovered the popular mood when he began his first speech to the crowd with the customary, in his case perhaps the instinctive word, 'Comrades.' The booing and whistling which followed taught him a quick lesson: he abandoned any vocabulary or hint of continuity with communism, whether of the hated Ceauşescu-type or of Dej's model (which had certainly been far from popular in its day). Instead, Iliescu began to emphasize the Front of National Salvation's spontaneous origins from the People. Later he claimed, 'The Front was born in the midst of the people, it is a creation of the people and it serves the people: *the Front equals the People.*'[4] This claim had unfortunate echoes of the old slogan 'Ceauşescu – the Party – the People', but at the time it went down well.

Inside the conference room, which increasingly resembled a command centre, more uniformed figures appeared, including Stanculescu in the company of Victor Ardeleanu, the head of the feared Securitate anti-terrorist unit, USLA, which was supposed to be made up of the last-ditch defenders of the *Conducator*. The comings-and-goings and the excited atmosphere were recorded for posterity – a student with a video camera had been filming the historic events apparently unobserved in all the confusion. When Iliescu saw the camera at last, he ordered it to be switched off and the cameraman removed. When the film surfaced on French television, Iliescu and Petre Roman strenuously and implausibly denied its authenticity. (At the end of August 1990, two other stars of the video, Brucan and Militaru, confirmed its authenticity in an attempt to discredit the old guard.) But these events, the real revolution, were not seen by the Romanian people or the world-television audience at the time. Very different and much more dramatic pictures were capturing their imagination.[5]

From the evening of 22 December, terrible fighting seemed to engulf the major cities of Romania for three days. There were reports of helicopters dropping fanatical paratroops into

Timişoara; while in Bucharest itself the population was terrified by the sound of gunfire and the apparent ease with which gunmen moved through hidden tunnels to strike in one part of the city centre before disappearing only to renew their deadly mayhem somewhere else. Undoubtedly, there was real gunfire and genuine victims fell victim to bullets, but it is impossible to believe in the existence of any serious or co-ordinated opposition to the new regime. The way in which the television distributed grossly exaggerated casualty figures, as well as its imaginative descriptions of the destruction of Sibiu, suggest that behind the image of chaos which the pictures of events inside the television centre suggested, careful control was kept over what actually got onto the screens.

One of the first faces to appear with the news that 'the tyrant has fled. We are free' was the bearded figure of Gelu Voican-Voicalescu. He was one of the 'water' group of plotters, whose occupation as a geologist had brought him into contact with Iliescu, who was Minister of Waterworks, and the young hydro-engineer Petre Roman, whose father had been a senior Communist Party official. Volcan-Voicalescu had been involved in the strange affair known as the 'Transcendental Meditation Scandal' in 1982 when, along with more than thirty others (including the future Minister of Culture in the post-revolutionary government, Andrei Plesu), he was arrested by the Securitate on charges connected with the decision to suppress the cult of yoga in Romania. It is proof of Ceauşescu's paranoia that he even felt threatened by a group of people practising yoga together.[6] Some observers have claimed to see the hand of Ceauşescu's antagonist, Andropov, behind this whole affair, but if he was, then clearly his hand was carefully hidden from Brucan and the others who were looking to Moscow for help in their plots against Ceauşescu at around the same time.[7]

Gelu Voican quickly established a system of control within the television station, which extended to censorship of what could be broadcast. After the first hour or so, the chaotic scenes played out in front of the television cameras and avidly watched throughout Romania bore increasingly little relationship to what was going on behind the scenes. Even Dumitru Maziliu had to hand the text of a declaration which he intended to broadcast to Silviu Brucan before it was cleared for transmission.

The crowd's calls to defend the TV centre from Ceauşescu-loyalists and the hysteria engendered by gunfire from surrounding buildings were genuine enough: only their cause remains in doubt. Like the Central Committee building a couple of miles away in the centre of Bucharest, the TV station was apparently at the heart of ferocious fighting, but although the buildings around it and on the other side of the street were gutted by gunfire and flames, the TV station itself was marked by only a few bullets. In front of the Central Committee building there were still the television cameras and the lights which had been set up for Ceauşescu's ill-fated speech the day before. Although they made obvious targets for snipers, they were not hit – nor was the massive building much defaced by the shooting: a few windows were broken, perhaps from within, and a few holes could be seen in daylight on it, otherwise the surrounding buildings, especially the burning university library, were the only evidence of the counter-*coup* launched by the Securitate. Even allowing for their demonic fury, it seems odd that the fanatical 'terrorists', as they quickly became known, should have concentrated their fire on the library rather than the seat of government.

The revival of fighting was necessary to clear the streets and to disperse the crowds, leaving the Front free to cement its control of the political situation. It certainly served that end. However, the very fact that the Front controlled the country in reality, with the exception of a few upstairs rooms from which increasingly desperate snipers occasionally shot, made the question of the fate of the fallen dictator and his wife more urgent. Of course, the revival of the sounds of battle also helped to make the ever-increasing casualty figures seem more plausible. The events in Timişoara were widely believed to have cost 4,000 lives before 22 December. Soon that figure had been exaggerated to 10,000. In the capital it was reported at least as many had died. By Christmas Day, the Front's spokesmen were talking of 60,000 dead. What the Ceauşescu-loyalists were committing was genocide.

In fact, only a few hundred people had been killed in the week's events. 'Only a few hundred' that is, in comparison with the scores of thousands alleged to have died. Of course, throughout the rest of Eastern Europe, hardly anyone had been killed and not a shot fired in anger as communism collapsed there. But in Romania Ceauşescu's control had been too strong and Gorbachev's influence too weak for there to be a 'Velvet Revolution' like the one which had been engineered in Czechoslovakia a month earlier. No doubt Nicolae and Elena Ceauşescu would have sacrificed thousands of lives to preserve their power, but in fact they fell before they could do so.[8] Once they were safely dead, the Front progressively lowered its estimates of the dead and wounded. But the claim that the couple had murdered thousands was necessary to justify their summary execution. After all, once they were dead, the 'resistance' could stop.

In any case, popular anger probably would not have tolerated their survival, but more to the point, Ceauşescu had sufficient evidence of the involvement of key subordinates in the plot against him to blow the gaff on Iliescu and his comrades. The plotters' presentation of themselves as the spontaneously chosen representatives of the Romanian people in arms might take a battering if Ceauşescu ever appeared in a public court. They needed to dispose of such uncomfortable witnesses, but they also had to satisfy the yearning for justice. A simple assassination would not do. If the couple were just butchered, the reputation of their killers would not survive long either at home or abroad. Due process was needed, but also a trial that could not get out hand. Stanculescu provided a suitable scenario.

Not everything had gone to plan that Friday afternoon. The helicopter pilot, Malutan, had panicked, as had many others. It seems that he received contradictory orders and when he tried to clarify the position with the commander of the airforce, that august personage left him in the lurch. With Ceauşescu's loyal bodyguard suspicious of his radio messages, the pilot had to switch off the radio and rely on his own initiative. The confused state of mind of his passengers helped him to disburden himself of them. Then had followed Nicolae and Elena's pointless roaming of the Oltenian plain in hijacked Dacia 1300s as their two guards jumped ship one after the other. Eventually, exhausted and bewildered, their unwilling driver had been able to deliver them up to the incredulous local police in an agricultural institute on the outskirts of Tirgovişte who in turn handed them on to the garrison at Tirgovişte where they were to spend their last hours together.[9]

The barracks at Tirgovişte had probably been selected as a suitable detention centre not only for Nicolae and Elena Ceauşescu but for the rest of their comrades in the Political Executive Committee of the Romanian Communist Party when Stanculescu had begun to prepare a coup against them. Of course, events had overtaken any plotting and the conspirators had been thrown into operation by the demonstrations starting in Timişoara the weekend before. Accompanied by Virgil Magureanu (the old Securitate expert on the West, and on Romanian dissidents in exile there), a group of military judges, lawyers, and a squad of special troops, including executioners, Ceauşescu's last Defence Minister flew by helicopter to Tirgovişte to supervise the demise of his former patrons.

The proceedings against the desposed couple were marked by grotesquerie on all sides. Neither Nicolae nor Elena seemed able to comprehend what was being done to them, and their judges, who doubled as prosecution and jury, hardly maintained the dignity of the court nor did they strike the correct solemn note for the awesome task they had taken on. The prosecution failed to detail the couple's true crimes: the deliberate impoverishment of the country; the sacrifice of a generation's well-being; the suppression of all dissent and the brutality towards their opponents; the humiliation of an entire people for year upon year. Instead the judges concentrated on ephemera and trivia (when they were not remarking sarcastically on Elena's scholarly pretensions). No doubt, even Stanculescu had once trembled in their presence and curried favour with them and now wanted to show the contempt that he and all their courtiers had really felt during years of fawning and grovelling to them. But he tolerated abuse of the couple by his subordinate judges and prosecutors which was petty and irrelevant to the great occasion: if Elena accused her judges of being absurd rhinoceroses, they gave as bizarrely as they got, making the extravagance of her *toilette* one of the chief counts against her.

Of course, many ordinary Romanians, impoverished and hungry after years of their oppression, were enraged to discover the details of their rulers' wasteful lifestyles, but by pandering to public indignation over what were in reality trivial abuses compared with the general results of Ceauşescu's rule the new leadership missed the chance of holding a worthwhile trial. Tyrants may be murdered but they are rarely called to account for their crimes. Certainly, the trial staged by Stanculescu did not meet any of the criteria of due process. Worse than that, it was counter-productive: the trial and the shabby end of the Ceauşescus almost aroused sympathy for them.[10]

The two old people sat under the gaze of the video camera which never showed the faces of their judges. It was probably not fear of reprisals by Ceauşescu loyalists which made the judges decide to preserve their anonymity, but their desire not to be recognized by those who would know their past service to the doomed defendants. The couple oscillated between refusing to recognize the court and exploding in indignation at what they regarded as the most insolent or absurd allegations. When they were accused of stashing away an untold fortune in Switzerland, they demanded 'Proof!' It has been alleged that Stanculescu was one of the chief executors of the Ceauşescus' foreign accounts which he replenished during his frequent trips abroad.[11] If so, he should have been in a position to confute the protestations of innocence on the couple's part. On the other hand, to have revealed how much he knew about their secret accounts would have exposed how closely involved with the 'tyrant' he had been.

The Ceauşescus' indignant denials of having any foreign bank accounts at all should not be believed, even if the accounts did not contain the billions of dollars routinely alleged. During the same cross-examination (if that is the correct term for the proceedings), they calmly claimed that their children lived in ordinary flats 'like anyone else'. The complete divorce between what they knew to be true and the picture which they still insisted on presenting to the world, even in the face of death, was remarkable. They had lived the lie for too long to renounce it now. Instead, they preferred to insist on Nicolae's constitutional rights as head of state and the armed forces or to repeat the wonders of the hospitals or housing they had built for Romanians.

When film was first released of the trial, the fallen *Conducator* seemed to have taken leave of his senses. Extracts given to the Western media suggested a ranting and irrational figure completely out of touch with what was happening. Much of that impression was undoubtedly true, but it was not the complete explanation of his splenetic fury. Sitting in front of him, invisible to the television viewer, was the man whom he had appointed Minister of Defence on the morning of 22 December and into whose hands he had entrusted the safety of his wife and himself: General Victor Atanasie Stanculescu.

Stanculescu's presence no doubt confirmed Ceauşescu's delusion that he was merely the victim of a plot and that the crowds denouncing him had been arranged by his rivals within the Communist élite. When asked why he had fled by helicopter from the Central Committee building, Ceauşescu replied that the question would be better directed to the man who proposed the idea. This answer suggested to an audience in ignorance of Stanculescu's role in the matter or his presence as a judge that Ceauşescu's mind was not entirely clear.

Even if Nicolae Ceauşescu's mind was far from balanced, his physical health was remarkable for a man of his age who had experienced a disastrous turn of events. When the doctors examined him in accordance with the law to determine whether he was fit to stand trial and to face execution, they were astonished by his condition. Apart from his diabetes, Nicolae Ceauşescu was not suffering from any problems worth recording. Like his wife, he came from a family of long-lived peasants. The news that in the face of death, Nicolae Ceauşescu's blood pressure was normal set off a tremor through many Romanians. Had he survived the revolution and suppressed it, he could have lived for decades more!

When the soldiers began to bind the couple's arms in preparation for their execution, Elena cried out that she had been like a mother to them. Was this simply the deranged cry of a deluded woman who was basking, even *in extremis*, in the title of 'Mother of the Nation', or did she recognize her guards from previous, happier days when soldiers had stood to attention in her presence? Rumour has it that the troops controlling the barracks in Tirgovişte were a special unit, perhaps the most special unit of all in the Romanian armed forces. Whatever was the case, she was determined not to be separated from her husband, as she had told their judges, 'We want to die together.'

According to the official version, Nicolae and Elena Ceauşescu were shot by firing squad on Christmas Day. In his last moments, he was supposed to have started to sing the anthem of the communist movement, The Internationale, while she wailed. The video film released a little while afterwards showed the couple being led towards a wall before cutting to the sound of a hail of gunfire. Spokesmen for the new regime said that every man in a three-hundred-strong unit had volunteered to join the execution squad. The Ceauşescus' defence counsel recalled an undisciplined volley of shots – apparently many soldiers began shooting before the official order was given, or added their bullets to those of the official firing squad.

The video film quickly dispelled rumours that Nicolae and Elena had somehow survived their downfall. Unfortunately, as evidence about how they met their fate, the film is inconclusive. French pathologists cast doubt upon the official version that both the Ceauşescus were killed in a hail of gunfire. Studying the film, they suggested that although both bodies, particularly Elena's, bore the marks of severe automatic fire, these wounds had been inflicted after death. The attempts by the new regime to portray the Ceauşescus as suffering a well-deserved fate at the hands of popular justice raised more questions than they answered.

Was it likely that professionals of the calibre of Victor Stanculescu and Virgil Magureanu would really have left the little matter of the execution of their former master and mistress to a badly disciplined group of teenage conscripts as the official version has it? If the troops guarding the barracks in Tirgovişte were composed of élite members of the presidential guard, it is unlikely that their commanders would have permitted such a chaotic execution. It is far more likely that Nicolae and Elena Ceauşescu were executed by a bullet in the back of the neck in the standard fashion of the Soviet bloc. Then it was thought expedient that the people's anger at the fallen tyrants should be given public expression. The wild firing on the sound-track of the video of the Ceauşescus' last minutes may have been a necessary fiction to cover up the embarrassing fact that they had died in a way more reminiscent of a palace *coup* than a popular revolution. Is it not odd that scores of soldiers did not come forward to claim their share in the glory of killing the hated couple? I cannot find a single instance despite the lucrative rewards which an ordinary private might expect from sensation-hungry foreign journalists.

Gelu Voican was put in charge of disposing of the bodies. After the execution, in an unconscious parody of the immortalization which the couple probably had planned for themselves, the two corpses were embalmed. The plotters had not yet decided how to dispose of their remains. Rumours were spread that they had been cremated and their ashes scattered over the Black Sea. Gelu Voican and a girlfriend led the military party which took the bodies back to Bucharest and buried them incongruously enough among the graves of those who died apparently fighting to overthrow them. Their graves were covered with concrete to make discovery rather than resurrection more difficult, but not before the bearded Gelu Voican imposed a final indignity on the scientific, atheistic corpses by pronouncing the traditional Christian words, 'From dust you came and to dust you return.' There were neither mourners nor flowers. Nicolae and Elena Ceauşescu went to hell unregretted.

Epilogue

Where Are They Now?

If we want things to stay as they are, things will have to change.
Guiseppe Tomasi Di Lampedusa

Nicolae and Elena Ceauşescu went to their deaths alone. Most observers who had anticipated their fall had expected it to coincide with a general massacre of the clan. Few Romanians would have given Nicu Ceauşescu, for instance, much chance of surviving long in the hands of a crowd. Yet, despite one attempt to knife him, and a few bruises, Nicu was unscathed by the disintegration of his world. His brother and sister too passed into custody without mishap – though Zoia's dog was not well-treated. Their uncles and aunts were all tracked down in hours, at most a couple of days, and removed from the risks of popular revenge. Only Uncle Marin lost his life in the days of revolutionary turmoil, and that was in Vienna, where the possibility that he might escape and seek asylum perhaps encouraged others to act summarily – particularly if he proved unco-operative about handing over the combinations of the safety-deposit boxes which he operated on behalf of his brother and sister-in-law. If agents of the rebels controlled the Romanian Embassy in Vienna (and the lack of personnel changes since suggests they might well have done), then Marin would have outlived his usefulness whether he handed over the necessary codes or not. But perhaps the official version is true: unlike his brothers and sister, Marin despaired of life after Nicolae, and gave way to the temptation of suicide.

The members of the politburo and political leadership also resisted any thought of self-immolation. Postelnicu handed over the ornate Syrian pistol, which Assad had once given him, with a show of incompetent subservience which was entirely in character: 'Please, don't shoot, comrade . . . I mean, sir.' At the trial of the four leading members of the inner circle – Postelnicu, Manescu, Dinca and Bobu – which was hastily arranged at the end of January 1990, Postelnicu revealed his cravenness with a thoroughness which his fellow defendants could not match – try as they might. The quality of the charges and evidence was much the same as at the trial of their master and mistress. They all pleaded guilty to crimes from genocide to failing to ensure the supply of rubber teats for babies' bottles. The charge of genocide had long since lost its credibility when attached to the death throes of the regime which had cost hundreds of lives: horrible but hardly genocide. The charge was not laid against them for their role in destroying the health and well-being of millions of Romanians. Since each defendant played his part by confessing in the appropriate places to whatever he was charged with, they would probably have admitted such a charge too – and with justice.

Accepting his general guilt, as the other three also did, Postelnicu sought to relativize his own responsibility by arguing that he had only become Minister of the Interior at an advanced age and had really never got to grips with his portfolio apart from his responsibility for the fire-brigade! He had to admit to ordering the shootings in Timişoara and the removal and incineration of the victims – but he had only passed on 'Her' orders. Postelnicu's utter cravenness rendered the trial grotesque. Until a few weeks before, he had been the overseer of a vast and terrifying security apparatus, which Romanians had believed omniscient and ruthless; now he was a pathetic shell of a human being, degrading himself before the court and the television viewers, as he had once done before Nicolae and Elena Ceauşescu.

Manea Manescu joined in the charade of mutual incrimination and self-incrimination. Postelnicu was a 'beast' and the 'hatchet-man of the dictator'. He himself had only kissed 'Their' hands on parting at Snagov because they had been kind enough to take him with them in the helicopter. Manescu had also suffered at 'Their' hands: Elena had forbidden him to accept an honorary doctorate from the University of Rostock – there was to be only one scholar in the government.

Emil Bobu was the only prize exhibit at the show trial to show any hint of resistance to the hectoring judges. When the chairman of the tribunal, a military judge not unfamiliar with the passing of the death-sentence under his previous employers, was demanding to know why he had obeyed the criminal and insane orders of the tyrant, Bobu blurted out, 'Because if I hadn't I would have found myself where I am now!' He did not add 'and in front of the same judges': it was unnecessary. Bobu was guilty. The three other men in the dock with him were guilty, but they should not have been alone. They now sit out life-sentences in Jilava prison where so many innocent opponents of the Communist Party used to suffer.

Later in the autumn of 1990, the other members of the politburo, the once grand-sounding Political Executive Committee before whom all other Romanians trembled, appeared for trial. Among the twenty-three defendants was Paul Niculescu-Mizil, the only one of their number to have played any role in the new regime, albeit briefly. A few days after the start of the trial, in the haphazard way in which the new regime ran justice, they were joined by Iulian Vlad, the last head of the Securitate under its old name. A first hint of serious differences between President Iliescu and Premier Petre Roman came during the trial when Roman called on the judges to take into consideration the defendants' long careers of service to the dead dictator, not least that of Colonel-General Vlad. In fact, at the end of the trial in March

1991, the judges found only eighteen of the twenty-three defendants guilty and handed out light sentences averaging two years in prison. All the offences related specifically to the events of December 1989.

By then interest in past politics had waned. The audience for televised show trials, even that of Nicu Ceauşescu, dwindled as the prosecutors and judges strove to narrow the courts' terms of reference and to concentrate only on the last days of the old regime. Everybody in Romania knew the implications of Petre Roman's demand that the careers of the old Party leaders should be judged as a whole. Roman himself had never played any part in the government of the country (unlike his late father), but Ion Iliescu had been Ceauşescu's right-hand man. He had been a colleague of the defendants until 1984. Other prominent leaders of the National Salvation Front had served both Dej and Ceauşescu at the very centre of Communist power. They had helped destroy democracy after the war and to collectivize agriculture or to administer the Securitate. A judgement even on the past twenty-five years would damage their standing in allegedly post-Communist Romania.

Before the elections for president and parliament on 20 May 1990, the opposition to the Front had issued the so-called Timişoara Declaration. This Declaration by the rebellious citizens of Tökes's old parish demanded that in the forthcoming elections no one who had held high office in the Communist Party should be eligible for election, least of all to the post of president, for ten years. Everyone knew that was completely unacceptable to the acting president, Ion Iliescu, the former Second Secretary of the Romanian Communist Party.

In the country at large, Iliescu had one great trump card against the nascent anti-Communist opposition that struggled to organize itself after years of repression. Whatever his critics might say about him and his past, Iliescu had shot Ceauşescu (and Elena), which was one huge political advantage. If Gorbachev had been able to say at any time during his tenure of office that he had shot Stalin only six months ago, his popularity would have soared. Almost every Romanian had wanted Nicolae and Elena Ceauşescu dead; some even complained that their end was not gruesome enough. The man who arranged their executions was bound to become a national hero.

However much the opposition groups tried to raise Iliescu's politburo past and that of some of his colleagues, or to scrawl graffiti renaming the 'FSN' (National Salvation Front) as 'Front for the Salvation of the *Nomenklatura*', they could not escape from the simple fact that for most Romanians the overthrow of Ceauşescu and the end of his humiliation of them was sufficient cause to vote for Iliescu and his Front.

Of course, Iliescu and his colleagues were anxious to dispel any public perception of themselves as new-style old communists. This was all the more necessary precisely because in practice they relied on the middle and lower ranks of the old *nomenklatura* to continue running the country. In fact, according to Silviu Brucan, they tried to encourage Ilie Verdeţ to re-establish the Communist Party soon after the revolution. Ostensibly, this was because every trend of opinion is entitled to take part in politics in a democracy, but clearly it would have served the Front's purposes to have the Party back on stage: after all, how could the Front be accused of being the Communist Party under a new name, if the old Party was still alive and kicking?

Most Romanians voted for Iliescu in May 1990. Whether 86% of the voters did so must be a matter of conjecture. Some independent election observers reported fraud, around Iaşi for instance, but my own observation was that the voting was conducted fairly in the Maramureş and probably in most places. A few days before the elections, Iliescu told the foreign observers at a televised meeting, which enabled him to address the country too, that he knew that if he received a huge percentage (more than 75% for instance), Westerners would find it difficult to accept the ballot as fair. This comment was probably directed at local Front organizers: the boss was telling them not to use the heavy mob or fraud, because he was going to win in any case. Unfortunately, in some places, the 'boys' did not get the message, so they turned out the traditional 97% 'Yes-vote'.

Iliescu knew that he could win on the day by fair means because he was the inheritor of an almost fifty-year-old legacy of intimidation and deceit which persuaded most people to go along with the powers that be, which in this case they also were grateful to for ridding them of the previous incumbent. The effects of Ceauşescu's rule had been either to suppress any organized internal opposition or to scatter his opponents abroad as harmless emigrés. By holding 'democratic' elections only five months after Ceauşescu's execution, Iliescu gave his opponents little time to organize and coordinate themselves, let alone to make themselves known to the people. In any case, the Front kept the most important propaganda media – television and radio – under its strict control.

Iliescu's chances in the elections were also greatly helped by the fact that the émigré opponents of communism could not agree among themselves on a single candidate against him. After the revolution, the old pre-communist political parties tried to re-establish themselves. Both the National Liberal Party and the National Peasant Party chose émigrés as their candidates: the Liberals' Radu Câmpeanu had been expelled from the country in the mid-1970s as a 'liberal' gesture by Ceauşescu; the Peasants' candidate, Ion Raţiu, had gone into exile fifty years before the revolution of 1989 and had refused to live in Communist Romania. Both Câmpeanu and Raţiu had honourable records of struggling against Western indifference to publicize the plight of their fellow countrymen under Ceauşescu, but they were mortally handicapped by their years of enforced absence from the country. Most Romanians instinctively looked for a leader who had shared the 'Epoch of Light' with them.

Unfortunately for the opposition, like many émigrés of all political hues, the exiled Peasants and Liberals had quarrelled with each other and often among themselves. Their failure to present a united front fatally weakened any attraction or political plausibility they might have had. The FSN's experienced agitators, like Brucan, who had played an important role in the 1946 elections, knew how to exploit the opposition's confusions and divisions. It was natural after so many decades of complete suppression of political activity that all sorts of people emerged from the totalitarian darkness blinking into the light of freedom and anxious to set up a party to express their own personal, long-held beliefs. Soon after December 1989, there were scores of parties representing every conceivable trend, but often with few members. Undoubtedly, some of these parties were set up by the Front's supporters to disorientate the public. Several Liberal parties appeared, as did parties appealing to the peasants. Some of these were genuine, if eccentric, organizations but others were merely extensions of the Front, a tactic used in the period after 1944 by the Communists.

The Front also infiltrated its own supporters, often former Securitate agents, into the parties. It also tried to suborn their members. Influential Liberals were offered posts in the government if they defected. After the crushing defeat of the opposition in May 1990, when the FSN won more than two-thirds of the seats in the Grand National Assembly, some ex-oppositionists drifted over to the winning side. Dinu Patriciu, for instance, the former leader of the Liberal youth wing, has become Minister of Transport. Some people allege that this sort of coat-turning shows that the individual concerned was always a Securitate agent or a Front-man, but others see it as the unattractive revival of the cynical 'politicians' democracy' of the 1920s and 1930s when deals were done and jobs doled out to the boys regardless of the electorate's views or the politicians' ostensible political commitments. Whatever the cause – and it may well be a combination of several elements of a historically long-diseased body politic – it is an unattractive phenomenon which bodes little good for Romania.

Most of the few active dissidents from the non-Communist opposition to Ceauşescu who survived to see the revolution were not by nature would-be party politicians. On the contrary, they were academics, clergymen, or ordinary workers who simply possessed the courage and the integrity (which is easily said, but not easily comprehended) to say 'No' to the regime. After Ceauşescu's fall, they wanted to return to their normal lives after years of imprisonment, surveillance and harassment. Doina Cornea, for instance, the most famous dissident in Cluj, wanted to return to her work in the university as a lecturer in French literature. She hoped that the revolution would enable her to recover some of the lost years of study since her purging in 1983. Such people did not want to play a part in politics. In any case, they lacked the facilites to do so.

The émigré politicians had certain advantages over the internal dissidents. Mr Raţiu is a rich businessman. Others had contacts with Western helpers. They were able to import some of the paraphernalia of a Western political party into Romania. But they were still frustrated by officialdom which obstructed all Raţiu's efforts to import the equipment for an independent television station. The bureaucracy also hindered attempts by Western organizations to supply office equipment or even newsprint to the opposition parties. The offices of the Liberals or Peasants on the eve of the elections in May were a pathetic sight: a few old typewriters (no doubt with type-faces well-known to the Securitate) and primitive roneo-style copying machines were the sum of their equipment. They certainly had none of the computerized election equipment normal in the West. Of course, the Front had access to all the facilities of the government, which may have been old-fashioned by Western standards (after all no one needed computer-models to forecast election results before 1989), but were vastly superior to the combined facilities of the opposition.

Individuals like Doina Cornea had no office equipment or team to put into the field against either the Front or the émigré politicians. In any case, the dissidents had hoped to retire into their private sphere. By the time they began to organize themselves as a political force, it was too late to get involved in the electoral process. That did not stop the Front's press from denigrating the dissidents, many of whom were of course unknown to the public after years of censorship.

In April 1990, students in Bucharest began to form their own opposition to the Front. For much of the spring a motley group of protesters occupied the University Square in the centre of Bucharest where much of the fighting and killing had taken place on the night of 21–22 December. Hunger-strikes were held under the banner of the Timişoara Declaration's demand that Iliescu not stand for the presidency. But this new strand of opposition failed to excite much support around the country. Intellectuals, professional men like doctors, as well as students were disillusioned with the ability of old Communists to turn their coats, but the people at large did not get their message or accept it. However, the protests in the University Square presented a problem for the government: they threatened to throw up possible future leaders to rival the appeal of Iliescu. The philosophy student, Marin Munteanu, particularly threatened to become a charismatic opposition leader.

After the Front's victory at the polls, the protestors refused to disperse as the government had hoped. On the night of 13 June the police mishandled an attempt to clear the square by force. Instead of ending the protests, the police action sparked rioting against the newly elected government. It is symptomatic of Romania's unhappy state that what happened next has bred a wealth of plausible conspiracy theories. Some people argued that the secret police sent *agents provocateurs* among the crowd to incite violence in order to justify a crackdown. Whatever the truth of those allegations, the eruption onto the streets of Bucharest the next day of thousands

of miners from the Jiu Valley and elsewhere sent shock—
waves through the country and destroyed the public image
of the freshly elected and not yet inaugurated president
Iliescu.

Iliescu made two public-relations blunders: first, he
appeared on television appealing to the miners to come and
suppress his opponents and then he thanked them in front of
the cameras for doing a good job. The brutality of the vigilantes' action was well-recorded by the Western journalists
who were in Bucharest for the presidential inauguration. The
US government boycotted Iliescu's big day (the Western
Europeans attended though they also denounced the violence). Afterwards, Iliescu found himself in an isolated position. He became a kind of post-Communist Waldheim: no
Western state would invite him to visit. He had to make do
with paying calls on still-Communist Yugoslavia and then on
China, which did little to calm the exaggerated comparisons
between what the Chinese Communists had done to their
students in Tiananmen Square in June 1989 and what Iliescu
had encouraged in Bucharest a year later. In any case, Iliescu's
apparent condoning of 'people's justice' did a great deal to
damage his carefully promoted picture of himself as a man
who had fallen out with Ceauşescu over his enthusiasm for
the Cultural Revolution. The lynch-justice of the miners
against intellectuals resembled the Red Guards' kangaroo
courts in Mao's China too closely.

The miners' willingness to do Iliescu's bidding can be
explained by a series of complicated interconnecting factors.
At one level, for simple people in the provinces, leading often
degrading and brutalizing lives, he was the hero of December.
They did not like the urban intellectual élite. But they had
also been told tales by the official media and the old rumour-
mongers of the ex-Securitate about the demonstrators: they
were in the pay of foreigners who were going to take over
Romania's assets (such as they were) and to put the miners
out of work; they were drug-pushers and drug-abusers or
prostitutes; they were even accused of being in league with

the old Communists! At the same time, the union organizers and local officials who had been promoted in the Jiu Valley mining towns since 1977, as well as their secret police minders, were set in motion to bring the shifts direct from the pits to Bucharest. The state-owned railways provided the transport free of charge. With cudgels and rubber hoses, egged on by the government, the miners dispersed the protesters, smashed up the opposition parties' meagre headquarters and homes and then set about settling local people's private scores.

The miners' violence may well mark a turning point in Romania's history. Until they beat down the open expression of opposition to the new government, Iliescu and Roman were coasting along to achieving an important goal: respectability for their government in the West and therefore Western aid for rebuilding Romania's economy. They desperately needed hard cash to invest in modernization. Whatever Ceauşescu had left in the kitty after paying back Romania's debts was quickly spent in the period from January to the May elections, when the Front had imported a lot of goods and foreign fruit to create the impression of a rapid improvement in the stardard of living. By the summer of 1990, the cash had run out and Romania was quickly going into the red. The Western horror at the miners' brutality and Iliescu's condoning of it dashed any hopes of immediate hard-currency aid.

This disappointment also helped to bring out tensions within the Front. Already Brucan and Militaru had been forced out by a mixture of public distrust of men with well-known Communist and pro-Soviet pasts and their colleagues' ambitions and jealousies. In the summer and autumn of 1990, the tensions between the old-style Communists (around Iliescu and Bârladeanu) who had never really wanted to reform the economy and society, just to ditch the Ceauşescus, and the more practical and often younger men around Petre Roman came into the open. Roman became the advocate of a rapid market-orientated economic reform, which threatened to dismantle the old organization of society and therefore much of the continuing power of the *nomenklatura*. Only by making real changes could Roman hope to convince the West of his sincerity as a reformer and therefore of his credit-worthiness.

The West is not the only source of influence over Romania. Events in the Soviet Union are carefully watched in Bucharest. If Mikhail Gorbachev encouraged the downfall of Ceauşescu in the full flood of his reforming enthusiasm in 1989, the Soviet leader's apparent retreat from reform over the next eighteen months encourages the old-style Communists that their day may not yet be done and that the marketization of the economy can be frustrated with Soviet help. All the other former Eastern European members of the Warsaw Pact may have gone their own way but, ironically, Romania, the least compliant of the old members of the Soviet-led alliance, is now the only state in the region to have signed a security treaty with Moscow. Its contents remain undisclosed (at the time of writing).

It would be wrong to give the impression that nothing has changed in Romania since 22 December 1989. Of course, many things have changed: most of all the atmosphere is immeasurably lightened. Before the revolution, the pall of fear and suspicion was so strong that it could be felt even by Western visitors (though not every Western politician or diplomat came into contact with it). The sense of despair and futility which dogged the lives of Romanians has been lifted to a great extent. Even a manipulated revolution cannot continue to cast the old diabolical spells even if there are those who would like it to.

The penumbra of fear has gone, but in essence everyday life is still conducted as before. The same faces administer the same factories and offices. The names of the state and its institutions have been changed but their functions remain as before. Only at the top have new men come in, even though often with a dubious past. The dissident, Gabriel Andreescu, dismissively describes this situation as 'old brothel, new whores'.

Criticism of the turncoats is widespread. Many of the most degraded former flatterers of the Ceauşescus do not escape the lash of public memory. For instance, even the devout cannot forget the behaviour of the Patriarch of the Orthodox Church in the last days of Ceauşescu's power when he congratulated the *Conducator* for dealing with the 'hooligans' in Timişoara. As soon as it was safe to do so, the Patriarch, Teoctist, denounced Ceauşescu as a new child-murdering 'Herod'. Popular pressure seemed to succeed in forcing him to abdicate but, by Easter 1990, Teoctist had been restored since none of the next ranking members of the Orthodox hierarchy were any less incriminated. In fact, Teoctist's natural successor, the Metropolitan Antonius of Sibiu, was so discredited by his eulogies of the late ruling pair that he was completely unacceptable as a replacement. At Easter 1990, some of the faithful joked that Teoctist was obviously under the impression that it was Judas rather than Jesus who rose again.

The more eerie lights of the old order's propaganda machine soon recovered their voices, now free to express their real opinions without coating them in flattery of the 'Couple'. Unfortunately, their own views are simply an unvarnished version of their tirades of yesteryear. Corneliu Vadim Tudor and Eugen Barbu are pouring out chauvinist and anti-Semitic writings now in their own newspaper, *România Mare*, one of the first private enterprises established in post-Communist Romania. Adrian Paunescu was rescued from unaccustomed obscurity in September 1990 and appointed editor of *Zig-Zag*, a weekly which, until then, had been in opposition to the Front.

If all sorts of former Ceauşescu loyalists of the second rank remained in place or had taken up new but still influential positions, the family, of course, had fallen completely. Nicu Ceauşescu remarked after his arrest that he had taken comfort from the news that Ion Iliescu had taken power because he knew him as a 'friend of the family'. That friendship was long since played out. After his parents, Nicu was the most loathed figure in Romania in December 1989. But such was the speed of events and the transient nature of popular emotions that by the time the former Crown Prince of the regime came to stand trial for his own misdeeds as party boss in Sibiu, the public desire for vengeance had greatly waned.

At his trial, Nicu showed himself to be far from the mere drunken buffoon of popular legend. In fact, he used the widespread view of him as a permanent adolescent, who was never sober, to diminish his responsibility for the shootings in Sibiu at the time of the revolution. He claimed that when he ordered the police to take action, he was drunk and that when he sobered up, he rescinded the orders. As for the past, Nicu portrayed himself as a man who had tried to reason with his parents but could not influence their obstinate insistence on pursuing a self-evidently disastrous course, so he had given up. He too, like everyone else, was under the surveillance of the Securitate, he insisted. This was true, but he and his brother and sister were more the objects of maternal protection than sinister concern.

In the calmer atmosphere of the summer of 1990, Nicu also challenged the legal basis of his trial. He faced only two charges: genocide and the possession of an unauthorized firearm. It was not difficult to show that the government had abandoned its claim that the revolution had cost scores of thousands of lives and that therefore the genocide charge was nonsense. On the other hand, the judges clearly could not acquit him of that charge and convict him only on a technicality carrying a sentence of two years or a fine. Eventually, with that indifference to legal first principles which is the despair of any proper lawyer, the tribunal decided to compromise by sentencing Nicu to twenty years, which was neither the sentence for the offence he had not committed nor yet the penalty for the crime he had committed. Despite his confident performance at his trial, Nicu in fact was ill, suffering the effects of years of over-indulgence on his liver. He was saved from prison (for the time being) by the need to go into hospital for treatment. Perhaps an old family friend did help him out after all?

Although both Valentin and Zoia, Nicu's brother and sister, lost their privileges and many of their assets after the revolution, any idea of visiting the sins of their parents on them further was dropped. Their uncles and aunt, Elena, were less fortunate. Nicolae Andruţa was sentenced to twenty years for his role in the December events. His brothers, Ilie and Florin, disappeared into protective custody. Aunt Elena was charged with a host of corruption offences arising from her lordly rule of the family's home-town, Scorniceşti. Other relatives who had neither enjoyed the trappings of power nor shared the booty hurried to distance themselves from the core of the clan. Some were happy to sell discreditable and not always true stories about their infamous kin to the Western press. Unfortunate people who shared the surname 'Ceauşescu' but denied any relationship hurried to publicize the lack of connection between their families and the diabolical brood.

In 1991, the political situation in Romania became increasingly fluid as the heirs of Ceauşescu fell out and struggled to position themselves for continuing intrigue. A triangular power struggle continues between President Iliescu, Prime Minister Roman, and now Industry Minister, Stanculescu. It seems that they hold the fate of Romania in their hands in the face of a divided and ill-organized opposition. But, in fact, the problems facing Romania are beyond their capabilities, even if they devoted their energies wholly to the public good. Ceauşescu has left a legacy which cannot be quickly reversed or even improved.

Unfortunately in the eighteen months since the revolution, little has been done to remedy the disastrous legacy of Ceauşescu. The plight of orphans, the sick, and handicapped in Romania aroused enormous sympathy in the West immediately after the revolution, but the failure of the Romanian authorities to institute reforms of their own to improve conditions in hospitals and asylums has disillusioned many Western donors of charity. The corrupting effects on people's morals of forty years of ever-worsening shortages in a command economy wears down the good intentions of Western helpers. Even if they should not blame Romanian nurses or others who steal aid to provide for their own families, the Western aid workers cannot help feeling frustrated at the apparent futility of many of their efforts.

Elsewhere in Eastern Europe and the Balkans, people are coming to terms with the tremendous difficulty of dismantling a planned economy while at the same time trying to provide the everyday needs of the people. Everyone in the region knows the joke: it is easy to turn an aquarium into fish soup, but no one knows how to turn fish soup back into an aquarium. All the best brains in the region have yet to find a quick and painless formula.

At Christmas 1989, the Romanian Revolution had many of the features of an archetypal fairy-tale. Ceauşescu's pride met its fall so publicly and the dictator's face told the whole story, so it seemed. Yet unlike a fairy-story, the history of the rise and fall of the Ceauşescus does not come to a satisfactory conclusion. Of course, the evil old man and the wicked witch are dead, but unfortunately the boys and girls whom they killed have not sprung back to life. In fact, from beyond the grave the decisions taken by Nicolae and Elena Ceauşescu continue to distort the conditions of life in Romania. Every Romanian alive today has been and will continue to be conditioned by their rule. They left no legacy of good, but the evil they did lives on. What Nicolae and Elena Ceauşescu would have called their ideals may die – indeed, they have no believers today – but that makes little difference to the problems faced by Romanians now and for the foreseeable future. Unfortunately, Nicolae and Elena Ceauşescu's influence has a life of its own. It will survive long after future historians begin to revise the contemporary verdict on them.

Precisely because no one – certainly not the current rulers – will be able to reform Romania quickly and produce obvious improvements overnight, and because the inherited problems will fester, it is safe to predict that the ghosts of Nicolae and Elena Ceauşescu can look forward to a better press in the future than they had at the end of their lives. But even they cannot hope for 1978 to come back.[1]

Notes

Preface

1. See John Sweeney, *The Life and Evil Times of Nicolae Ceauşescu* (London, 1991), who explains Nicolae Ceauşescu's 'frenzy' as primarily a medical condition.

2. See Edward Behr, *'Kiss the Hand You Cannnot Bite': The Rise and Fall of the Ceauşescus* (London, 1991), especially Ryszard Kapuscinski's introduction, for the theme of all-perverting nationalism.

I

1. For the rituals associated with such meetings, see chapter VII and chapter X below. The poet, Helmut Britz, has assembled a fascinating collection of eye-witness accounts of the revolution in Romania, including his own testimony, see 'Augenzeugen, Augentäter: Texte zum Ceauşescu-Sturz' in *Neue Literatur* 41 (January–February 1990), 10–36; 57–136 for the events in Bucharest itself.

2. See Alexander Dubcek with Andras Sugar, *Dubcek Speaks*, translated by Kathy Szent-Gyorgyi (London, 1990). Also see Vojtech Mastny (ed.), *Czechoslovakia: Crisis in World Communism* (New York, 1972), 64 for Ceauşescu's visit to Prague on 15–16 August 1968.

3. See Mastny, *Czechoslovakia*, 85–86.

4. For the effect of Ceauşescu's televised words and of his aged and weary appearance on his people, see *Neue Literatur* 41 (1990); many Romanians felt that the television address on 20 December was the clear sign of the beginning of the end: flanked by his wife, Elena, and a group of strikingly moribund politburo flunkeys, Ceauşescu looked old and tired, and made a poor, repetitive speech.

5. Several participants as well as people who failed to go to the Palace Square noted this confusion.

6. The events in the square in front of the Party Headquarters have been described by many eyewitnesses and journalists; television, film, and radio soundtrack also record the events, but still they remain far from clear. This account was put together from discussions with people

present in the square and the vicinity, plus material supplied to me by others from eyewitnesses as well as *Neue Literatur* 41 (1990), 57–136.

7. Eyewitnesses.

8. See Caramitru's contribution to *Neue Literatur* 1 & 2 (1990), 59–62.

9. For the stenographic report of the meeting of the Political Executive Committee, also the closed-circuit television conference with the Communist Party bosses in each of Romania's forty-one counties, see *România Libera* (10 January 1990).

10. See *Neue Literatur*.

11. The green paint is still visible today. New anti-Ceauşescu slogans were painted up after the army changed sides on 22 December.

12. For an unflattering characterization of Vasile Milea, see Ion Mihai Pacepa, *Red Horizons* (London, 1988), 157–59.

13. See Thomas Ross, 'Schlüsselfigur' in *Frankfurter Allgemeine Zeitung* (13 February 1990); for Stanculescu's claims that he offered to resign on 19 December, see 'Je ne fuirai pas mes responsabilités' and 'L'armée roumaine dans le jeu politique' in *Libération* (19 November 1990).

14. For the involvement of the army in the management of the economy, see chapter IX below. Ceauşescu's trust in Stanculescu was such that he apparently made him one of the very few administrators of his secret funds deposited abroad. See Radu Portocala, 'Mieux qu'un compte bancaire' in *Le Point* (8 April 1991), 27.

15. See the series 'Cine destabilizea viata Timisoara?' in *România Libera* (24–27 January 1990).

16. See *Le Figaro* (31 January 1990).

17. The flight of the Ceauşescus has been described many times already in various languages. The most reliable and exhaustive versions seem to be 'Cum a vrut sa fuga Ceauşescu' in *Libertatea* (30 December 1989), ff., and John Simpson *Despatches from the Barricades; An Eye-Witness Account of the Revolutions that shook the World, 1989–90* (London, 1990), 228–253.

18. For the lack of evidence of any kind and on any count at the Ceauşescus' trial, see chapter XI below.

19. Nicolae Andruţa Ceauşescu led the officer-cadets from the Securitate training school at Baneasa into the city centre, but even if he was willing to shoot at the crowds, it would seem that they proved strangely reticent.

20. For Manescu's own account of his subservient gesture, see *România Libera* (29 January 1990).

21. See *Libertatea* (30 December 1989).

22. For the cult of Ceauşescu, see chapter VII below.

23. Many British television viewers will remember the spate of sightings and arrests reportedly made that Friday afternoon.

II

1. I am grateful to Norman Stone for the information concerning the Romanian Army's use of make-up.

2. For Andruţa Ceauşescu, see Mary Ellen Fischer, *Nicolae Ceauşescu: A Study in Political Leadership* (Boulder, Colorado, 1989), 25–26; also Michel-P. Hamelet, *Nicolae Ceauşescu avec ses texts essentiels* (Paris, 1971), 8–10. A photograph of Ceauşescu's parents appears in Robert Maxwell (ed.), *Ceauşescu, Builder of Modern Romania* (Oxford, 1983). Less flattering portrayals of the father were given to the press by family members like Andruţa's cousin, Florin Ceauşescu. For Hitler's family background, see Joachim Fest, *Hitler* translated Richard and Clara Winston (Harmondsworth, 1977); for Stalin's see Philip Pomper, *Lenin, Trotsky and Stalin: the Intelligentsia and Power* (New York, 1990).

3. For the ethnic composition of the newly united 'Greater Romania' in the interwar period, see Joseph Rothschild, *East Central Europe between the Two World Wars* (Seattle & London, 2nd edition, 1977), 284: Romanians made up 72% of the eighteen million inhabitants; Hungarians were 8%, Germans 4%, Jews also 4%; a *mélange* of gypsies, Ukrainians, Russians, Turks, Armenians, and at least eight other ethnic groups composed the rest of Romania's population. For an evocative memoir of childhood and youth in the *Romanized* Bukovina, see Gregor von Rezzori, *The Snows of Yesteryear: Portrait for an Autobiography* translated by H. F. Broch de Rothermann (London, 1990).

4. See Stephen Fischer-Galati, 'The Impact of the Russian Revolutions of 1917 on Romania' in Peter Pastor (ed.), *Revolutions and Interventions in Hungary and its Neighbor States 1918–19* (Boulder, Colorado, 1988), 303.

5. See Daniel Chirot, *Social Change: the Making of a Balkan Colony* (London, 1976), 157–158; also Henry L. Roberts, *Rumania: Political Problems of an Agrarian State* (New Haven, 1951); under Ceauşescu's regime, the Academy of Political and Social Sciences in Romania published five volumes on the revolt, *Documente privind marea rascolá a táranilor din 1907* (Bucharest, 1976–1987), but only two pages (vol. IV, 332–333) on the events around Scorniceşti itself.

6. For a convenient summary of the facts and figures of Romania's uneven economic development after 1918, see Joseph Rothschild, *East Central Europe between the Two World Wars*, 285 & 318–21. Romania had the most rapidly growing population in Europe in this period – 1.4% per annum – with more than two fifths of the population below the age of twenty. The fecundity of Andruţa and Alexandra Ceauşescu was not untypical.

7. See Pomper, *Lenin, Trotsky and Stalin*, 155.

8. See Hamelet, *Nicolae Ceauşescu*, 16.

9. See Pomper, *Lenin, Trotsky and Stalin*, 154 & 160–62.

10. See Enver Hoxha, *Reflections on China, 1973–1977* (Tirana, 1979), 150–53.

11. See *Flacara* (1 August 1990).

12. Quoted in C. B. Macartney, *Hungary and her Successors* (London, 1937), 327.

13. For the international reputation of the King's most famous mistress, Elena 'Magda' Lupescu, see the limericks inspired by her name, e.g.

> Let's hear it for Magda Lupescu,
> Who came to Roumania's rescue;
> It's a very grand thing
> To be under a king;
> Is anything better, I *esk* you?

(I am grateful to Dr John Kleeberg for making his compendious knowledge of similar rhymes available to me.)

14. Interview with Apostol. See also Fischer, *Nicolae Ceauşescu*.

15. For the Iron Guard, see Eugen Weber 'The Men of the Archangel' in *Journal of Contemporary History*, I (1966), 105–122, or Weber's 'Romania' in Eugen Weber & Hans Rogger (eds.), *The European Right* (Berkeley, 1966); also Zeev Barbu, 'Psycho-Historical and Sociological Perspectives on the Iron Guard, the Fascist Movement in Romania' in Stein Ugelvik Larsen et al. (eds.), *Who were the Fascists: Social Roots of European Fascism* (Bergen, 1980), 379–394. For the role of former Iron Guardists under Ceauşescu, see Michael Shafir, 'The Men of the Archangel Revisited: Anti-Semitic Formations among Communist Romania's Intellectuals' in *Studies in Comparative Communism* xvi (Autumn 1983), 223–243.

16. See note 15 above.

17. For the ethnic composition of the Party, see Shafir, *Romania*, 26.

18. For the Iron Guard attack on Jilava, see Hamelet, *Ceauşescu*, 35. See also Hamelet, *Ceauşescu*, esp. 2ff, and Maxwell, *Nicolae Ceauşescu, Builder of Modern Romania*, 29–31. For an officially approved hagiographic account, see Olimpiu Matichescu, *Doftana. Simbolul al eroismului revolutionar* (Bucharest, 1979).

19. For Ceauşescu's relations with the guards, see Fischer, *Nicolae Ceauşescu*, 30.

20. For Ceauşescu's eventual denunciation of the Pact, see chapter X.

21. For the documents kept secret in the Stasi headquarters in East Berlin about Honecker's past, see Ralf Georg Reuth, 'Erich Honecker, der zwielichtige Held', in *Frankfurter Allgemeine Zeitung* (16 November

1990). The pre-revolutionary Bolshevik party in Russia was deeply penetrated by *Okhrana* informers, including possibly Stalin himself, but that did not prevent Lenin's party coming to power. See John J. Dziak, *Chekisty: A History of the KGB* (Lexington, Mass. 1988), 4–10.

22. For Petrache, see Zeev Barbu, *op. cit.* above.

23. See *The Independent* (8 January 1990).

24. Quoted in Kenneth Jowitt, *Revolutionary Breakthrough*, 77.

25. Sometimes they united to destroy other Communist rivals, like Patraşcanu after 1948.

26. Interview with Pavel Câmpeanu.

27. By contrast, Scorniceşti became a town of about 30,000, but it was also under the thumb of Nicolae's sister, Elena Barbulescu. See chapter IV below.

28. For Elena Petrescu's school-reports, see *România Libera*.

29. See accounts of his trial in March, 1990.

30. For Iliescu, see below, especially chapters X–XII.

31. For the rivalries between 'native' and 'Muscovite' Romanian communists and also between personalities, see Ghita Ionescu, *Communism in Rumania*, especially chapters 7–9; also Shafir, *Romania*, 29–38.

III

1. For the situation in Bucharest around 23 August, 1944, see the classic memoirs of Ivor Porter, *Operation Autonomous: With S.O.E. in Wartime Romania* (London, 1989), 189–244; the Armenian-born British agent, Murad Mathossentz, covers the same ground in *The Black Raven*, translated by Irene Walton-Stiubey (London, 1988), 93–97.

2. Ghita Ionescu's account of the early Communist period remains essential reading for anyone concerned to understand the combination of fanaticism and duplicity which was the minuscule Romanian Communist Party and how it rose to complete power. See his *Communism in Romania, 1944–1962* (Oxford, 1964).

3. For an official Romanian account of the significance of Romania's change of sides in 1944, see Ilie Ceauşescu, Florin Constantiniu & Mihail E. Ionescu, *A Turning Point in World War II: 23 August 1944 in Romania* (Boulder, Colorado, 1985).

4. Interviews with Apostol, Maurer, and Brucan. See Robert King, *A History of the Romanian Communist Party* (Stanford, 1980); also Vladimir Tismaneanu's account of the early growth of the Party in 'The Tragi-Comedy of the Romanian Communist Party', in F. Fehér and A. Arato (eds.) *Crisis and Reform in Eastern Europe* (New Jersey, 1991), 121–74.

5. Elena's role at this time was, if anything, more modest than that of other senior wives.

6. For Stalin's overall ambitions in this period, see Vojtech Mastny, *Russia's Road to the Cold War* (New York, 1979); Hugh Thomas, *The Beginnings of the Cold War* (London, 1986); and Paolo Spriano, *Stalin and the European Communists*, translated by Jon Rothschild (London, 1985), 233–305.

7. See Milovan Djilas, *Conversations with Stalin*, translated by N. B. Petrovich (Harmondsworth, 1963), 107–109.

8. For Vyshinsky's role in Romania, see Arkady Vaksberg, *The Prosecutor and the Prey: Vyshinsky and the 1930s Moscow Show Trials*, translated by Jan Butler (London, 1990) 245–246 & 256–257.

9. Private information.

10. See Jon Halliday (ed.), *The Artful Albanian: the Memoirs of Enver Hoxha* (London, 1986), 117–118.

11. See *ibid.*, 123.

12. For the post-war show-trials, see George H. Hodos, *Show Trials, Stalinist Purges in Eastern Europe, 1948–1954* (New York, 1987).

13. See the local Slatina newspaper, *Glasul Adevarului*, cited in Joachim Siegerist, *Der Rote Vampir* (Hamburg, 1990), 38ff. Enver Hoxha's description of Dej's mobile armoury above makes clear how plausible this account of Ceauşescu's behaviour is. (See above.)

14. Interview with Apostol (October 1990).

15. Interviews with Silviu Brucan. See also Virginia Gheorghiu's forthcoming comparative study of the Romanian press in the period 1944–47 and 23 December 1989–1991.

16. See Ceauşescu, *Builder of Modern Romania*, 47.

17. For Ceauşescu's rise in the Party hierarchy, see Mary Ellen Fischer, *Nicolae Ceauşescu*, 35–81.

18. See Vladimir Tismaneanu, 'The impossible heresy of Miron Constantinescu' in *Survey* (1984).

19. For the Hungarian Revolution, see David Irving's controversial *Uprising!* (London, 1986). For an eyewitness account by a victim of Andropov's charm, see the memoirs of Sandor Kopasci, *In the Name of the Working Class* translated by Daniel and Judy Stoffman with a foreword by George Jonas (London, 1986), especially 28–32 and 235–237. The current chairman of the KGB, Vladimir Kryuchkov, was Andropov's First Secretary in Budapest in 1956. He remains 'very fond of Hungarian literature'. See Vladimir Kryuchkov, *The KGB must abide by the interests of the people* (Novosti: Moscow, 1989), 30.

20. Ion Maurer still denies that there were disorders in Transylvania and the Banat in November 1956. He also says that there was no collusion between the Soviet authorities and their Romanian hosts, claiming that Dej's government (in which he was Minister of the Interior) was 'not informed' by the Soviet authorities about their actions

in the case of Imre Nagy. (Interview with Ion Maurer, September 1990.)

21. Kadar's successor as General-Secretary of the Hungarian Socialist Workers' Party, Karoly Grosz, was kind enough to describe Kadar's rueful state of mind at the end of his life and to recall for me what the Party élite in Hungary knew of the events of 1956. (Interview, November 1990.)

22. See the memoirs of Ion Pacepa, Ceauşescu's chief intelligence adviser who defected to the West in 1978, *Red Horizons* (London, 1988), 356–361. His anecdote about the moans and chilblains of the keeper of the safe house and his wife, twenty years on, requesting early retirement for all they had suffered during the torture of Nagy has a truly accurate ring. The Romanian controller on the spot of the Nagy group appears to have been Valter Roman, the father of the present Romanian Prime Minister, Petre Roman. See Vladimir Tismaneanu, 'The Tragicomedy of Romanian Communism' in Feher and Arato, *Crisis and Reform in Eastern Europe*, 169 note 74.

23. Interview with Brucan. See note 15 above, for references to Ceauşescu's early slavishly pro-Soviet speeches and newspaper articles. All the Old Guard – Maurer, Apostol, Brucan – agree that Dej had turned against Ceauşescu at the end of his life, but they are also apologists for Dej's regime, which was their period of greatest influence. It is useful for their own self-esteem to argue that the regime only became brutal *after* 1965.

24. In the end, Draghici found himself among the 'outs' along with Apostol and the rest. See chapter VI below.

25. For Stalin's bugging of his colleagues and rivals in the mid-1920s, see Boris Bazhanov, *Bazhanov and the Damnation of Stalin*, translated with a commentary by David W. Doyle (Athens, Ohio, 1990), 39–40: 'I found him [Stalin] on the telephone – but listening, not talking . . . The phone was part of an automatic system [*vertushka*] installed on Lenin's orders. He had thought it dangerous to let the telephone 'girls' listen in on important and secret conversations. A separate unmanned automatic system had therefore been installed . . . Only Central Committee members, People's Commissars and their deputies, and of course Politburo full and candidate members, had these phones . . . It didn't take long to realize that a phone 'central' [tap] had been installed on his [Stalin's] desk. It enabled him to listen to all the other officials who had automatic phones. Those others, of course, thought *their phones were secure* because no girl operators were involved. They spoke freely on their lines, and *so Stalin could hear all their secrets*.' [Emphasis added.] By the later 1970s, Elena Ceauşescu, too, had her own bugging system next to her office so that she could listen to the Romanian élite's private conversations in the same way. See Pacepa, *Red Horizons*, 172.

26. See chapter X below.

27. For Dubcek's hopes that Kadar or Tito would back the Prague Spring, see Alexander Dubcek with Andras Sugar, *Dubcek Speaks*, translated by Kathy Szent-Gyorgyi (London, 1990), 54–62; Dubcek's close collaborator recalls that Kadar asked the naïve man on 17 August 1968, 'almost desperately: "Do you *really* not know what kind of people you are dealing with?"' See Zdenek Mlynar, *Nightfrost in Prague: the End of Humane Socialism* (London, 1980), 157. For Tito's real attitude to 'socialism with a human face' see Marko Milivojevic, *Descent into Chaos: Yugoslavia's Worsening Crisis* (IEDSS, London, 1989), 23.

28. See *Dubcek Speaks*, 57–58.

29. *Ibid.*

30. See *Newsweek* (8 January 1990), 16. See also Vladimir Tismaneanu, 'Ceauşescu's Socialism' in *Problems of Communism* 34 (January–February, 1985), 60.

31. For Ceauşescu's reforms, see Shafir, *Romania*. For Silviu Brucan's emphasis on how far Gorbachev seemed to be following the Romanian model, see his article 'Contradictions Along the Road to Reform' in the *International Herald Tribune* (6–7 August 1988).

32. There is no published biography of Iliescu, and he is ungenerous in granting interviews, but it is rumoured in Bucharest that the Labour MP, George Galloway, is intending to write one.

33. Interview with Kiraly.

34. For Madame Mao, see Ross Terrill, *The White-Boned Demon: A Biography of Madame Mao Zedong* (New York, 1984). For Ross Terrill's views before the fall of Jiang Qing and the Gang of Four, see Simon Leys, *The Burning Forest: Essays on Culture and Politics in Contemporary China* (London, paperback edition, 1988), 188–197.

35. For the machinations behind the fall of Lin Biao, see Simon Leys, *op. cit.*, 138–47. I seem to recall that Radio Peking, in its more colourful period, described Lin Biao as 'a piece of shit which even a dog would not sniff'.

36. For Ceauşescu's speech, see *Lumea* (21 April, 1989), 8. For Deng's attack on the Gang of Four's subordination of science to the demands of ideological rigour, seen general editor Robert Maxwell, *Deng Xiaoping: Speeches and Writings* (Oxford, 1984), 40–53. See especially page 45, for Deng's emphasis on the need for 'a large contingent of scientific and technical personnel who are both *"red and expert"* . . . The Gang of Four made the absurd claim that the more a person knew, the more reactionary he would become.' If we want to understand one of the reasons why Deng is still in power and Ceauşescu is not, pages 47–48 reveal Deng telling the Party apparatchiks to let scientists get on with their research work: 'We cannot demand that scientists and technicians . . . study

stacks of books on political theory . . . and attend meetings not related to their work.' But he insisted that scientists should not stray into politics of their own accord either.

37. For Nicu Ceauşescu's illusions on 22 December 1989, see Epilogue below.

38. It was since been imitated by Mikhail Gorbachev in the Soviet Union, albeit in different circumstances. See Brucan, *International Herald Tribune* (6–7 August 1988).

IV

1. For the fate of Elena's mother, see *The Times* (9 January, 1990) and Camelia Kalamar, 'Am intrat primii in Casa din Primaverii' in *Zig-Zag* (19–26 June, 1990).

2. For Zhivkov, see note 13 below.

3. For Saddam's background and his views on family life, see Samir al-Khalil, *Republic of Fear* (London, 1990), especially 77–78.

4. For the values of the Mafia, see Norman Lewis, *The Honored Society*, (London, 1984). For a sympathetic view of the origins of the Mafia, see Eric Hobsbawm, *Primitive Rebels* (Manchester, 1972).

5. See Arshi Pipa, 'The Political Culture of Hoxha's Albania' in Tariq Ali (ed.), *The Stalinist Legacy* (Harmondsworth, 1984), especially 459. Pipa was the relative in question, who had in fact been taught French at school by the young Hoxha. For Enver Hoxha's account of this murderous episode, see *The Titoites* (Tirana, 1982).

6. For rumours of a recent coup attempt in Democratic Korea, see *Die Welt* (9–10 February 1991).

7. Stalin made his attitude towards Pauker clear at a meeting with Dej and Apostol towards the end of his life. (Interview with Apostol.)

8. For the wives of the Romanian leaders, see Tismaneanu's characterization, in 'The Tragicomedy of Romanian Communism' in Ferenc Feher & Andrew Arato (eds.), *Crisis and Reform in Eastern Europe* (New Brunswick, NJ, 1991), 152.

9. See Michael Voslensky, *Nomenklatura: Anatomy of the Soviet Ruling Class*, translated by Erich Mosbacher (London, 1984).

10. Marin Ceauşescu's role must remain a matter of hypothesis, but it has been widely rumoured. Since the autumn of 1989, the German press has carried almost daily accounts of the corruption of the East German *nomenklatura*'s way of life and its methods of obtaining Western goodies.

11. For a cynical view of Swiss banking and money-laundering, see Jean Ziegler, *Die Schweiz wäscht weisser* (Hamburg, 1990).

12. See Boris Yeltsin, *Against the Grain: An Autobiography*, translated by Michael Glenny (London, 1990), 132.

13. For Todor Zhivkov, see Carl Gustaf Ströhm, 'Todor Schiwkov denkt über sein Leben nach' in *Die Welt* (30 May, 1990) and Tim Judah, 'Zhivkov confesses socialist sins and seeks West's mercy' in *The Times* (28 November, 1990), and the accounts of his trial in March 1991. Georgi Markov, *The Truth that Killed* (London, 1983) is a description of life at the top in Communist Bulgaria.

14. See Robert Maxwell (gen. ed.), *Nicolae Ceauşescu, Builder of Modern Romania*, 121.

15. For Ceauşescu's keeping of the option of Nicu's succession, see *Newsweek* (21 August 1989).

16. See Vladimir Tismaneanu, 'The Tragicomedy of Romanian Communism'.

17. Elena's bedroom furniture, see *Adevarul* (26 December 1989).

18. See Ivan Volgyes, *Politics in Eastern Europe* (Chicago, 1986), 153.

19. For Petre Borila, see Vladmir Tismaneanu, *Personal Power and Elite Change in Romania* (Philadelphia, 1989), 56 note 35; see also Shafir, *Romania*, 26.

20. See John Sweeney, *The Life and Evil Times of Nicolae Ceauşescu* (London, 1991) for a characterization of Valentin as the 'good' and Nicu as the 'bad' prince.

21. Pacepa's memoirs contain several episodes of Nicu's drunken debauchery. As an official of the Romanian Communist Youth Organization, Nicu hardly bothered to disguise his impatience to get away from boring meetings and get on with life. For instance, in the mid-1980s, Nicu was officially president of the United Nations World Youth Year (1986), but he barely deigned to go to open meetings with his colleagues from around the globe, let alone sit through them. (I am grateful to the then leader of the Dutch Labour Party's youth-wing, A. Melkert, for talking to me about that period.)

22. Nadia Comanecj's spectacular deflection from Romania a few weeks before the revolution in 1989 was a major propaganda defeat for the regime.

23. Interview with Sergiu Celac.

24. For the most often quoted account, see René de Flers, 'Socialism in one Family', in *Survey* (1984). Edward Behr, *Kiss the Hand You Cannot Bite* (London, 1991) seems to have followed this exaggerated version of Ceauşescu's formidable nepotism. Vladimir Tismaneanu is a better-informed guide to the family in politics and has whittled down the number of immediate members of the Ceauşescu–Petrescu clan.

25. For a characterization of Andrei, see Pacepa, *Red Horizons*. Sergiu Celac regarded his former minister as essentially a cynical nihilist (interview); in a series of newspaper interviews, Violetta Andrei has defended

her husband, insisting on his ignorance of Ceauşescu's crimes and their own fear of persecution by the Comrade.

26. See Pacepa, *Red Horizons*.

27. See *Le Figaro* (30 January 1990).

28. See Manescu's statement in *România Libera* (26 January, 1990).

29. See the classic defence of corruption at the last bastion of human liberty in a would-be totalitarian society, Alain Besançon, 'Eloge de la corruption en Union soviétique' in *Présent soviétique et passé russe* (Paris, 1986), 291–318.

30. For the local tyranny, grotesque corruption and pathetic love affairs of Elena Barbulescu, see 'Doamna de Scornicesti' in *România Libera* (6 March, 1990) and 'Barbulestii–Tiranii din Olt' in *Adevarul* (20 January, 1990). See also Rasvan Popescu & Alin Alexandru, 'Ce mai fac boierii 'Epocil de Aur' in *Express* (30 August 1990).

V

1. See his interview in *Le Figaro* (11 July 1990).

2. Unfortunately, a complete list of the foreign honours bestowed upon Nicolae and Elena Ceauşescu up to December 1989 does not survive, but a modest sample of one hundred and ten can be found in Robert Maxwell (gen. ed.), *Nicolae Ceauşescu, Builder of Modern Romania and International Statesman* (Oxford, 1983), 162–166.

3. For the April Statement of the (then) Romanian Workers' Party, see Shafir, *Romania*, 177.

4. Interview with Silviu Brucan. He presented a paper on the likely consequences of a split with Moscow to the politburo and was present for (at least part of) the discussion.

5. See Tismaneanu, 'The Tragicomedy of Romanian Communism'.

6. See Christopher D. Jones, *Soviet Influence in Eastern Europe. Political Autonomy and the Warsaw Pact* (New York, 1981), 209.

7. See Ion Mihai Pacepa, *Red Horizons* (London, 1988), 177.

8. See Pacepa, *ibid.*, 73. Leonard Schapiro has pointed out how the generous whim of a despot is misinterpreted in the West, with a good example from Khruschev's visit to New York in 1959. An elderly Lithuanian couple who had not seen their son since the end of the Second World War begged Khruschev to let their son out of the USSR. The Soviet leader told Gromyko 'Make the arrangements.' Schapiro comments: 'The reunion of families is, of course, an excellent thing. But I was appalled by this story – though I found it difficult to get some of my friends to share my indignation [with] . . . this power of an autocrat over the destiny of one of his subjects.' See G. R. Urban (ed.), *Stalinism: Its Impact on Russia and the World* (London, 1982), 414.

9. Most of the academic studies of Romanian politics published in the last three years ignore Pacepa's memoirs, e.g. Mary Ellen Fischer, *Nicolae Ceauşescu*. But Sergiu Celac, who owes Pacepa no favours, told the author that he regards the book as basically truthful: 'You should ask what Pacepa left out.' Clearly, Pacepa's portrait of himself as an anti-Communist of long-standing is absurd, but the flaws in his self-portrait and the vulgarity of the book's style and content should not rule it out as a source. Surprisingly, Vladimir Tismaneanu is also dismissive of the central theme of Pacepa's book and for once seems to underrate the multilaterally developed duplicity of Ceauşescu. See 'The Tragicomedy of Romanian Communism' in Ferenc Feher & Andrew Arato (eds.), *Crisis and Reform in Eastern Europe* (New Brunswick, 1991), note 26, pages 159–160.

10. See Anatoly Golitsyn's books for a Soviet defector on this theme. See James Sherr, *Soviet Power: the Continuing Challenge* (London, 1987) for the central importance of 'deception' in Soviet military thinking.

11. For Ilie Ceauşescu's role, see *International Herald Tribune* (11 January 1990).

12. See Henry Kissinger, *The White House Years* (Boston, 1979), 156; see also Stephen E. Ambrose, *Nixon: the Triumph of a Politician 1962–1972* (New York, 1989), 107–108 & 288 for Nixon's belief that the Soviet Union would be put on the defensive by his opening to China via Romania. For Nixon's continuing association with Ceauşescu, see his memoirs (1985). The former US president seems to have been involved in a complicated deal worth US$181 million to broker the supply of uniforms to the Iraqi Army from Romania. See Adel Darwish & Gregory Alexander, *Unholy Babylon: the Secret History of Saddam's War* (London, 1991), 153.

13. See Shafir, *Romania*, 182.

14. For Romania's growing dependence on trade with the Soviet Union and the Comecon bloc, see Vladimir Socor, 'Romania's slide into economic submission' in Vojtech Mastny (ed.), *An Annual Soviet/East European Survey, 1985–1986* (Durham, North Carolina, 1987), 77–83.

15. For Ceauşescu's Soviet medals and relations with Gorbachev as well as Gromyko, see *Frankfurter Allgemeine Zeitung* (6 October 1988).

16. For the later phase of the US courtship of Ceauşescu, see the memoirs of Reagan's ambassador to Bucharest, David Funderburk, *Pinstripes and Reds: An American Ambassador Caught between the State Department and the Romanian Communists, 1981–1985* (Washington, D.C., 1987); as late as 1985, Henry Kissinger's vicar on earth, Helmut Sonnenfeldt, dismissed Western critics of Ceauşescu's regime as 'influenzed by Hungarian propaganda', quoted in *Frankfurter Allgemeine Zeitung* (15 July 1988).

17. See Henry Kissinger, *The White House Years*, 704 & 714.

18. For the differences between Western and Soviet and Eastern European understandings of 'détente', see P. H. Vigor, *The Soviet View of War, Peace and Neutrality* (London, 1975) and James Sherr, *Soviet Power: the Continuing Challenge* (London, 1987).

19. Lord Callaghan's remarks were broadcast by BBC Radio Four's 'World This Weekend' programme, 31 December 1989; see David Steel, *Against Goliath: David Steel's Story* (London, 1989; 1991 paperback edition), 194 on David and Judy's dog-breeding: 'One I gave to President Ceauşescu of Romania as a thank-you after an official visit. By all reports, at the time of writing, it still lives in the presidential palace and is a favourite of the elderly autocrat. The Romanian embassy in London has to dispatch tins of its favourite food and biscuits in the diplomatic bag'; also page 247 for how Steel renewed his acquaintanceship with 'a beaming President Ceauşescu' at Tito's funeral in 1980 and was able to ask 'how my dog was getting on'. For Steel's enthusiasm for Romania in the late 1970s, see *Lumea* (May 1978).

20. See Tony Benn, *Office Without Power: Diaries 1968–72* (London, 1989), 79. Unlike his contemporaries in office on both sides of the House of Commons, Mr Benn has not sought to distance himself from an embarrassing episode by pleading a 'hazy' memory or by withdrawing his diary. However much one may disagree with his judgements, Mr Benn's *glasnost* must put historians of this period in his debt. Neither Lord Callaghan nor Dr David Owen, the Prime Minister and Foreign Secretary at the time of Ceauşescu's state visit to Britain, have cast any light upon the background to this peculiar period in Anglo-Romanian relations.

21. See Benn, *Office Without Power*, 21.

22. *Ibid.*, 25.

23. *Ibid.*, 80. After dinner with the present president of the Romanian Senate, Alexandru Bârladeanu, then chief economic planner under Ceauşescu, Mr Benn enjoyed the charms of Bucharest twenty years before Ceauşescu sent in the bulldozers: 'It was a beautiful evening and . . . quiet except for the sound of orchestras from different restaurants . . . I hadn't realized what a beautiful city Bucharest is.' *Ibid.*, 77.

24. *Ibid.*, 79–80.

25. *Ibid.*, 77.

26. *Ibid.*, 100, 97.

27. *Ibid.*, 354.

28. Private communication to the author..

29. See Robert Hughes, *The Red Dean: the Life and Riddle of Dr Hewlett Johnson, 1874–1966* (Worthing, 1987), 191; for the Dean's admiration

of Dej's Romania, see Hewlett Johnson *Eastern Europe in the Socialist World* (London, 1955), 179–206.

30. For Mervyn Stockwood's dithyramb, see *The Times* (12 June 1978); for his exploits as an undercover cleric – too secret too long, perhaps – see Roland Rudd, 'God's Scarlet Pimpernel' in *The Sunday Correspondent* (31 December 1989).

31. See Richard Clogg, 'Let us now praise a famous woman', in *New Scientist* (20 January 1990), 65.

32. See 'Letters' in *The Times* from Jessica Douglas-Home, *et al.*, (23 November, 28 November, and 3 December 1988).

33. See his letter to *New Scientist* (3 February 1990), 73.

34. For the Central London Poly's belated proceedings to strip Elena Ceauşescu of her honorary professorship, see 'Professor Elena is put on trial' in *Evening Standard* (12 January 1990).

35. See 'Zimbabwe heads towards one-man one-party rule' in *The Sunday Telegraph* (28 January 1990) and the *Neue Zürcher Zeitung* (12 June 1990).

36. For those who enjoy fairy-tales for grown-ups, see World Bank, *Romania: Industrialization under Socialist Planning* (Washington, D.C., 1979); for the corrective, see Peter Bauer's article in *The Wall Street Journal* (10 August 1979). In 1977, Professor Marvin Jackson told the US Congress that Romania had achieved growth of 6% in the years 1966–1970, which he thought 'a substantial achievement by world standards, one that would have pleased most developing countries'. (Report to Congress, quoted in Mary Ellen Fischer, *Nicolae Ceauşescu*, 177.) Today, Professor Jackson is still promoting growth in the new Eastern Europe, one hopes just as enthusiastically.

37. For Ceauşescu's visit to the USA, see Pacepa, *Red Horizons*.

VI

1. See *Scînteia* (4 August 1977).

2. For the events of 1972, see Robert King, *A History of the Romanian Communist Party*, 111. As late as the beginning of December 1989, Ceauşescu used this tactic for one last time when he criticized the quality of the work of several of his leading colleagues in the Central Committee. See chapter X below.

3. Much of my account of the events of August 1977, in the Jiu Valley is based on interviews with miners and their families in the region in June 1990. For the perspective of the Hungarian minority on the strike, see Zsolt Csalog, 'Ceauşescu and the miners. István Hosszú's Story' in *New Hungarian Quarterly* 30 (Winter 1989), 5–11.

4. Memories about these changes were still bitter, thirteen years on.

5. Csalog ('Ceauşescu and the miners') argues that Dobre mishandled

the situation from the beginning by treating Ceauşescu with respect, even calling him 'the Romanian people's favourite son'. For information about Dobre's future career. I am grateful to Silviu Brucan and several acquaintances of Dobre who prefer not to be named.

6. For Ceauşescu's measures after the strike, see Robert L. Farlow, 'Romania', in R. F. Staar (ed.), *Yearbook of International Communist Affairs* (Hoover Institution: Stanford, 1978), 60–61.

7. See Ion Mihai Pacepa, *Red Horizons*, 133–37.

8. For Liliana Cojacaru's story, see *Romania Today* (June 1989), 35.

9. I am grateful to Claudiu Secassiu for his eyewitness account of the events.

10. See the *Independent* (28 November 1987).

11. For Babes, see *Sunday Times* (March 1989). The BBC broadcast 'Holiday 89' on the day his death was announced. The Romanians had stage-managed the BBC's visit so effectively that the programme's presenter informed the audience of would-be tourists that religious freedom was not only tolerated in Romania but written into the constitution.

12. For Ceauşescu's later economic policies, see chapter IX below.

13. For food exports, see Paul Gafton, 'Economic Malaise and Remedies' in Vojtech Mastny (ed.), *An Annual Soviet/East European Survey 1985–1986* (Durham, North Carolina, 1987), 305–09.

14. For Ceauşescu's methods of dealing with economic difficulties and grievances, see Vlad Georgescu, 'Romania in the 1980s', in *Eastern European Politics and Societies* 1 (1988).

15. For Trofin, see his son's articles in the Constanza newspaper, *Contrast*, in September–October 1990. I am grateful to Mircea Trofin for talking to me about his father in October 1990.

16. For the circumstances of his father's death, interview with Mircea Trofin. The Trofin family were disappointed that Iliescu neither voted against his old friend's political humiliation by Ceauşescu when it came before the Central Committee nor attended his funeral.

17. See Georgi Markov, *The Truth that Killed* (London, 1983), 37–38.

18. For Ceauşescu's comment, see 'Exposé on Questions of Socio-economic management', a supplement to *Romania Today* (May 1988).

19. A full history of the Securitate's methods of changing the minds of dissidents has yet to be written, but Ion Vianu, a psychiatrist and victim of his own refusal to collaborate in torture, gave terrible evidence to the Human Rights Commission of the European Parliament on 17 February 1989. See note 24 to chapter IX below for the scientific research performed under Elena Ceauşescu's aegis into lobotomizing the religious believer, etc.

20. See Shafir, *Romania*, 170.

21. See Pacepa, *Red Horizons*, 154, and Shafir, *Romania*, 17.

22. See Matei Pavel Haiduc, *J'ai refuse! de tuer. Un agent secret roumain revêle les dessous de l'affaire* (Paris, 1984). For the extent of Romanian espionage in France, see Thierry Wolton, *Le KGB en France* (Paris, 1986), 159–182 and 384–400.

23. For Ceauşescu's preference for RADU, see Pacepa, *Red Horizons*, 143–49. Unusually many members of the RFE Romanian service staff in Munich developed cancers, and at least three died, in the 1980s, arousing suspicions that they were being poisoned by the DIE.

VII

1. I am grateful to Anthony Daniels for drawing this poem to my attention and to James Alison for lending me his copy so I could quote from Cardenal's *Marilyn Monroe and Other Poems* translated by Robert Pring-Mill (London, 1975), 47. It is a comment on human frailty that though the poet, Cardenal, could penetrate to the heart of the desire to humiliate the ruled which the Nicaraguan dictator's cult of himself epitomized, the political activist Cardenal was simultaneously describing Castro's Cuba as 'the kingdom of heaven on earth' despite the universal presence of the *commandante en jefe*. But then Julien Benda, who first exposed the *trahison des clercs*, the infatuation of intellectuals with fascism in the 1920s, himself endorsed Stalin's show-trials a decade later. Is anyone immune to double-standards?

2. *Scînteia* (27 April 1968), cf. Anneli Ute Gabanyi, *Die Unvollendete Revolution: Rumänien zwischen Diktatur und Demokratie* (Munich, 1990), 42).

3. For the Palace of the People, see chapter VIII below.

4. For Maurer and Bârladeanu's comments, see Richard Van Allen (ed.), *Yearbook of Communist Affairs, 1968* (Stanford, 1969), 510.

5. For the XI Party Congress, see Vladimir Tismaneanu, 'Ceauşescu's Socialism' in *Problems of Communism* 34 (January–February 1985), 63.

6. Like other Communist rulers, Ceauşescu liked to send telegrams as much as to receive them. Whenever flying on one of his state visits, he would fire off greetings to the heads of state whom he passed over and he continued to remember them long after they lost office. Sir Zelman Cowen, the former Governor-General of Australia, told me that while he was still in office he received birthday congratulations from heads of state from all over the world, including the Queen, but after he retired to Oxford as Provost of Oriel, the telegrams dried up until in the end in 1989 he received only three – from Todor Zhivkov, Erich Honecker, and Nicolae Ceauşescu.

7. I was present during the session as a witness. Mr Newens' colleague,

Richard Balfe, the chairman of the Great Britain–Ethiopia Society, could not understand what all the fuss was about: he thought Romania sounded like a right-wing paradise – 'a ban on abortion and a hereditary monarchy'. Mr Balfe's forte of cynical wit came out again in his defence of another Balkan tyrant. Not long before the downfall of Bulgaria's Todor Zhivkov, the irrepressible Balfe and two of his Labour MEP colleagues, Alf Lomas and Barry Seal, wrote to the *Independent* (25 July 1989) in defence of Zhivkov's regime to deny that the Bulgarian Communists were driving scores of thousands of Turks out of the country of their birth and ancestors and into exile in Turkey: hadn't human rights campaigners complained about restrictions on travel rights in the Communist bloc, 'everyone [now] enjoys the right to leave Bulgaria . . . What does the West want?' The continental press was not amused by *les travaillistes britanniques* (see *Libération*, 23 February 1989), though it has to be said that the Christian Democratic group in the European Parliament sent a delegation headed by the gullible German Christian Democrat, Egon Kleptsch, to Romania in 1989 which met President Ceauşescu and found nothing wrong.

8. For a description of the museum and its ideological function (which was replicated in every other Romanian museum of whatever sort in its own salon of homage), see Paul Simionescu & Hubert Padiou, 'Comment la musée national de Bucarest racontait l'histoire' in Alain Brossat (ed.), *A l'Est la mémoire retrouvée* (Paris, 1990), 212–228.

9. See Valentin Pelosse, 'Le mémorial de Josip Broz Tito' in Brossat (ed.), *A l'Est la mémoire retrouvée*, 229–245. For Kim's cult of himself, even of his childhood playgrounds, see the Polish film, *The Parade* (1988).

10. See 'We Don't Have Empty Shelves' in *Newsweek* (21 August 1989), 15.

11. See Anneli Maier, 'Ceauşescu Family Succession?' in Vojtech Mastny (ed.), *An Annual Soviet/East European Survey 1985–1986* (Durham, North Carolina, 1987), 320; also Vladimir Tismaneanu, 'Byzantine Rites, Stalinist Follies: The Twilight of Dynastic Socialism in Romania' in *Orbis* (Spring 1986), 82; and Mary Ellen Fischer, 'Women in Romanian Politics: Elena Ceauşescu, Pronatalism, and the Promotion of Women' in Sharon L. Wolchik & Alfred G. Meyer (eds.), *Women, State, and Party in Eastern Europe* (Durham, North Carolina, 1985), 123. For a rationale behind the cult, see Mary Ellen Fischer, 'Idol or Leader? The Origins and Future of the Ceauşescu Cult' in Daniel Nelson (ed.), *Romania in the 1980s* (Boulder, Colorado, 1981).

12. For Madame Mao, see Ross Terrill, *The White-Boned Demon: A Biography of Madame Mao Zedong* (New York, 1984).

13. Pacepa's *Red Horizons* is full of examples of Elena's spying on the

peccadilloes of her husband's flunkeys and her promotion of the least
worthy of them, like Vasile Milea.

14. See Vladimir Tismaneanu, 'Byzantine Rites, Stalinist Follies: The
Twilight of Dynastic Socialism in Romania' in *Orbis* (Spring 1986), 72.

15. See *Neuer Weg* (7 January 1989).

16. See Anthony Daniels, *The Wilder Shores of Marx* (London, 1991),
for many insights into the psychological mechanisms of 'real existing
tyranny'.

17. For Enver Hoxha's views on Dej, see chapter III above. See Milovan
Djilas in conversation with George Urban in *Encounter* (September 1988).

18. For the posthumous cult of Lenin in the Soviet Union, the source
and model of all future cults of living beloved leaders, see Nina Tumarkin, *Lenin Lives! The Lenin Cult in Soviet Russia* (Cambridge, Mass.,
1983) and Alain Brossat, 'Le culte de Lénine: le mausolée et les statues'
in Alain Brossat (ed.), *A l'Est la mémoire retrouvée* 165–197.

VIII

1. For Aristotle's views on the connection between public works and
tyranny, see *The Politics* V, xi, translated T. A. Sinclair, revised and
re-presented by Trevor J. Saunders (Harmondsworth, 1957; 1986 print-
ing), 345, where he also quotes Periander of Corinth's famous advice to
would-be tyrants to treat their potential rivals as tall stalks of corn, 'Lop
off the eminent and get rid of the men of independent spirit.'

2. See Paul Morand's classic *Bucarest* (Paris, 1935). In fact, a fairer
comparison seems to be between Brussels and Bucharest. Both have the
monuments and grand aspirations to an imperial past that never was:
today, they are both disfigured by the elephantine buildings of mega-bu-
reaucracy.

3. See, for instance, Véronique Soulé, 'Ceauşescu crève le coeur de
Bucarest' in *Libération* (25 November 1987) to get an idea of the growing
alarm in Western Europe about the demolitions. Britain was longer in
catching on to the devastation. I remember a fruitless conversation with
an editor of BBC 1's *Panorama* about Ceauşescu's policies as late as
September 1988.

4. For the Prince of Wales's speech, see 'Devouring the Soul of a
Nation' in *The Times* (28 April 1989). Ceauşescu's reply appeared in the
form of a double-page advertisement in the *Observer* (30 April 1989)
under the headline 'ROMANIA – SUCCESSFUL INDEPENDENCE',
which talked about 'energy saving schemes' and other euphemisms for
degrading the quality of life to provide resources for the 'systematization'
of the country.

5. For Saddam's architectural tastes, see Timothy Clarke, 'Arms and

the Man' in *The Guardian* (4 February 1991), a review of Samir al-Khalil's *The Monument: Art, Vulgarity and Responsibility in Iraq* (London, 1991). For a survey of the first generation of totalitarian architecture, see Franco Borsi, *The Monumental Era: European Architecture and Design 1929–1939*, translated by Pamela Marwood (London, 1987).

6. For Le Corbusier's cult of the generous and far-seeing tyrannical patron, see Peter Hall, 'Metropolis 1890–1940: Challenges and Responses' in Andrew Sutcliffe (ed.), *Metropolis, 1890–1940* (London, 1984), 34. From another architectural school altogether, consider Léon Krier's recent letter to Prince Henri of Luxembourg: 'History shows us that with the passage of time it is not so much the individual artist who is remembered as the sovereign who marks an epoch or style with his personality and his vision. Thus it can be said that Louis XIV, Philip II and Federick-William IV were the real architects of Versailles, the Escorial and Charlottenhoff.' Quoted in *Architectural Design: Imitation & Innovation*, guest editor Lucien Steil (London, 1988), 59.

7. See his speech to the National Council of the Socialist Democracy and Unity Front in *Scînteia* (24 December 1980), cf. Paul Gafton, 'Romania's Socialist Agriculture' in Vlad Georgescu, *Romania: 40 Years (1944–1984)* (New York, 1985), 38 note 8, for Ceauşescu's comment to the Central Committee in February 1984 that '. . . for the future of a people what is decisive is not the amount of consumption, but the amount of accumulation.'

8. See *Libération* (25 November 1987).

9. For 'Ruinenwerttheorie' see Albert Speer, *Inside the Third Reich*, translated by Richard and Clara Winston (London, 1970), 97: 'By using special materials and applying certain principles of statics, we should be able to build structures which *even in a state of decay*, after hundreds or (such were our reckonings) thousands of years would more or less resemble Roman models.'

10. For a survey of the recent devastation of Paris, see Harald A. Jahn, *Das Neue Paris* (Vienna, 1990).

11. For the sake of comparison the diameter of the dome of St Peter's in Rome is a little less than fifty metres, but then Pope Julius II was modest on God's behalf. Hitler intended to build on a still vaster scale than Ceauşescu: his dome (on the proposed Great Hall in Berlin at the head of the Boulevard of the Victory of National Socialism) was to be 275 metres across. (See Speer, *Inside the Third Reich*, 222–223.)

12. For an official account of the occasion, see *Romania Today* (September 1988), 3.

13. Nicu Ceauşescu must have been a bitter disappointment to his father since, unlike Kim Jong Il, he showed no traits of architectural

megalomania: Nicu's vices were private. For the North Korean regime and its rebuilding of Pyongyang and the younger Kim's role, see Adrian Lyttleton in *Communist Studies*. Compare with the Ministry of Love's pyramid in Orwell's *1984*.

14. For the demolitions in Moscow, see Kathleen Berton, *Moscow: An Architectural History* (London, 1977; second edition, 1990), 222ff: the Spassky Cathedral was demolished to make way for a Palace of Soviets, topped by a gigantic statue of Lenin, and housing conference halls with a seating capacity of 20,000 and 8,000 respectively. Only the hole dug for the foundations survived the Second World War and is now used as a swimming pool. See also R. A. French, 'Moscow, the Socialist Metropolis' in Andrew Sutcliffe (ed.), *Metropolis, 1890–1940* (London, 1984), 355–379, especially 373, for the ever-growing shortage of accommodation in Stalin's ever-more rebuilt Moscow: down from 5.7 square metres per capita in 1926 to 4.8 square metres in 1956 (officially each individual was 'entitled' to 9 square metres). The population of Bucharest is similarly squeezed into new blocks, but the exact figures have not been published.

15. For Zhdanov's definition of the architect's role, see Andrzej Turowski, 'Town Planning and Architecture' in Serge Fauchereau (ed.), *Moscow, 1900–1930* (Fribourg, 1988), 215.

16. Quoted in Turowski, *ibid.*, 212–213.

17. Quoted in Sophia M. Miskiewicz & Aaron Trehub, 'The Chronic Housing Deficit' in Vojtech Mastny (ed.), *An Annual Soviet/East European Survey, 1985–86* (Durham, N.C., 1987), 180; see also Dan Ionescu, 'Housing as a Political Tool' in *Radio Free Europe Research: Romania Situation Report* 12 (6 November 1987).

18. Quoted in *Romanian News* (22 July 1988).

19. For the style of life of the *nomenklatura*, see chapter IV.

20. See Vladimir Paperny, 'Moscow in the 1930s and the Emergence of a New City' in Hans Günther (ed.), *The Culture of the Stalin Period* (London, 1990), 229–239.

21. See C. V. Wedgewood, *Richelieu* (Harmondsworth, 1968), 123.

22. So immense was the demand for domestically quarried stone and marble, for instance, that graves in Romania in the 1980s were often unfinished. See *Neuer Weg* (29 January 1990).

23. Several architects and planners have talked to me about the choice of Anca Petrescu. She also took part in a BBC World Service programme about the Casa Republicii (28 March 1990). Despite the necessarily different viewpoints, their stories hold together convincingly.

24. For Mussolini's demolition of seventeen Roman churches and many other buildings, see Alex Scobie, *Hitler's State Architecture: The Impact of Classical Architecture* (London, 1990), 10.

25. See Mark Almond, *Decline without Fall*, 37 note 10, for an example of the indifference to the human cost of demolition.

26. The great day had been put off so often that many suspected Ceauşescu was superstitious about completing the project, afraid that it would end his life's work, but 23 August was a suitable date in the Romanian revolutionary calendar. Other monster projects had schedules which loomed into the distant future. There were intended to be many more grand openings.

27. Information from those involved in the design at various levels.

28. I was shown this on a tour of the building in April 1990.

29. This gives some idea of how useless the building is for any practical, let alone profitable, purpose.

30. For the cult of Lenin and the ghoulish purposes underlying that first communist embalming, see Nina Tumarkin, *Lenin Lives! The Lenin Cult in Soviet Russia* (Cambridge, Mass., 1983). See also chapter VII above.

IX

1. For the full text of the *Manifesto*, see David Fernbach (ed.), *MARX: the Revolutions of 1848* (Harmondsworth, 1973), 87.

2. See Albert Speer, *Inside the Third Reich*, translated by Richard and Clara Winston (London, 1970). Speer describes the reasoning behind the Nazis' demolition of historical monuments as follows (*ibid.*, 429), 'Away with castles and churches; after the war we'll build our own monuments! In part this impulse sprang from the feeling of inferiority toward the past that the party bigwigs had. But there was another element in this feeling, as one of the *Gauleiters* explained when he was justifying his demolition order to me: Castles and churches of the past were citadels of reaction that stood in the way of our revolution.'

3. See text of the *Manifesto* in Fernbach (ed.) *MARX: the Revolutions of 1848*, 71.

4. See *ibid.*, 71–72.

5. See Leon Trotsky, *Literature and Revolution*. Also *Brief History of the Revolutionary Activities of Comrade Kim Il Sung* (Pyongyang, 1969), 116.

6. See Albert Speer, *Inside the Third Reich*.

7. For the early Communist aspirations to modernize and systematize all aspects of life, see the texts in William Rosenberg (ed.), *Bolshevik Visions: First Phase of the Cultural Revolution in Soviet Russia* (2nd edition, Ann Arbor, 1990), II, especially pages 153–219.

8. For the origins of the then Romanian Workers' Party's breach with Moscow, see Ghita Ionescu, *Communism in Rumania, 1944–1962* (London, 1964), 318ff.

9. See *Agerpress* release (4 March 1988) and 'Exposé on Questions of Socioeconomic Management, Ideological and Political Educational Work, and the International Situation at the Meeting of the Executive Political Committee of the Central Committee of the Romanian Communist Party', supplement to *Romania Today* (May 1988).

10. For the functioning of the Second Economy, see Horst Brezinski and Paul Petersen, 'The Second Economy in Romania' in Maria Los (ed.), *The Second Economy in Marxist States* (London, 1990), 69–84.

11. See chapter VI above.

12. Recently, Cuba's Castro has echoed Ceauşescu's appeals to Romanians to substitute pedal-power for petrol-consuming motor cars, even going so far as to propose a 'Kampuchean solution' to Stalinist Cuba's economic problems. See Hildegard Stausberg, 'Kuba fällt zurück in einen Steinzeit–Kommunismus' in *Frankfurter Allgemeine Zeitung* (18 March 1991).

13. See the *Independent* (28 November 1987).

14. See *Newsweek* (21 August 1989).

15. Christian Mititelu of the BBC Romanian Service kindly supplied me with an analytical list of affected areas.

16. See *Züricher Tages-Anzeiger* (15 July 1988) for quotations from *Scînteia* about the reaction of local people to the demolitions supervised by Ceauşescu in Ilfov county. 'The move was easier for the young people of the villages of Buda and Ordreanu than for the elderly . . . .Although the people now live in civilized conditions in their new houses, it is difficult for them to give up the customary way of life which they pursued in villages.' (My copies of *Scînteia* for the first two weeks of July were confiscated at the Episcopi Bihar frontier crossing into Hungary by Romanian border guards, who clearly regarded me as unfit to have the Party paper in my possession.)

17. See Shafir, *Romania*, 143.

18. See the illustration in Ivan Völgyes, *Politics in Eastern Europe* (Chicago, 1986), 90.

19. See *Romania Today* (July 1988) and *România Libera* (8 February 1986).

20. See *Scînteia* (11 February 1986).

21. See Robert Bidelux, *Communism and Development* (London, 1985), 147.

22. See *Ceauşescu, Builder of Modern Romania*, 113.

23. See *Ceauşescu, Builder of Modern Romania*, 117–118.

24. See the various articles under the collective title, 'Revolutia stiintifico-tehnica si Formarea Omolui nou' ('The scientific-technical revolution and the formation of the New Man') in *Era Socialista* (30 July 1988), 30–35.

25. See Kligman, *Wedding of the Dead*, 8.

26. See *Ceauşescu, Builder of Modern Romania*, 113.

27. See 'Exposé', note 9 above.

28. See Kligman, *Wedding of the Dead*, 249.

29. Nicolae Ceauşescu's words are quoted in Ilie Ceauşescu, *Transylvania: An Ancient Romanian Land* (Bucharest, 1983), 3 & 38.

30. See Ceauşescu's interview with Manfred Schell, 'Es gibt keine Schablone für den Sozialismus' in *Die Welt* (30 December 1988).

31. See Shafir, *Romania*, 122.

32. Compare this with the golden age of Stalin's iconoclasm, when visiting fellow-travellers, like the First Viscount Stansgate, found more Christianity in the newly established 'museums of scientific atheism' than in the few remaining Orthodox churches left open.

33. Quoted in Kathleen Barton, *Moscow: An Architectural History* (London, 1990), 240.

34. See Joachim Siegerist, *Der Rote Vampir*, 350. Father James Alison, OP, has exorcized the perimeter of the building.

35. I am especially grateful to Marianna Celac for patiently discussing the architectural problems of Romania with me from February 1988 onwards. See also Dinu Giurescu, *The Razing of Romania's Past* (New York, 1989) for a thorough listing of the buildings destroyed by Ceauşescu until the last few months of his rule.

X

1. For a description of the XIV Party Congress, see 'Absage Ceauşescus an Reformen' in the *Neue Zürcher Zeitung* (22 November 1989) and 'Ceauşescu is adamant: He'll resist' in *International Herald Tribune* (21 November 1989).

2. For Yasser Arafat's presence, see *Scînteia* (22 November 1989); also *Le Monde* (22 November 1989) for a typically caustic Plantu cartoon. For the absence of any other distinguished delegates, see 'Land der lebenden Toten' in *Der Spiegel* (20 November 1989), 192.

3. See Nigel Hawkes (ed.), *Tearing Down the Curtain: the People's Revolution in Eastern Europe* (London, 1990), 95.

4. For a detailed discussion of the new Front's appeal to the Party Congress to 'take the last opportunity to avoid bloodshed' by sacking Ceauşescu, see 'Un Front de salut national demande aux délégués de limoger M. Ceauşescu' in *Le Monde* (26 October 1989). Both Silviu Brucan and Gheorghe Apostol told me that they saw the letter of the Six as having a decisive impact on Romanian opinion. For the controversy about the origins of the post-revolutionary National Salvation Front, see below.

5. For the trial and execution of Ochoa and informed speculation about the underlying reasons for it, see *Le Monde*.

6. For the Six's letter, see *Libération* (13 March 1989) and *Le Monde* (13 March 1989), Silviu Brucan has been particularly helpful about the background to the letter.

7. Interview with Apostol.

8. Information from Brucan. See also the details of plotting among the generals in *Cuvintul* (5–11 February 1991), 4–5.

9. For an unflattering characterization of Milea, see Pacepa, *Red Horizons*, 157–59.

10. See Pacepa, *Red Horizons*, 192–195.

11. For well-informed speculation about Iliescu's future, see *Der Spiegel* (6 November 1986); for Ceauşescu's comment to the Political Executive Committee, see *România Libera* (26 January 1990).

12. See *Newsweek* (21 August 1989). For part of the Securitate's dossier on Brucan dealing with his foreign contacts, see *Expres Magazin* (20–26 February 1991), 9.

13. Interview with Brucan.

14. Silviu Brucan was able to see Apostol's testimony after Ceauşescu's fall. Personal information to the author.

15. Interview with Brucan.

16. For early interest in the Tökes affair, see 'Siebenbürger Pfarrer Tökes soll schweigen' in *Frankfurter Allgemeine Zeitung* (4 October 1989) and *Neue Zürcher Zeitung* (27 October 1989).

17. For Deng's praise of Ceauşescu, see *The Guardian* (14 May 1989).

18. Interview with Grosz.

19. See Alain Jacob, 'Questions sur la genèse d'une révolution' in *Le Monde* (6 January 1990). For my views on the general balance between popular protest and Soviet influence in the revolutions of 1989, see Mark Almond, *Retreat to Moscow: Gorbachev and the East European Revolution* (IEDSS, London, 1990).

20. For the view of Romania as an exception to the general rule, see Timothy Garton Ash, *We the People, The Revolution of '89 Witnessed in Warsaw, Budapest, Berlin & Prague* (Cambridge, 1990), 141.

21. See *Agerpress* text (31 December 1988), 3.

22. For the involvement of West German companies in this field, see *Der Spiegel* (1990–91), *passim*.

23. For Ceauşescu's inadequate conventional military forces, see Robert Van Tol and Jonathan Eyal, 'The New Romanian Navy: A Weapon without a Target?' in the *RUSI Journal* (March 1987). Ceauşescu made great propaganda play of the fact that half his troops were deployed in industry or agriculture. Their fingers were not on the trigger. Ceauşescu wanted to put his on the nuclear button.

24. Quoted in *Scînteia* (18 December 1985), cf. Anneli Ute Gabanyi, *Die unvollendete Revolution*, 102.

25. See *Current Digest of the Soviet Press* 49 no. 21 (1987), 13.

26. See Karen Dawisha, *Eastern Europe, Gorbachev and Reform: the Great Challenge* (Cambridge, 1988), 171.

27. See Christopher D. Jones, *Soviet Influence in Eastern Europe. Political Autonomy and the Warsaw Pact* (New York, 1981), especially 209; also Pacepa, *Red Horizons*, 201–202.

28. See *Scînteia* (7 May 1967).

29. See *Frankfurter Allgemeine Zeitung* (8 July 1988); also Charles Gati, 'Gorbachev and Eastern Europe' in *Foreign Affairs* 65 (1987), 961.

30. See Zeev Barbu, 'Psycho-Historical and Sociological Perspectives on the Iron Guard' in Larsen (ed.), *Who Were the Fascists* (Bergen, 1980), 380. For Ceauşescu's statements, see Vlad Georgescu, 'Romania in the 1980s: the Legacy of Dynastic Socialism' in *East European Politics and Societies* (1988), and Vladimir Tismaneanu, 'Byzantine Rites, Stalinist Follies' in *Orbis* (Spring 1986). For the deviations, see Ceauşescu, 'Exposé', in *Romania Today* (May 1988).

31. See 'Dieselbe Fabrik entsteht in Rumänien' in *Der Spiegel* (8 May 1989), 166–69; also 'W. German link with Romanian missiles' in *Independent* (9 May 1989).

32. For Kim's comments, see *Lumea* (November 1988).

33. Only a week after the Congress, Ceauşescu told the Central Committee to put the country 'in absolute order', see *The Times* (4 December 1989). For Ceauşescu's purging of several senior figures in the last days before the outbreak of the revolution, see Professor Katherine Verdery, 'Romania, Reluctant Domino' in *International Herald Tribune* (16–17 December 1989). Ironically, none of these last victims of 'rotation' played any part in Ceauşescu's downfall. Professor Verdery was prophetic enough to envisage on the eve of the Timişoara events that the crushing of a 'spontaneous demonstration' might provoke a 'world reaction of outrage and precipitate the end of [the] dictatorship'. For events in Timişoara, see Florin Medelet & Mihai Ziman (eds.), *O Cronica a Revolutiei din Timisoara, 16–22 Decembrie 1989* (Timişoara, 1990). For the stenographic report of Ceauşescu's tele-conference on 17 December, see *România Libera* (9 January 1990).

34. For a thoroughly disillusioned interpretation of the Romanian Revolution, see Michel Castoux, *Un mensonge gros comme le siècle: Roumanie, histoire d'une manipulation* (Paris, 1990). Annely Ute Gabanyi, *Die unvollendete Revolution*, 132ff. At the time of the XIV Congress in November, several Soviet and Yugoslav journalists and tourists with valid visas were turned back at the Romanian border. See *Le Figaro* (21 November 1989).

XI

1. See *Zig-Zag* (27 May 1990).

2. For Brucan's praise of Stanculescu's expert assistance during the crucial days of the revolution, see the sketch of the General in the *Frankfurter Allgemeine Zeitung* (13 February 1990).

3. For the fall of Maziliu, see the coverage in *The Times* or *Independent* at the end of January 1990. Maziliu's case brings out the difficulty of finding an untarnished dissident in a system like Ceauşescu's. He was both a dissident who had used his position with the UN Human Rights Commision to publicize the appalling situation inside Romania, especially for the young and sick, but also could not have been based in Geneva in the first place had he not been trusted by the regime and have proved his reliability in the past. Furthermore some observers think that Maziliu precipitated his own downfall by appearing to shift his support behind crowds critical of Iliescu. See Sylvie Kaufmann, 'Les divergences s'accentuent au sein du Conseil du front de salut national' in *Le Monde* (16 January 1990).

4. For Iliescu's doxology of the Front of National Salvation, see *Le Monde* (31 January 1990).

5. On 23 August 1990, Brucan and Militaru published an interview describing the manoeuvrings before December 1989. Both by then had fallen from power. Silviu Brucan was kind enough to give me a copy of the text. For my comments and Michael Shafir's thorough notes on it and Mr Brucan's own authorized translation, see 'Romania: Was there a coup?' in *East European Reporter* (Autumn/Winter 1990), 74–77.

6. For an internal Securitate list of the members of the 'transcendental meditation group', see *Zig-Zag* (11–17 September 1990).

7. See Anneli Ute Gabanyi, *Die Unvollendete Revolution*, 102ff, for an interpretation difficult to square with Brucan's account of Soviet reticence about helping the anti-Ceauşescu plotters inside the Romanian Communist élite.

8. The orders to use firearms given at the Political Executive Committee's meeting on 17 December were ambiguous, but everybody in that sort of regime understood euphemisms about 'all necessary measures'. Elena's outbursts were more to the point. See *România Libera* (10 January 1990).

9. See 'Cum a vrut sa fuga Ceauşescu' in *Libertatea* (30 December 1989).

10. Doina Cornea, who had no reason to regret the passing of either Nicolae or Elena Ceauşescu, remarked that he was the only participant who showed any trace of dignity. The text of the trial-video has been widely published: I have used especially the extensive documentation

in the series 'Timpul dezvaluirilor: Procesul dictatorilor Ceauşescu' in *Dimineaţa* (16 March–4 April 1990) and 'Procesul sotilor Nicolae si Elena Ceauşescu, un Proces al Commujnismului însuşi' in *Europa* (August 1990).

11. See *Le Point* (7 April 1991).

Epilogue

1. David Edgar's review of two other biographies of Nicolae Ceauşescu in the *Guardian* on 15 April 1991 was perhaps a harbinger of rehabilitation: according to Edgar, Ceauşescu had tried to insulate Romanians from the rigours of the world market economy. Quite right! He could not have put it better himself.

Further Reading

Anyone interested in current developments in Romania is dependent on the vagaries of the British press. For accounts of developments since December 1989, see Mihnea Berindei, Ariadna Combes & Anne Planche, *Roumanie, le livre blanche: La Réalité d'un pouvoir néo-communiste* (Paris, 1990); Anneli Ute Ganbanyi, *Die unvollendete Revolution: Rumanien zwischen Diktatur und Demokratie* (Munich, 1990), edited by Vladimir Weissmann (Copenhagen, 1990); or Mark Almond, 'Romania since the Revolution' in *Government and Opposition* 25 (1990), 484–496. The journal *East European Reporter* and Radio Free Europe also provide regular expert analyses.

Select Bibliography

Romanian Published Sources

Books

Anonymous, *Omagiu Tovarasului Nicolae Ceauşescu* (Bucharest, 1973).
Anonymous, *Un Ctitor de Istorie u Epoca de Aur. Omagiu Conducatorlui Iubit* (Craiova, 1988).
Ceauşescu, Nicolae, *România pe drumul construirii societatii socialiste multilateral dezvoltate* (Bucharest, 1970 onwards), 30 volumes.
Matichescu, Olimpiu, *Doftana, Simbol al Eroismului Revolutionar* (Bucharest, 1979).

Newspapers and Magazines

Adevarul (Bucharest; see also *Scînteia*)
Alutus (Rimnicu Vîlcea)
Atlas, Cluiul Liber (Cluj-Napoca)
Avîntul (Braşov)
Contrast (Constanta)
Express (Bucharest)
Flacara (Bucharest)
Gazeta de Vest (Timişoara)
Lumea (Bucharest)
Neuer Weg (Bucharest)
Opinia Publica (Bucharest)
Palaţul de Justitie (Bucharest)
Phoenix (Bucharest)
Plus (Bucharest)
România Libera (Bucharest)
Scînteia (including *Scînteia Poporlui*, Bucharest; see also *Adevarul*)

Tineretul Liber (Bucharest)
Tribuna. Saptaminal de Cultura (Cluj-Napoca)
Viata Armatei (Bucharest)
Zig-Zag (Bucharest)

Books and Articles

Benn, Tony, *Office Without Power, Diaries 1968–72* (London, 1988; paperback edition 1989).

Brown, J. F., *Eastern Europe and Communist Rule* (Durham, N.C., 1988).

Catchlove, Donald, *Romania's Ceauşescu* (Tunbridge Wells, 1972).

Crowther, William, 'Romanian Politics and the International Economy' in *Orbis* (Fall, 1984), 553–574.

Eyal, Jonathan, 'Why Romania could not avoid bloodshed' in Gwyn Prins (ed.), *Spring in Winter: the 1989 Revolutions* (Manchester, 1990), pp 139–62.

Fischer, Mary Ellen, *Nicolae Ceauşescu. A Study in Political Leadership* (Boulder, Colorado, 1989).
'Women in Romanian Politics: Elena Ceauşescu, Pronatalism, and the Promotion of Women' in Sharon L. Wolchik & Alfred G. Meyer (eds.), *Women, State and Party in Eastern Europe* (Durham, 1985), pp 121–137.

Gabanyi, Anneli Ute, *Die unvollendete Revolution: Rumänien zwischen Diktatur und Demokratie* (Munich, 1990).

Fischer-Galati, Stephen, *The New Romania: From People's Democracy to Socialist Republic* (Cambridge, Mass., 1967).

de Fleurs, René, 'Socialism in One Family' in *Survey* 28 (Winter 1984), 165–174.

Funderburk, David, *Pinstripes and Reds: An American Ambassador Caught between the State Department and the Romanian Communists, 1981–1985* (Washington, DC, 1987).

Georgescu, Vlad (ed.), *Romania: 40 Years (1944–1984)* (New York, 1985).

Georgescu, Vlad, 'Romania in the 1980s: The Legacy of Dynastic Socialism' in *East European Politics and Societies* 1 (1988).

Gilberg, Trond, *Nationalism & Communism in Romania: the Rise and Fall of Ceauşescu's Personal Dictatorship* (Boulder, Colorado, 1990).

Giurescu, Dinu *The Razing of Romania's Past* (New York, 1989).

Hamelet, Michel-P., *Nicolae Ceauşescu* (Paris, 1971).

Hoxha, Enver, *The Artful Albanian* edited by Jon Halliday (London, 1986).

Ionescu, Ghita, *Communism in Romania, 1944–1962* (London, 1964).

Select Bibliography

Jackson, George D. Jr., *Comintern and Peasant in Eastern Europe, 1919–1930* (New York, 1966).

Jelavich, Barbara, *History of the Balkans* vol II ('The Twentieth Century') (Cambridge, 1983).

Jowitt, Kenneth, *Revolutionary Breakthroughs and National Development: The Case of Romania, 1944–65* (Berkeley & Los Angeles, 1971).

King, Robert, *History of the Romanian Communist Party* (Stanford, 1980)

Kligman, Gail, *The Wedding of the Dead. Ritual, Poetics and Popular Culture in Transylvania* (Berkeley & Los Angeles, 1988).

Maxwell, Robert (gen. ed.), *Nicolae Ceauşescu: Builder of Modern Romania and International Statesman* (Oxford, 1983).

Olschewski, Malte, *Der Conducator Nicolae Ceauşescu: Phänomen der Macht* (Vienna, 1990).

Pacepa, Ion Mihai, *Red Horizons* (London, 1988).

Pastor, Peter (ed.), *Revolutions and Interventions in Hungary and its Neighbor States, 1918–1919* (New York, 1988).

Sampson, Steven, 'Is Romania the next Poland?' in *Critique* xvi (1983), pp 139–144.

'Rumours in Socialist Romania' in *Survey*.

Shafir, Michael, *Romania. Politics, Economics and Society: Political Stagnation and Simulated Change* (London, 1985).

Siegerist, Joachim, *Ceauşescu. Der Rote Vampir* (Hamburg, 1990).

Socor, Vlad, 'Eyewitness on the 1977 Miners' Strike in Romania's Jiu Valley' in *Radio Free Europe Research Background Report* (13 August 1986).

Tismaneanu, Vladimir, 'Ceauşescu's Socialism' in *Problems of Communism* 34 (January–February, 1985), 50–66.

'Byzantine Rites, Stalinist Folies: The Twilight of Dynastic Socialism in Romania' in *Orbis* (Spring, 1986), 65–90.

Personal Power and Elite Change in Romania (Philadelphia, 1989).

'The Tragicomedy of Romanian Communism' by Ferenc Fehér & Andrew Arato (eds.), *Crisis and Reform in Eastern Europe* (New Brunswick, NJ, 1991), 121–74.

van Tol, Robert, & Eyal, Jonathan, 'The New Romanian Navy: A Weapon Without a Target?' in *RUSI Journal* (March, 1987), 37.

Wolton, Thierry, *Le KGB en France* (Paris, 1986), especially pp 384–400.

Western Newspapers and Academic Journals

Daily Telegraph (London)
Die Welt (Berlin)
Dissent (Philadelphia)
East European Reporter (London)
Frankfurter Allgemeine Zeitung (Frankfurt-am-Main)
Guardian (London)
Independent (London)
Le Figaro (Paris)
Le Monde (Paris)
Le Monde diplomatique (Paris)
Le Point (Paris)
Libération (Paris)
Neue Literatur (Bucharest)
Neue Zürcher Zeitung (Zürich)
New York Times (New York)
Observer (London)
Orbis (Philadelphia)
Problems of Communism (Washington DC)
Radio Free Europe: Romanian Situation Report (Munich)
Studies in Comparative Communism
Süddeutsche Zeitung (Munich)
Sunday Telegraph (London)
Sunday Times (London)
Survey (London)
Telos (Chicago)
Times (London)

Index

Index

All Chapmans books are available at your local bookshop or newsagent, or can be ordered direct from the publisher. Indicate the number of copies required and fill in the form below.

Send to: **Chapmans Publishers Ltd**
141/143 Drury Lane
Covent Garden. WC2B 5TB.

or phone: **071 379 9799 quoting title, author and**
Credit Card number.

Please enclose a remittance* to the value of the cover price plus: 60p for the first book plus 30p per copy for each additional book ordered to a maximum charge of £2.40 to cover postage and packing.

*Payment may be made in sterling by UK personal cheque, postal order, sterling draft or international money order, made payable to Chapmans Publishers Ltd.

Alternatively by Barclaycard/Access:

Card No.

Expiry date: _____

Signature: _____

Applicable only in the UK and Republic of Ireland.

While every effort is made to keep prices low, it is sometimes necessary to increase prices at short notice. Chapmans Publishers reserve the right to show on covers and charge new retail prices which may differ from those advertised in the text or elsewhere.

NAME AND ADDRESS IN BLOCK LETTERS PLEASE

Name _____

Address _____

_____

_____

Post code _____ Tel. no. _____